Organizational
Creativity

Praise for *Organizational Creativity: A Practical Guide for Innovators & Entrepreneurs*

"Simple, deep, entertaining and useful—that rare combination can be found in this engaging book. A must-read for anyone interested in innovation and creativity. I enjoyed it and strongly recommend it."

—*Sergio Fajardo, Ph.D. in Math, UW-Madison;*
Mayor of Medellín (2004–2007) and
Governor of Antioquia (2012–2015), Colombia

"*Organizational Creativity* is one of the most lucid, thoughtful, and insightful books on how organizations can leverage creativity to produce innovative results. The "know-do-be" theme and the engaging writing style convincingly articulate ways to develop creativity skills and traits. Anyone interested in fostering innovation in organizations needs to read this book."

—*Srikant M. Datar, Arthur Lowes Dickinson*
Professor of Business Administration,
Harvard Business School;
Coauthor of Rethinking the MBA:
Business Education at a Crossroads

"Another insightful contribution to understanding creativity from Buffalo's International Center. The significance of creativity for innovators and entrepreneurs is badly in need of such clarification."

—*Tudor Rickards, Emeritus Professor,*
Creativity and Change Management,
Alliance Manchester Business School,
University of Manchester

"*Organizational Creativity* is a wonderful book—so engaging, enlightening, and inspiring that readers will hardly notice how much they are learning. It gives a guided tour through each stage of the innovation process, from identifying and defining the most important problems to generating breakthrough ideas to successfully implementing the best solutions. Aspiring entrepreneurs, innovators, and business leaders will find here the keys to nurturing not only their best ideas but also their most creative selves."

—*Teresa Amabile, Professor and Director of Research,*
Harvard Business School;
Coauthor of The Progress Principle

"Creative thinking is widely considered a 21st-century skill. To best prepare students for today's complex work world, colleges and universities must find pedagogically sound practices that promote creative thinking. Here at Sheridan we have adopted, with great success, many of the principles, methods, and tools described in *Organizational Creativity*. There is little doubt that these strategies are contributing to our students' creative-thinking capabilities."

—*Mary Preece, President & Vice Chancellor,*
Sheridan College, Ontario, Canada

"Educational experts and business leaders throughout the world have consistently cited creativity, innovation, and entrepreneurial skills as vital for professional success in this century. At the Universidad Autónoma de Bucaramanga we have used the contents of this book to help guide a powerful institutional intervention to make our university the first creative campus in Latin America. As a result, our students now have strategies to release the utmost potential they have within them."

—*Alberto Montoya Puyana, President,*
Universidad Autónoma de Bucaramanga, Colombia

Sara Miller McCune founded SAGE Publishing in 1965 to support the dissemination of usable knowledge and educate a global community. SAGE publishes more than 1000 journals and over 800 new books each year, spanning a wide range of subject areas. Our growing selection of library products includes archives, data, case studies and video. SAGE remains majority owned by our founder and after her lifetime will become owned by a charitable trust that secures the company's continued independence.

Los Angeles | London | New Delhi | Singapore | Washington DC | Melbourne

Organizational Creativity

A Practical Guide for Innovators & Entrepreneurs

Gerard J. Puccio
Buffalo State–State University of New York

John F. Cabra
Buffalo State–State University of New York

Nathan Schwagler
The Dalí Museum, St. Petersburg, Florida, USA

Los Angeles | London | New Delhi
Singapore | Washington DC | Melbourne

FOR INFORMATION:

SAGE Publications, Inc.
2455 Teller Road
Thousand Oaks, California 91320
E-mail: order@sagepub.com

SAGE Publications Ltd.
1 Oliver's Yard
55 City Road
London EC1Y 1SP
United Kingdom

SAGE Publications India Pvt. Ltd.
B 1/I 1 Mohan Cooperative Industrial Area
Mathura Road, New Delhi 110 044
India

SAGE Publications Asia-Pacific Pte. Ltd.
3 Church Street
#10-04 Samsung Hub
Singapore 049483

Acquisitions Editor: Maggie Stanley
Developmental Editor: Neda Dallal
eLearning Editor: Katie Ancheta
Editorial Assistant: Ashley Mixson
Production Editor: Jane Haenel
Copy Editor: Mark Bast
Typesetter: C&M Digitals (P) Ltd.
Proofreader: Christine Dahlin
Indexer: Terri Morrissey
Cover Designer: Janet Kiesel
Marketing Manager: Ashlee Blunk

Printed in the United States of America

Library of Congress Cataloging-in-Publication Data

Names: Puccio, Gerard J., author. | Cabra, John F., author. | Schwagler, Nathan, author.

Title: Organizational creativity : a practical guide for innovators & entrepreneurs / Gerard J. Puccio, Buffalo State, State University of New York, John F. Cabra, Buffalo State, State University of New York, Nathan Schwagler, University of South Florida Dali Museum.

Description: Thousand Oaks, CA : SAGE, [2018] | Includes bibliographical references and index.

Identifiers: LCCN 2016051144 | ISBN 9781452291550 (pbk. : alk. paper)

Subjects: LCSH: Creative ability in business. | Creative thinking. | Problem solving. | Technological innovations.

Classification: LCC HD53 .P83 2018 | DDC 658.4/094—dc23
LC record available at https://lccn.loc.gov/2016051144

This book is printed on acid-free paper.

17 18 19 20 21 10 9 8 7 6 5 4 3 2 1

Brief Contents

Detailed Contents

PART III. BEING: WAYS TO SUSTAIN YOURSELF AS A 21ST-CENTURY INNOVATOR

Introduction

Purpose and Design of This Book

We begin this book with an exercise in creative thinking. Ponder this: What do Bob Dylan and James Dyson have in common? To be fair, to answer this question, you must first be familiar with these two individuals. Most will easily recognize the name Bob Dylan, but in case not, he is an American singer, songwriter, artist, writer, and Nobel Prize winner. Dylan's recording career has spanned more than 50 years, during which time he has sold more than 100 million records. As for James Dyson, have you ever dried your hands in a public bathroom that had the Dyson Blade mounted on the wall? James Dyson is a British inventor, innovator, and entrepreneur.

So, what do a famous musician and an entrepreneur have in common? The answer is creativity. Both have been successful professionally because of their creativity, but more than that, both are ardent creativity advocates as well.

Dylan and Dyson recognize the power of a creative idea and encourage others to address significant issues in their lives through the deliberate application of creative thinking. Bob Dylan, for example, was recently named founding patron of the University of Auckland's Creative Thinking Research Fund and is the inaugural creative laureate of that university's Creative Thinking Project. This project promotes a deeper understanding of the creative process, to encourage wider participation in creative thinking and to promote creativity as being crucial to individual and community success, well-being, and development.[1] As Jenny Dixon, chair of the Creative Thinking Project and deputy vice chancellor of the University of Auckland, stated,

> Creative thinking drives success. Creativity is a proven force for cognitive development, academic achievement and social and economic innovation. Being creative strengthens neural pathways and generates connections. It opens up worlds of possibilities and change.[2]

James Dyson is quick to attribute his success as an entrepreneur and innovator to his prowess as a creative thinker. In fact, Dyson is a passionate spokesperson for the importance of organizational creativity and creativity in education. Indeed, he has put his money where his mouth is by establishing a foundation to support the next generation of innovative engineers. Dyson makes a close connection between creativity and the invention process, and in the following excerpt from a *Wall Street Journal* interview, it is easy to detect how important he believes creative thinking is for organizational success.

I think if you have a general atmosphere of creativity, of wanting people to come up with ideas and not rejecting them when they do—but trying them out and seeing how they work—and of generally employing engineers who are creative and scientists who are creative, and if you have the reputation of following good ideas through, however unusual and however strange they look, then I think you attract people who are creative and who want to do their best creatively. So I don't think there is any magic potion. I think it is simply having the right attitude internally—that you are there to create things.[3]

Creativity, and to be more specific creative thinking, has always been important. In fact, you could say creativity is a basic human need. In Franken's popular book on human motivation, he argues that humans are driven to create for at least three fundamental reasons:

- Need for novel, varied, and complex situations;
- Need to communicate ideas and values; and
- Need to solve problems.[4]

Given the pace of change in the 21st century, it could be argued—and we do so in this book—that creativity and creative thinking are necessary for success now more than ever. Indeed, the World Economic Forum recently published a report on workplace trends in which they forecast that in 2020 creativity will become the third most important job skill (complex problem solving will be number one).[5] Bob Dylan's own words capture well life in our times: "There is nothing so stable as change." What Dylan's quote does not capture is the pace of change. For instance, the case has been made that a student pursuing a 4-year technical degree will discover that nearly 50% of the knowledge acquired in the first year of study will be out of date before graduation.[6] In the early 21st century, creative thinking has become a survival skill.

In 2008, Harvard Business School, perhaps the preeminent business school program in the United States, celebrated its 100th birthday. Three Harvard Business School professors, Datar, Garvin, and Cullen, used this milestone to reflect on how current and future business education might better meet students' needs. Their book, *Rethinking the MBA: Business Education at a Crossroads*, highlights what they see as the unmet needs associated with business programs. Included in their list of unmet student needs is "acting creatively and innovatively," which they describe in the following way: "finding and framing problems; collecting, synthesizing, and distilling large volumes of ambiguous data; engaging in generative and lateral thinking; and constantly experimenting and learning."[7] Perhaps influenced by this work, or in recognition of the innovation economy that defines modern-day life, the Association to Advance Collegiate Schools of Business (AACSB) updated its accreditation standards around the three themes of innovation, impact, and engagement.[8] To that end, as of 2013 the AACSB standards for general business programs at the master's degree level now include thinking creatively. And, we would strongly suggest, creativity and creative thinking are basic skills for undergraduate students to master as well.

Whereas the field of creativity studies has enjoyed more than 6 decades of research and practice, relatively few business programs, let alone colleges and universities, have incorporated the key insights and best practices from this field into their curricula. This book shares knowledge and practices drawn from the field of creativity so that business school students, as well as any program that prepares students to join or create their own organizations, might reignite and further develop their capacity to think creatively and to produce innovative outcomes. Indeed, a model of entrepreneurial competencies and cognitive skills reads like the classic description of a creative person: energetic, open to risks, unafraid of failure, and intuitive; demonstrating a need for achievement, an internal locus of control and the ability to work with change; capable of fluent idea generation; and ultimately, flexible and original thinking.[9] What the field of creativity education and studies has shown us is that these attitudes and skills are highly teachable. The goal of this book is to expose the reader to knowledge and tools aimed at improving these and other creativity-related skills and traits.

The reader will quickly recognize that this book has adopted a tone that is not typical for most textbooks. Because of a creativity exercise the authors self-administered, one that placed us in the user's experience—the student reader—we decided to adopt a writing style designed to speak directly to the audience. Why? Ultimately, creativity is both an act of doing and being, not simply knowing or dreaming. We wanted to engage the reader in a manner that we hope will lead to personal transformation and growth. To that end, you will find the book uses an active voice and often speaks directly to you—the reader.

Besides writing in an engaging voice, we also included "thought starters" in the text to invite the reader to interact with the ideas presented in this book. Adults learn best and retain the most information when their minds are actively involved and provoked. You will get more out of this book if you use these thought starters. The thought starters are designed so that the reader can pause to interact with some of the main concepts in the book by generating reactions, thoughts, reflections, and connections. When you see a thought bubble, we encourage you to actively engage with that particular concept by capturing your thoughts in the margins of the book or elsewhere. Effective creative thinkers find it easy to make associations. Each thought bubble provides an opportunity to practice associative thinking, thereby allowing you to further develop your creative-thinking skills.

Recognizing that some learners learn best through visual stimuli, we include original sketches by the famous surrealist artist Salvador Dalí. We selected Dalí's work for several reasons. First, as a surrealist artist Dalí attempted to communicate abstract concepts, such as emotions and the cognitive processes associated with the unconscious, human characteristics and qualities that often go unnoticed and unobserved but have a profound impact on our lives. Like surrealist artists we endeavor to help our readers become more aware of the emotions and cognitive processes that make up creativity. For many, a heretofore-unconscious experience once grasped can transform your life—positioning you to be an innovator or entrepreneur. Second, Dalí, like all successful creatives, deliberately engaged in the creative process. Whereas he is famous for his large canvases, he had to play with many ideas before arriving at these final products. His sketches provide insight into his creative process, and show how he tinkered with ideas, played with alternatives, made unusual connections, and refined original ideas into workable solutions—aspects of the creative process that we all can master.

Finally, the structure of the book is unique as well. Datar and his colleagues from the Harvard Business School recommend that effective business programs, and we would suggest any educational or training program, should balance three components: knowing, doing, and being. Knowing, which is the focus of most programs, is concerned with transmitting facts, frameworks, and theories. Doing relates to practices that develop skills and capabilities. Being is concerned with ongoing personal development and integration that sustain beliefs, values, and attitudes in a way that allows one to model the way for others. This book uses these components in a fractal manner, in that these components repeat themselves. Specifically, the chapters are organized into these three categories, starting with what we "Know" about creativity (Part I). We then move to the "Doing" chapters that focus on practices associated with effective creative thinking (Part II). In the spirit of integration, we close with chapters in the "Being" section aimed at helping you to sustain your creative behavior. Additionally, each chapter is structured using the same framework. All begin with what we *know* about the topic addressed in that chapter. This material is followed by recommendations for activities you might *do* to develop skills relative to the chapter's topic. Finally, each chapter concludes by exploring ongoing actions aimed at sustaining the newfound skills and behaviors (i.e., *being*). All chapters end with a case study designed to provide a real-world example of concepts explored in that chapter.

We believe creativity is an essential life skill. Our goal is to provide the necessary background information (knowing), along with proven creative-thinking strategies (doing) that, when internalized (being), help the reader bring about creative breakthroughs that are valuable to an organization (either an existing organization or a start-up). Through developing and improving these creative-thinking skills, the reader will be prepared to serve as a creative leader, someone who successfully facilitates organizational creativity.

With this aim in mind, our book is intended to accomplish two primary objectives: (1) to guide readers on a journey through the creativity essentials (intellectual, cognitive, affective, and behavioral) needed to position themselves as creative assets in the organizations they serve—whether they be for-profit or not-for-profit or existing or start-up ventures—and (2) to support instructors in their efforts to prepare students for successful intrapreneurship and entrepreneurship in the age of innovation.

Acknowledgments

Collectively the authors wish to express their deep appreciation to their colleagues at the International Center for Studies in Creativity, Buffalo State. This unique group of professionals teaches, studies, and promotes creative thinking and creative problem solving on a daily basis. By living what we teach, we have created a rare environment, a work climate characterized by colleagueship and friendship. Thanks, Mike, Marie, Selcuk, Susan, Cyndi, Roger, Deb, Lee Ann, Jo, and all our wonderful adjunct lecturers—you make coming to work a joy! And a special thanks to our former graduate assistant, Molly Holinger, for creating the learning activities in this book.

As the International Center for Studies in Creativity begins its 50th year at Buffalo State, we wish also to acknowledge the founding faculty members, Drs. Sid Parnes and Ruth Noller. We stand on the shoulders of these giants. We also want to express our gratitude for the ongoing support on the part of the Buffalo State administration, especially Associate Dean Rita Zientek, Dean James Mayrose, Provost Melanie Perreault, and President Katherine Conway-Turner.

Finally, we wish to thank those whose feedback was instrumental in shaping the final version of this book. Jasmine Hodges, our writing coach, provided feedback that was both invaluable and inspirational. Maggie Stanley, business and management acquisitions editor for SAGE, guided this book from inception to realization. Mark Bast, our copy editor, whose attention to detail was truly impressive. And to the team of reviewers who pored over early drafts of our manuscript.

Lizabeth Barclay, *Oakland University*

Sara Beckman, *University of California, Berkeley*

H. David Chen, *Saint Joseph's University*

Gary Coombs, *Ohio University*

AnnMarie DiSiena, *Dominican College of Blauvelt*

Lesley Dowding, *Coventry University*

Susan Fant, *University of Alabama*

Michael Littman, *SUNY Buffalo State*

Patrick Lee Lucas, *University of Kentucky*

Enrique Mu, *Carlow University*

Patricia K. O'Connell, *Lourdes University*

Jim Olver, *College of William and Mary*

Tudor Rickards, *University of Manchester*

Rajesh Sharma, *University Centre Croydon*

April J. Spivack, *Coastal Carolina University*

Eric M. Stark, *James Madison University*

Paul D. Witman, *California Lutheran University*

Amy Zidulka, *Royal Roads University*

Authors' individual acknowledgments follow.

G. J. Puccio

It is an illusion to think that a creator can be successful without the love, support, and energy of others. I wish to express my deepest appreciation to those very special people in my life who inspire me: Gabe, Anthony, Pam, Ben, and my mother—Teresa Puccio.

J. F. Cabra

I owe a debt of gratitude to Jennifer Greer, my editor. You helped turn some of my chapters into something I could be proud of. To my sister Claudia, you are a wonderful sister, and I thank you for your many words of cheer. To my treasured friend Cyndi Burnett, thank you for your many encouraging walks. Let me also give special thanks to Dr. Alberto Montoya, president of the Universidad Autónoma de Bucaramanga, and dear friend Cesar Guerrero, for supporting this work. To Dr. Sergio Fajardo, we asked for half an hour of interview time from your busy gubernatorial schedule, and you unselfishly gave us 2 hours! I owe gratitude to my academic advisors Reg Talbot and Andy Joniak. From you stem my love of scholarship. To my children, Michael and Annalise, you inspire my creative spirit. And finally, to my father, Gonzalo Cabra, and mother, Adela Cabra, thank you for serving as beautiful role models. You gave up enormously to come to the United States long ago, and in pursuit of your dreams, you helped me to pursue mine. This book is a testament to your many sacrifices. You left me a heritage of hard work and perseverance.

N. Schwagler

For Joshua, my compass.

To my parents for providing an imaginative youth sufficient distance to experiment and scratch elbows, knees, and pride—and for always being there when a hug, a creative whack on the side of the head, or a solid debriefing conversation was needed.

To Trish and Bobby (and Max) for the privilege of your company and the opportunity to think and to write in your sacred space; Dr. Stephanie Andel for teaching me about grace, voice, and the importance of standing up for what you believe in; and Carissa and Grant for the refreshing reminder that *play is the way*.

To the Dalí Museum family for teaching me about artistry and the importance of ensuring that artistic expression remains a creative cornerstone of our educational practices—and to its executive director, Dr. Hank Hine, for believing in me and sharing a belief that an art museum is an unsuspecting yet ideal location for a creativity and innovation services laboratory.

Family, friends, colleagues, and mentors. Students. Scientists. Artists. Builders. Hustlers. Innovators. Creative misfits of atypical types, and for all who believe in the depths of their being that we can be better humans with imagination and effort: my heart and this book to you.

About the Authors

Gerard J. Puccio is department chair and professor at the International Center for Studies in Creativity, Buffalo State. Gerard has written more than 60 articles, chapters, and books. His most recent book, *The Innovative Team*, coauthored with Chris Grivas, is a fable about a team that turns around a dysfunctional situation through the use of proven creative-thinking tools. In 2011 he and his colleagues, Marie Mance and Mary Murdock, published the second edition of their widely adopted book *Creative Leadership: Skills That Drive Change*.

Gerard is an accomplished speaker and consultant; he has worked with major corporations and universities. Some of his recent clients include the BBC, the Smithsonian Institute, BNP Paribas, Rubbermaid, and Coca-Cola. In 2013 Dr. Puccio was selected by the Teaching Company as one of America's Great Lecturers and as such was invited to design and deliver a course composed of 24 video sessions. This "Great Course," titled *The Creative Thinker's Toolkit*, was released in January 2014.

Among other responsibilities, Gerard serves as a distinguished visiting scholar at Sheridan College, Oakville, Canada, and is a member of the selection committee for the Toy Hall of Fame at the National Museum of Play.

John F. Cabra is an associate professor at the State University of New York College at Buffalo's International Center for Studies in Creativity where as part of a team he focuses on teaching, assessing, and researching the science of creativity. John specializes in facilitating and accelerating scientific and interdisciplinary innovation as part of his work through Knowinnovation. John has written journal articles, book chapters, and books in the areas of business, technology, engineering, and creativity.

In recognition for his work, he was awarded the President's Award for Excellence in Teaching, the State University of New York Chancellor's Award for Excellence in Teaching, and grants from the National Science Foundation and the State University of New York. John is also a Fulbright Scholar. He served his Fulbright at the Universidad Autónoma de Bucaramanga, Colombia.

Some organizations that have benefited from John's training and organizational development expertise include IBM, Pfizer, Kraft Foods, Coca-Cola, British Home Office, National Science Foundation, NASA, Drexel University, Penn State University, Purdue University, and the Ohio State University.

Dr. Cabra held internal consulting positions for American Airlines in the fields of training and development, employee relations, and organizational development. Before joining American Airlines, he was a training and organizational development specialist for Fisher-Price.

Nathan Schwagler is a founding codirector of the Dalí Museum Innovation Labs, where he serves as lead program designer and executive facilitator. Before joining the museum, Nathan served as the nation's first business school "Creative in Residence" at the University of South Florida, St. Petersburg, where he designed and delivered courses on creativity and innovation and new venture creation. His students were back-to-back-to-back national champions in the Collegiate Entrepreneurs' Organizations' business simulation competition, and his three-member startup academic department was recognized as the top Emerging Entrepreneurship Education Program across the entire United States by the United States Association for Small Business and Entrepreneurship (USASBE) in 2013.

As a consultant, Nathan has supported more than 150 organizations, including Abbott Labs, Transamerica Insurance, DuPont Chemical, Novartis, the Miller/Coors Brewing Co., the Converse Shoe Co. (NIKE), the Tampa Bay Rays, the Home Shopping Network, Bloomin' Brands, Raymond James Financial, and thousands of innovators as they've deployed their innovation capabilities to drive business outcomes.

Nathan holds a BA in psychology and a master of science degree in creativity from SUNY–Buffalo State and a master of science degree in entrepreneurship from the University of South Florida. He is a published author of peer-reviewed and popular press articles.

Knowing

Creativity Knowledge to
Support a 21st-Century Innovator

CHAPTER 1

Innovation Wired
You Evolved to Create

Learning Goals

After reading this chapter, you will be able to do the following:

- Use a scientifically based argument to defend the view that all humans are creative
- Explain the lessons that can be extracted from evolution and how these lessons translate into strategies for innovators and entrepreneurs
- Contrast two fundamentally different forms of creativity: eminent creativity and everyday creativity
- Appraise the degree to which you actively work to enhance your innate creativity through practice, passion, and play
- Formulate a plan for improving your creative thinking by using journaling and/or in-and-out note taking on a regular basis

Knowing—You Were Born to Be Creative

Creativity Lessons From Evolution

The question is not whether you are creative. *You are*! The better question is, am I living up to my creative potential? And, assuming there is always room for growth, a natural follow-up question is, in what ways might I be able to enhance my creativity? This opening chapter uses information extracted from science, biology, and anthropology to demonstrate that all humans with normally functioning brains are endowed with creative thinking and therefore possess the ability to create. Our species alone has the imagination and the dexterity to make complex tools and to produce new technology. Creative thinking is the competitive advantage of our species; thus, through evolution this competitive advantage has been selected for and developed through the millennia.[1] You were born creative, and we contend that you can enhance your success as an innovator and entrepreneur if you tap into your innate creativity. To that end, we use lessons from evolution to present the first set of tips you can follow to extend the natural creative talent you already possess.

Let's be honest about our species. When you compare humans to other animals with whom we share planet Earth, it is plain to see that humans are not the fastest, strongest, or biggest. Humans cannot fly away from danger nor hide underwater (at least not for very long). Even though the human body is not particularly well insulated from cold temperatures or designed to efficiently cool down in blistering heat, our species has found a way to expand around the globe and to inhabit a wide range of climatic conditions. How is this possible? To what quality can we attribute such adaptability and flexibility? If it is not strength and speed, nor other forms of physical prowess, could it be the size of our brains? It is not size alone, however, for humans cannot claim to have the largest brains; the prize for size belongs to elephants and some whales. What is unique about the human brain is its rare and valuable cognitive ability—creative thinking. Humans may not be fast, strong, or big, but humans can employ imagination in a way that leads to mental and behavioral flexibility that, through experimentation and evaluation, leads to novel solutions.[2]

It is likely that the mental ability to generate creative solutions was present in its nascent state in prehumans and then developed in ever-expansive ways from early humans through to the creative minds now found in modern humans. Although human evolution did not advance along a straight line, with competing branches often existing at the same time, evolutionary psychologists have concluded that developments in the size and structure of the human brain over time led to corresponding increases in the complexity of products generated by the evolving *Homo* species.[3]

In 1974 an unusually complete skeleton of a species that served as a forerunner to humans was found in Tanzania, Africa. The skeleton, nicknamed "Lucy," had been preserved in sediment for more than 3.6 million years. Lucy and others from her species, called *Australopithecus afarensis*, were about the size of chimpanzees and walked upright. These diminutive creatures survived for about 700,000 years, from about 3.6 million years ago to about 2.9 million years ago, an impressive longevity for an animal so small and fragile. Imagine the frightening conditions this prehuman species must have faced, an easy meal for any number of four-legged animals and birds of prey. It is likely that the mental conditions that eventually blossomed into the highly functioning creative brains humans enjoy today were beginning to form in Lucy's mind. According to science writer Douglas Palmer, Lucy and her tribe lacked sharp teeth, claws, and speed; however, they made up for these physical deficiencies with cooperation, communication, and creative intelligence—exemplified by the use of sticks and stones as weapons.[4]

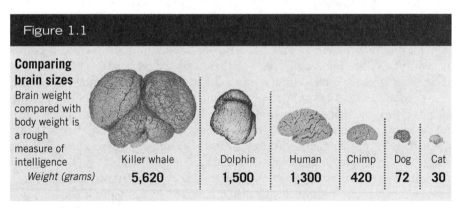

Figure 1.1

Comparing brain sizes
Brain weight compared with body weight is a rough measure of intelligence

	Killer whale	Dolphin	Human	Chimp	Dog	Cat
Weight (grams)	5,620	1,500	1,300	420	72	30

Source: Bellville/MCT/Newscom

There are animals today that use objects found in nature as tools. Sea otters, for instance, use rocks to crack open crabs, mussels, and oysters. Chimpanzees strip the leaves off small branches to fish for termites and ants. Early humans carried out similar forms of practical problem solving that eventually led to what anthropologists refer to as the creative explosion in human civilization about 50,000 years ago. At this critical breakpoint, humans moved from applying imagination to solving practical problems, like finding food to eat, to applying imagination in all sorts of interesting ways, such as burial rituals and art.

Let's look at some examples of the tools created through the imaginations of the earliest human species. The first tool made by humans is called the flaked tool (approximately 2.6 million years ago). With a brain capacity of about 50% of modern humans', the *Homo habilis* broke fine-grained rocks into sharp-edged flakes to split open fruit and nuts. The process of manufacturing this tool—and we do mean manufacturing, in that these early humans had to first locate the materials and then fashion these tools from them—required a degree of higher-level thinking. The flaked tool lasted about 1 million years, then like all creative ideas, it was surpassed by a new and improved idea—the hand ax.

Homo ergaster, with a brain 75% the size of that of modern humans, is credited with the development of a symmetrically shaped tool that was easier to hold while striking objects (approximately 1.76 million years ago). The pear-shaped design had a sharp point and edges on one side and a blunt end, held in the palm of the hand, on the other. Some experts argue that this more complicated, all-purpose tool is evidence of increasingly more complex mental functions in humans. Geneticist Morriss-Kay, for example, suggests that the multistep manufacturing process associated with the hand ax illustrates the emergence of mental operations unique to the human species, such as being able to see "in the mind's eye."[5]

The life cycle of the hand ax endured over 1 million years. Although we are endowed with great imagination, it may be difficult to imagine any product created today that will still be in use in half the life cycle of the hand ax, that is, 500,000 years from now. In today's world, manufactured products go through fundamental redesign every 5 to 10 years, whereas technologically based products experience significant redesign every 3 to 6 months.[6] How long do you think it will be before you consider that phone in your pocket so outmoded that an upgrade becomes necessary? Contrasting the life cycle of these early creative products to those of today highlights the increase in the pace of change as driven by human creativity.

With each successive human species came more sophisticated tools. And with *Homo sapiens*, the modern human being, the expanding use of imagination eventually led to a tipping point referred to as the creative explosion, that is, a dramatic increase in the complexity and diversity of human artifacts dating back to about 50,000 years ago. In a relatively short span of time, 10,000 to 20,000 years, the human imagination began to produce art (e.g., cave paintings and figurines), sew clothing, create musical instruments, construct purpose-built shelters, and develop elaborate social rituals such as those associated with burial.

Given that the brain reached its present volume with the emergence of *Homo sapiens* roughly 200,000 years ago, it might occur to you that the creative explosion lagged far behind the emergence of the modern human—a gap of more than 100,000 years. Why was there such a lag between the appearance of the fully modern human and the diverse application of creativity? Following are some insightful explanations of human evolution that connect to our contemporary understanding of creativity and underscore, we believe, how humans have been wired to be creative.

Development of the Fully Creative Brain: Use Your Whole Brain

Some psychologists, scholars, and archeologists believe that whereas the thinking skills associated with creativity were present in early *Homo sapiens*, these skills continued to be refined as the modern human evolved. It took time for modern humans to learn to direct their thinking. Humans are self-aware and can think about their own thinking. For the creative process, it is especially important that humans manage to balance and move back and forth between two basic forms of thinking—divergent and convergent thinking.[7] Divergent thinking is an exploratory form of thinking, looking for possibilities, identifying in our mind's eye what might be, generating novel responses, and making associations. For example, the Dalí sketch included in this chapter reflects this artist's ability to see in his mind's eye a *strange* new possibility. Though drawn in 1936 this sketch looks a lot like augmented-reality goggles used by today's gamers. Convergent thinking is testing, evaluating, refining possibilities, and exploring ways to make our novel ideas valuable. To create, humans need to be able to engage in both forms of thinking and to direct their thinking so they apply these skills effectively. Cognitive scientist Liane Gabora argues it is exactly this process of switching between these two forms of thought that makes up the fundamental approach used by successful creative people today:

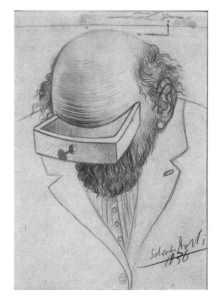

Salvador Dalí, *Freudian Portrait of a Bureaucrat*, 1936 pencil on paper, image: 10 5/8 in × 7 3/4 in.

© Salvador Dalí, Fundació Gala-Salvador Dalí, Artists Rights Society (ARS), New York 2017

© Salvador Dalí Museum, Inc.

> When tackling a problem, they first let their minds wander, allowing one memory or thought to spontaneously conjure up another. This free association encourages analogies and gives rise to thoughts that break out of the box. Then, as these individuals settle on a vague idea for a solution, they switch to a more analytic mode of thought.[8]

Another significant shift in thinking believed to have contributed to the creative explosion is an ability called cognitive fluidity.[9] It has been argued that before 50,000 years ago human thinking tended to be domain specific; that is, our thoughts were isolated to specific areas of knowledge—silos, if you will—that did not interact with each other. For example, Steven Mithen, a professor of archeology, describes three fundamental domains or areas of intelligence that were mastered by *Homo sapiens* and likely Neanderthals as well.[10] These were social intelligence, natural intelligence, and technical intelligence. Domain-specific thinking is a form of vertical thinking in which a person builds up knowledge in isolated areas. By contrast, cognitive fluidity is a form of flexible thinking in which a person is able to develop new insights and ideas by cross-fertilizing thoughts from different domains.

This ability to connect ideas across areas of knowledge is crucial to the creative process and helps to drive innovation. The way termites build their mounds, which are the tallest structures on Earth (when comparing the builders' size to the size of the building), inspired an African architect who built highly efficient energy buildings. Ships' propellers provided the solution for powering heavier-than-air flying machines. Facebook was inspired, in part, by the idea of a collegiate yearbook. Without cognitive fluidity, our creative thinking, problem-solving, and innovation efforts would be severely limited. Steve Jobs seemed to be abundantly aware of how the ability to cross-fertilize thoughts contributes to innovative success. As he observed, "I think part of what made the Macintosh great was that the people working on it were musicians and poets and artists and zoologists and historians who also happened to be the best computer scientists in the world."[11]

It took time for the human brain to develop the capacities to effectively engage in divergent thinking, convergent thinking, and cognitive fluidity. The good news is that, thanks to your ancestors, you are endowed with these same abilities, and through this book you will learn to take advantage of these innate thinking skills.

Emergence of Pretend Play: Be Childlike

Some scholars argue that cognitive abilities alone were not sufficient to cause the widespread application of our creative potential. It has been suggested that humans also had to develop a creative attitude to maximize the ever-increasing horsepower of their brains. Let's look at an analogy: Two drivers may have equally powerful engines in their cars, but the one who has the willingness to explore the full power of that engine is likely to win in a head-to-head race. By contrast, the risk-averse driver is likely to be cautious, thereby underusing the full horsepower at his or her disposal.

In a similar way, our brains need an emotional partner that does not constrain creative thinking. Philosopher Peter Carruthers eloquently argues that this creative attitude comes easily to us as children.[12] Children suspend their judgment, thus allowing their imaginations to roam unfettered. This ability to remain emotionally open, not to prematurely eliminate a novel idea, is crucial to divergent thinking, that is, the production of novel options and ideas. Without the emotional ability to remain open, to suspend our judgment temporarily, our thinking would not venture into new areas. Carruthers suggests the kind of pretend play humans engage in as children is crucial for adult creativity. After the emergence of *Homo sapiens*, and before the creative explosion, it is believed that our modern ancestors needed to hone their ability to engage in pretend play. It was the attitude of playful thinking that unshackled the human capacity for divergent thinking; judgment limits possibilities, whereas an attitude of suspended judgment promotes unlimited possibilities. As Carruthers states, "The cognitive prerequisites for pretence were in place at least at the advent of language, I suggest; but actually *engaging* in frequent pretend play in childhood served to practice and enhance our imaginative abilities."[13] As with our ancestors, this has implications for both your own creativity and how you might best position yourself as a catalyst for innovation and entrepreneurial endeavors. To fully leverage your creative-thinking skills, you need the right attitude—a willingness to suspend your judgment and engage in pretense—and you need to practice this attitude regularly. Without it, your imagination will be constrained, limiting the number and range of possibilities for innovative ideas and solutions.

Sexual Selection Favored Creative Partners: The Drummer Effect

There is an urban legend that musicians and other creative types find it easier to attract mates. Perhaps there is some truth to this belief, in that scholars have suggested that over time creativity and creative problem solving were qualities that rendered one a more appealing mate.[14] And one recent study has provided evidence for this claim.[15] Analysis of a questionnaire completed by more than 400 adults in England revealed a strong relationship between creative activity and success in mating. Specifically, those research participants who reported greater levels of creative productivity in poetry or art also reported having had greater numbers of intimate partners.

What might account for the relationship between creativity and sexual attraction? First, it's conceivable that individuals who were more creative and more effective at creatively solving problems were more likely to survive and thus reproduce. In this way creative tendencies were passed along, compounding with each successive generation. Second, it has been argued that individuals looking for mates will prefer effective problem solvers, who are likely to ensure a more secure future. As Carruthers suggests, the selection of more creative partners results from the "human capacity to detect the casual connection between creative thinking, on the one hand, and problem-solving success, on the other."[16] So there seems to be some support for the belief that creativity does intersect with sexual selection, and if this is the case, then it could be reasoned that over time creativity and creative problem solving are traits that have been passed down from one generation to the next—once again supporting the point that creativity is innate.

Numerous reports on workplace skills include creativity and innovation as essential for professional success. Like our early ancestors who recognized that a good mate is one who can problem-solve, today's organizations recognize that their survival depends on attracting employees who are creative thinkers. Therefore, honing your creative problem-solving skills can make you a more attractive match for organizations in a hypercompetitive world.

This is not a lesson in evolution; if it were, we would be guilty of treating the subject too lightly. Rather, our goal was to demonstrate that the story of human evolution is a story of creativity and that within this story, a major plot line has been creativity's contribution to the survival of the human species. Furthermore, our creativity doesn't just help us to survive but also to thrive. Unlike any other species on the planet, humans can imagine and create a diverse range of products, from tangible objects like technological products that let us leave Earth and explore our galaxy to intangible products like culture, music, art, laws, and more.

Let us be very clear: We suggest that our creativity was initially designed to enable the relatively weak human species to survive. Once the ability to imagine novel solutions was well entrenched in our practical problem-solving abilities, humans expanded the application of imagination in other interesting ways. As Morriss-Kay suggests, "Without these survival-enhancing functional origins, it is unlikely that we would have the neural equipment to create art."[17] This line of thinking fits well with Charles Darwin's view on the modes of transition in organs; that is, an organ designed for one purpose can evolve toward other functions. This may be exactly what has happened to the human brain and to imagination. Initially the function of the brain was to apply creative thinking to solve the practical problems related to survival, that is, finding food to eat and avoiding becoming food for others. Then through the evolution of this organ, the human brain, the power of imagination expanded and broadened beyond immediate problems of survival and has been employed in a way that has literally shaped the world we live in today.

Like no other species, for better and for worse, humans have created the very conditions within which we live. It's sort of circular. For most of human history, imagination allowed humans to adapt to the environment. More recently, the expanded application of imagination has resulted in changing the very conditions of our environment. Consequently, humans must apply their creative thinking in both their personal and professional lives to respond more and more quickly to the changing conditions brought about by their own creativity. The pace of change that humans must adapt to is unlikely to slow down. The more humans create, the more they are required to use their creativity to adapt.

Thought Starter
Innate Creativity

Creativity is primal. It is in all of us. As part of the human race, you came into this world with both the mental and emotional prerequisites to be creative. Like the inexplicable primal response to the beat of a drum or the innate sensation of danger when standing on the edge of a precipice, all humans have been wired through evolution to create. Whereas our understanding of human evolution continues to develop with new scientific discoveries, we feel certain that humans have survived for more than 2.5 million years because of our unique ability to creatively solve problems. Moreover, we believe, as do other educators and business leaders, that due to the rapidly changing conditions in the 21st century, which are being driven by human creativity, everyone will need to call on this primal skill to continue to survive and thrive.

Before we leave the topic of evolution, there are other lessons important to creativity that can be drawn from Charles Darwin's teachings.[18] The following are a few we wish to highlight. We start with the most fundamental of concepts and then elaborate with two specific insights that the study of evolution gives us into creativity.

Change Is Natural: The Only Way to Stop Changing Is to Become Extinct

Evolution teaches us that change is constant and not just in our natural world. Everything around us, including ourselves, is in a constant state of flux. Society, the economy, technology, and knowledge are perpetually changing. Because of this universal principle, organizations and individuals that do not actively evolve will watch their success erode and eventually become extinct. Recent examples of organizations that did not continue to evolve include Blockbuster, the brick-and-mortar video rental giant that was too late in joining the online movement, and Kodak, the leader in film photography that actually created the first digital camera in the 1970s but was late transitioning over to this new technology. And, because change is ongoing, if such innovative organizations as Redbox and Nikon do not continue to evolve, you can bet they too will slowly evaporate. Ideas, like species, are always evolving, with new ideas replacing old ideas. In this way, creativity has a destructive quality to it. As new and better ideas emerge, they displace old ideas. For individuals to remain current and to continuously add value to their organizations, they too must be ever vigilant in facilitating their own evolution. In an era of unprecedented change, those who stop evolving may not literally become extinct, but they will quickly become irrelevant.

Novel Variation Is the Stuff of Life: Without Novelty, There Is No Growth

Evolution is the balance between two forces, the generation of novelty and the selective retention of those alternatives that are most adaptable to the environment. Both are necessary, but there is an implied and very important sequence to evolution. The first ingredient in evolution is the production of novel variations, the new alternatives without which there would be no change, at least not creative change. Darwin highlighted the important impact of novelty:

> Consequently, in the course of many thousand generations, the most distinct varieties of any one species of grass would have the best chance of succeeding and of increasing in numbers, and of supplanting the less distinct varieties; and varieties, when rendered very distinct from each other, take the rank of species.[19]

In the previous quote, replace the word *grass* with the word *ideas*, and you will easily recognize how novelty ushers in entire new industries or completely new trends. To add value to an existing organization, you need to sow the seeds of ideas.

For it is ideas, those that solve problems and those that create new opportunities, that sustain an organization. And for those interested in entrepreneurship, it is again novel ideas that help to distinguish new start-ups, which lead to new industries and markets.

Let's be a little less lofty and consider novelty and its role in an individual's life—your life. Think about the degree to which you explore new ideas and experiences. Novelty is important in our lives for at least two reasons. First, by continuously experimenting with novel ideas, individuals discover and grow. Second, novel ideas and experiences can serve as stimulants for breakthrough ideas. Time and time again, we hear stories of people developing creative ideas because of a connection stimulated by exposure to a novel experience. So if you want to be sure to stimulate ongoing growth and new thinking, make it a regular habit to try new things and to learn about new topics. We hasten to add that there are important physiological benefits to seeking out novel ideas and experiences. Current research shows that those who remain actively curious live longer, healthier, and more fulfilling lives.[20]

Everything Is a Prototype: No Idea, Product, or Person Is Ever Complete and Perfect

One of the hard lessons given to us by evolution is the fact that every idea and product is always under development; it is never complete. Just as past species gave rise to subsequent species, ideas and products serve as bridges to future ideas. Darwin captured this point well when he stated, "Almost every part of every organic being is so beautifully related to its complex conditions of life that it seems as improbable that any part should have been produced perfect, as that a complex machine should have been invented by man in a perfect state."[21] This is a real risk for those organizations that lead their respective markets, because it can be difficult not to fall overly in love with your product line, thereby failing to see what might come next. This is why it is sometimes easier for organizations that are not market leaders to be innovative, because with distance they can sometimes more easily see ways to improve or leapfrog their competitors' products and services. This is equally applicable to entrepreneurs, who are less apt to be wedded to past ideas. We say this is a hard lesson because the recognition that everything is a prototype suggests that organizations can never really stop creating. The research is clear: Those companies that have stood the test of time are always experimenting and exploring, pursuing what might be thought of as continuous creativity.[22] Great companies reinvent themselves. And in the 21st century, when it is expected that people will change jobs up to 11 times before retirement, people will need to reinvent themselves as well.[23]

Everyday Creativity

In the previous section we made the case that because of human evolution you have been gifted with cognitive and emotional skills that make you creative. Still, some of you may doubt this. As professionals in the field of creativity, the three authors of this book often have people tell us they are not creative. Conversations when meeting someone new usually go like this: "Hi, nice to meet you," they begin. This is almost always followed up by, "So what do you do for a living?" A typical response from any of the three of us is, "I teach, train, and study creativity." Our unusual occupation sometimes stuns the unsuspecting stranger, generally followed by the comment, "Oh, I'm not creative." Now, we just covered the fact that everyone with a normally functioning brain is wired to be creative, so in both theory and practice it is impossible for anyone to "not be creative" whatsoever. This is akin to saying, "I've never used my imagination or solved a problem in an interesting way in my entire life," which is highly unlikely.

We suspect that there are two reasons for the "I'm not creative" response. The first is that some people are under the false impression that creativity is strictly about excelling in some artistic way, for instance, writing poetry and playing music. This is a narrow view, for the use of imagination to produce novel solutions and new knowledge is applicable to any field of endeavor.

The second reason we believe people so quickly judge themselves as not being creative is the comparison of themselves to great creators like Pablo Picasso, Dean Kamen, Ernest Hemingway, Bill Gates, Leonardo da Vinci, J. K. Rowling, Wolfgang Amadeus Mozart, Steve Jobs, Kid Cudi, Maya Angelou, and Thomas Edison, to name a few. In our culture we raise great creators to legendary status, and therefore it would be presumptuous for someone to put himself or herself in the same class as these individuals. The reflexive "I'm not creative" response denies our humanity, and it ignores a very important kind of creativity called everyday creativity.[24]

In the field of creativity studies, a distinction is made between eminent creativity and everyday creativity, sometimes referred to as "big C" creativity and "little c" creativity, respectively. Big C creativity refers to those who become socially recognized for their creative products and performance. Little c creativity refers to creative acts that occur on a daily basis, for example, making a good meal, solving a problem at work, or planning a party. This is the kind of creativity that all humans display on a regular basis and the type of creativity that clearly demonstrates that all humans have been born with the capacity to be creative.

The main difference between big C and little c creativity is the scope of impact. That is, big C creativity is appreciated by, and impacts, a large number of people, whereas little c creativity is useful to the individual or to those most closely associated with the individual. Despite popular beliefs, eminent creators are not born with some special talent that makes being creative any easier than it is for the rest of us.

Thought Starter
Little c creativity

But wait, you say, what about people like Mozart, the boy genius who began composing music at age 5 and publicly performing on the violin and piano at age 8? When he was 17, he was appointed as a court musician in Salzburg and went on to produce more than 600 compositions before his premature death at age 35. Wasn't Wolfgang Amadeus Mozart special? Didn't he come into the world as a gifted creative genius? Right? Wrong! Mozart may have had some advantages, but it's not because he was gifted with innate creative genius from conception. At least two factors contributed to his big C creativity. First, he had a domineering father who literally wrote the book on violin instruction. In fact, Leopold Mozart's book was published the year Wolfgang was born.[25] Leopold started little Wolfgang on an intensive training program at the age of 3. Leopold also had a heavy hand in Wolfgang's early compositions, editing and revising these works. Second, Wolfgang worked hard at being creative. Even though Mozart is held up as a child prodigy, the reality is that he worked very hard, practicing for hours on end and tirelessly revising his musical compositions. His incredible work ethic is visible in the large body of compositions he generated in a short career. Mozart did not simply produce a small number of works; instead, he was prolific, and this approach paid off when his first masterpiece came at the age of 21. This was about 40% of the way into his lifetime body of work, or about 16 years after it is said that he began writing music. Instead of being a child prodigy, perhaps Mozart really was a late bloomer, in that Howard Gardner's research on eminently creative individuals shows that it takes about 10 years of hard work to yield a first big C creative product.[26] What is unusual about Mozart is that he had a much earlier start than the rest of us.

From the Mozart example, and from studying other great creators, we can learn some valuable lessons about how to maximize the creative potential we all possess. To make it easy to remember, we call this the 3 Ps of creativity.

Practice

Evolution occurs naturally over time, with the chance emergence of novel variation and the retention of those variations that are most adaptable. However, evolution can be sped up and directed. It's called breeding. Humans can, and do, intercede and manipulate evolution. For example, that's why we have such a great variety of dogs, apples, and so many other domesticated animals and plants. As with evolution, humans can move their creativity from the natural creativity that they brought into the world to more deliberate creativity. This is perhaps the most important difference between eminent creators and everyday creators: Eminent creators deliberately work on their creativity.

Let's take Benjamin Franklin as an example. He was a founding father, businessman, and inventor, another person who must have been destined by birth to be a creative genius, right? Here's a small example of how he was deliberately creative. To perfect his writing skills, Franklin would study his favorite articles in a publication called the *Spectator*. Days later he would reconstruct the article in his own words. He would then compare his version to the original article, making corrections as necessary. Franklin didn't stop there; next he would translate these articles into rhyme and then back into essay form. This dedication to perfecting one's creative skills is not unusual and is found in most, if not all, great creators. They commit to their creative process and work hard at applying their creative talents. And guess what? The creative-thinking skills they possess and the creative process they follow can be used on an everyday basis. Indeed, the skills taught in this book are the very same types of skills used by great creators.

Passion

Great creators are passionate about their work. This passion fuels their creativity and enables them to persist, to continuously practice their skills and refine their work. Generally they are driven by intrinsic rather than extrinsic rewards. That means they pursue an idea, problem, or performance for its own sake, for the joy and stimulation that come from complete immersion in the creative process. It's not that extrinsic rewards, such as monetary gain and fame, are unimportant, but these are not the primary driving forces of their creativity. In fact, research shows that when people focus on extrinsic rewards, it distracts them and undermines their creativity.[27] Want to maximize your creativity? Focus on those areas in life about which you are most passionate.

Play

The young of all mammals engage in the kind of play that develops skills necessary to survive.[28] The offspring of cats play by stalking, pouncing, and wrestling. As we noted earlier, human offspring play by engaging in pretense. Pretend play requires an ability to suspend one's judgment, to entertain the belief that all things are possible. This ability to suspend one's judgment plays a crucial role in the creative process of great creators, and for all of us. Much learning and discovery comes through play. It allows us to experiment without pressure, to try something new.

In this chapter we have tried to lay down some important foundational concepts and principles for this book. First and foremost is the assertion that all humans with normally functioning brains have the cognitive and emotional prerequisites to be creative. Creativity comes naturally to all of us, or at least when we were young it did. Whereas some of us are able to retain our natural creativity, for many of us it has eroded over time (more on how our creativity is lost in the next chapter).

The good news is that all of us can build on our natural creativity. It is possible to leverage the natural, hard-wired, deep-seated aspects of creativity that Mother Nature bestowed on us. In this respect, creativity is just like breathing. All humans breathe, no thinking necessary—it's natural. There are times, though, when we want to take this natural activity and be more deliberate about our breath, such as when playing a musical instrument, singing, running, or meditating. Just as we can learn strategies and practice ways to be more deliberate about breathing, we can improve on our natural creativity by learning and practicing deliberate creativity methods. In this way, it is possible to move our creativity from chance to on demand. Sometimes it's not convenient to wait for lighting to strike; sometimes you need to be like Benjamin Franklin and go out and catch it (as he did with lightning and his own creativity). In the next section you will learn a deliberate creativity tool that can assist you in moving from creativity by chance to creativity on demand.

Reflect back on the concepts of big C and little c creativity. In your own words, define big C and little c. Generally, it is easy to think of examples of products and people that demonstrate big C, for example, Mark Zuckerberg, Elon Musk, Larry Page, and Oprah Winfrey, to name a few. Oftentimes, however, we overlook the numerous instances of little c in our daily lives. Take some time to reflect on how you and others demonstrate acts of little c creativity on an everyday basis. See how many examples you can capture, again, both your own and others'. What insights does this provide you in terms of your own creativity? Given the examples you identified, in what ways does this help you to develop a deeper appreciation for creativity? Big C and little c are not necessarily a dichotomy; how might practicing creativity on little c acts help to enhance big C?

Doing—Tuning in to the Creativity Already Inside of You

Idea Journal and In-and-Out Note Taking

The first tool we wish to introduce is straightforward and effective and starts by having you simply tune into the creativity already happening inside of you. Many great creators keep track of their thinking through note taking, journals, and sketchbooks. Da Vinci's notebooks are famous for their innovative ideas. Whereas da Vinci's journals are held in great esteem, the award for most prolific journal writer might go to Picasso, who generated 175 notebooks of his draft ideas from 1894 to 1967. Perhaps the prize for the most unusual notebook goes to Andy McCluskey, who used his bedroom wall to capture all sorts of ideas, such as song lyrics, song titles, and poetry. McCluskey, along with Paul Humphreys, founded one of the most successful British new wave bands of all time, Orchestral Manoeuvres in the Dark (OMD). OMD has sold more than 40 million records, and one of their best-known hits is "If You Leave," written for the movie *Pretty in Pink*. Despite his mother's disapproval, the wall in McCluskey's bedroom launched this songwriter's career.

Capturing your ideas via written or electronic journal, in words and visuals, creates three immediate advantages. First, by capturing your ideas you relieve your memory from having to hold onto the idea, thus freeing the brain to refine and build on the concept or to generate new insights. Second, capturing your ideas allows you to cross-fertilize your thinking. Once captured, it becomes easier to cross-reference, double-check insights, and to connect two or more ideas into even bigger breakthroughs. Finally, by capturing the insight you stand a better chance of retaining it for future use. Ever have a sudden insight, perhaps in the middle of the night or during some routine activity, and then later can't remember that big idea? Sure, most of us have had this "aha" moment. You might believe the insight is so profound that it will never be forgotten, so you don't stop to capture it. Alas, the brain moves on, and what was a brilliant insight soon becomes an irretrievable memory. Why take that chance? Instead, use a laptop, pocket notebook, the memo function in your phone, or some other tool to immediately capture the idea. Mimic da Vinci and Picasso by being systematic about capturing your ideas. Create different electronic files, notebooks, or sketchpads for different categories of ideas and projects.

Journaling doesn't need to wait for a precise time or a fixed schedule. Our minds wander naturally. Have you ever noticed in a classroom or meeting or while reading that other ideas and thoughts besides the content under examination or discussion come to mind? We suggest that you can take advantage of the fact that your mind is always working. A tool we recommend is called in-and-out note taking. This tool allows you to tune in to the creativity that is naturally occurring in your mind. With in-and-out note taking you create space wherever you are taking notes to capture two types of notes, that is, your "in" thoughts and your "out" thoughts. Your in thoughts are the specific details you want to remember in terms of the content being presented in the meeting, classroom, or book. Out thoughts refer to the thoughts and ideas that come to you while your mind is wandering. Sometimes these thoughts are a simple recollection of something you need to do, but often they are creative ideas and possibilities that are sparked by the content being presented to you. A standard approach for capturing in and out thoughts is to divide a sheet of paper, actual or electronic, into two columns. One column is labeled "In Thoughts," and the other is labeled "Out Thoughts." Notes are then placed in the appropriate column. Find a system to organize your in thoughts, and commit to reviewing your out thoughts and following up on those that pose the greatest value for you. As a reminder, we have placed thought starters throughout this book to encourage you to engage in "out" thinking. The thought bubbles should serve as cues for you to tune into your own creative thinking and to challenge yourself to see what associations you might make with the main concept featured in that particular thought bubble.

Thought Starter
In-and-Out
Thinking

Learning Activity
Practice Imaginary Play

Leonardo da Vinci used his journal as a tool to capture his imaginative thoughts. Begin a journal and make your first entry an exercise in imagination. Imagine that 5 years into the future you are the head of a thriving start-up. What does your start-up do? What is your role as CEO? Who works there? Where is it located? What does the office space look like? Whose lives might be made better as a result of your start-up? What trends does your start-up leverage? Envision the start-up of your dreams without editing or worrying about practicalities. Allow yourself to dream; practice visionary thinking and imaginary play by exploring the limitless possibilities. Start your entry and then add to it over time. How does your dream expand and change? What were the benefits of distilling your imaginative thoughts into a written and/or visual form?

Being—Making Reflection a Habit

In-and-out note taking allows you to take advantage of the fact that your mind naturally makes connections. By practicing this form of note taking, you are in a better position to take advantage of your own creativity and to further enhance your ability to make meaningful associations. When creative imagination is ignored, the ability slowly wanes with time; journaling and in-and-out note taking are like exercise for your creative brain.

Our minds are wired to be efficient. Neuroscience shows that humans develop well-worn pathways along which our thinking travels.[29] These well-established neural pathways act like superhighways, allowing our thoughts to travel fast. However, creative breakthroughs often happen when people allow their thoughts to travel along new pathways. In-and-out note taking and journaling help us to slow our thinking down, to recognize and nurture side journeys. When you drive fast, you tend not to notice what is around you; however, when you slow yourself down, such as when you walk or bike, you become much more aware of your surroundings. Through in-and-out note taking you encourage your mind to become accustomed to seeking connections by opening up to side trips, then through journaling you allow your mind to more deeply explore and elaborate on these new journeys. This is a powerful set of tools for both intrapreneurs and entrepreneurs.

As an old friend of ours liked to say, "Learning without application achieves the same end as ignorance." We therefore want to encourage you to apply in-and-out note taking and journaling. With this goal in mind, we close the Being section of this chapter with the following two activities.

Learning Activities
Use In-and-Out Note Taking

Commit to using in-and-out note taking for 3 weeks. If you are a student, use in-and-out note taking in all your classes. If you are employed, use in-and-out note taking in the meetings you attend. After all, in the United States alone approximately 11 million business meetings are held daily—think of all the creativity that is being lost![30] To do in-and-out note taking, create two columns on your computer or sheet of paper. You decide what width works best for you in terms of whether you wish to dedicate more space to the "in" or "out" thoughts. Use the In column to capture notes related to the content being presented. Then use the Out column to tune in to the natural side journeys your mind takes while you participate in class or the meeting. In this column record your ideas, new insights, possible actions, things you need to do, and other miscellaneous thoughts. After 3 weeks, look over these notes and make decisions as to whether there are ideas and thoughts you need to follow up on in your Out column. Going forward, consider ways you can incorporate this tool into other areas of your life. After practicing this tool describe how it was beneficial.

Begin an Idea Journal or Idea Log

Create a system to capture your ideas. And be sure, because ideas appear at random and unexpected times, that this idea-capturing system is portable so that you can have it with you always. You can use the memo function in your smartphone, carry index cards, use a small notepad, or create a file in your laptop or e-reader. You may need to try several methods before you strike on one that works best for you. As in the in-and-out note-taking activity, commit to capturing your ideas for at least 3 weeks. And don't just capture the ideas; commit to reviewing, organizing, and elaborating on these ideas at least once per week. Use this time to do at least two things. First, expand on the ideas you like best. Second, organize the ideas. If you have ideas that relate to a project you are working on, organize these ideas so that they are clustered together. Additionally, if you are using in-and-out note taking at the same time, review those notes to see what ideas might need to be transferred into your idea journal. Because our minds are always working, we encourage you to make the idea log, as well as in-and-out note taking, an ongoing habit. Then, after 3 weeks, ask yourself these questions: In what ways was it valuable to deliberately capture your ideas in an idea log or journal? What did you learn about your own creativity (strengths and weaknesses)?

Case Study
The StartupBus

Introduction

According to the influential British artist David Hockney, "People tend to forget that play is serious." After interviewing Elias Bizannes, it's apparent that he's not among the forgetters. In 2010, a pint-fueled Bizannes pitched an idea to some friends at a San Francisco pub: rent a bus and go on an epic journey to the popular Austin, Texas–based South by Southwest music festival (SXSW). A seemingly innocuous idea on the surface but one with an interesting catch: to ride on the bus means you are agreeing to conceive, build, and launch a start-up company along the way!

Elias went to bed that night, largely writing the idea off as an alcohol-inspired impracticality. His beer mates, on the other hand, liked the idea so much they went home and mocked up a website for the road trip. With the website published, several additional friends jumped on board for the adventure, and, suddenly, their playful ideation had gained momentum and was morphing into something larger!

Soon thereafter, a popular technology website, TechCrunch, scooped the plot and published an attention-getting blog post about Bizannes's SXSW bus plan.[31] With this newfound social pressure, Elias felt he was on the hook to really make the trip into something special. With just a few short weeks to pull everything together—and with the help of his talented co-conspirators—Elias and company successfully orchestrated the world's first StartupBus.

Equal parts entrepreneurial boot camp and multiday business competition, the StartupBus is

(Continued)

(Continued)

a playful yet high-stakes "hackathon-on-wheels" designed to stretch participants to their limits (and perhaps beyond). The mission, should each "buspreneur" choose to accept it: brainstorm business concepts with complete strangers, converge on the best ideas, form implementation teams, and then turn the most promising ideas into functioning businesses. In 72 hours. On a bus.

Since 2010, the StartupBus has blossomed into an active, global community of technology-driven change makers. In 2010, a single bus left from San Francisco. In 2011, six buses rolled from all corners of the United States. In 2012, 11 buses—including a bus originating from Mexico City, Mexico—competed. Since then, in addition to maintaining the U.S.-based operations, additional global StartupBus challenges have been executed in Europe (twice), Australia, and Africa, and in 2015, the first India-based competition was launched.

Because of its unique style, ability to attract top talent, and track record of successes, StartupBus has been able to obtain high-profile sponsors such as Microsoft, Elance, Rackspace Hosting, and MailChimp. In addition, the investor community has supported the competition; notable investors are Dave McClure (of 500 Startups) and the popular technology blogger Robert Scoble.

Results

Most start-ups created on "the Bus" don't actually translate into postbus success, but, as Elias and his team would come to learn, that's not actually the point of the trip. The "secret sauce" lies with the development of people; StartupBus participants make lifelong friends, and, perhaps even more importantly, meet future collaborators and cofounders. As global director Mitch Neff says, "We're here to build people, not companies." A prime example of this is the connection of two buspreneurs from 2011 who would exit the bus and go on to cofound a grocery delivery service: Instacart. Since its 2012 launch, Instacart has proven its business model and solved several key technological and logistical challenges that had thwarted previous attempts at third-party grocery delivery. As a result, investors have backed them to the tune of at least $275 million, at a current company valuation of more than $2 billion! *Forbes* magazine recently awarded them the top spot on their "America's Most Promising Company" list for 2015.[32]

To be successful in the StartupBus competition, teams must organically form themselves around an interesting problem they want to solve or an idea that catches attention and gets others excited. From there, they must work toward meeting developmental milestones such as the creation of social media assets, website mock-ups, and mobile and/or web-based application prototypes. They collect early adopter/user feedback and use that feedback to iterate and improve their product, and they create and refine a compelling investor pitch showcasing their prototype(s) and business model. It's a start-up on steroids.

According to Bizannes, the goal is to create a learning journey for buspreneurs that challenges them to overcome obstacles and to practice the art and science of entrepreneurship while staring directly into the face of adversity. Constraints include but are certainly not limited to a fast-moving bus (ever try to type, design, or code on a moving bus?), interpersonal conflicts (ever try to collaborate with a team of complete strangers with different backgrounds and skill sets?), spotty Internet connectivity, device charging issues, time pressure and sleep deprivation, and pervasive uncertainty at the hands of organizer curveballs![33]

The combination of stressors can quickly take their toll, and this is precisely when participants realize what they're made of and what they're capable of achieving. The StartupBus teaches riders that there will always be more to do and that prioritization and execution are key. In the midst of it all, if you can find a way to be successful while enjoying the mania and not taking yourself (or what's going on around you) too seriously, then you are winning (by growing).

Why on earth would people subject themselves to this? According to StartupBus alumnus and bus conductor Greg Ross-Munro,

> The bus shows people a different way that they can live their lives; people don't always realize that you can have fun at work and be surrounded by inspiring and talented people who are amazing at what they do. Buspreneurs come (and come back) because it's an opportunity to work with people who are as equally competent and high achieving as they are. The bus truly gives people a taste of what it really means to be on a high-functioning team; they cannot forget how that felt, and if they do it right, they'll be able to bring a little bit of that back home for their next project.

The experience can be addictive (as demonstrated by repeat riders and the connectivity between alumni). StartupBus alumni are highly active and engaged on social media platforms after the competition is over. A contributing factor to this "stickiness" of the StartupBus experience is the deliberate commitment to playfulness. For example, one of the authors has participated in the StartupBus challenge (twice) and recalls one year where participants unknowingly got off the bus at Rackspace corporate headquarters (a converted shopping mall) and were secretly greeted by hundreds of company employees hiding behind the front doors waiting for the buspreneurs to walk in. Upon entry the employees began hooting, hollering, clapping, and cheering as loud as possible, and they showered their guests with company-branded swag and support and encouragement that was greatly appreciated after three long and difficult days on the road. We felt like rock stars, if only for a moment.

Ultimately the experience is intended to give participants an accelerated, deep dive into the entrepreneurial process, and it's designed in such a way that risk aversion cannot be a successful strategy; the competition unfolds so that the only way out is to seriously *play* your way out.

Closing

Five years in, the StartupBus leadership team (consisting of a dedicated core plus a revolving network of alumni volunteers) has helped thousands of people around the world locate and tap into their inner entrepreneur and to get a taste of what the entrepreneurial lifestyle is like, while

(Continued)

(Continued)

simultaneously embedding them into a community of practitioners and a network of potential cofounders. Indeed, the riders return to their respective homes (you famously have to find your own way because the buses are only a one-way trip to keep costs down!), but riders never return in quite the same condition as when they'd left. Greek philosopher Plato suggests, "Life must be lived as play," and, after riding, we know the StartupBus community is on board.

Discussion Questions: Knowing

1. In the landscape of entrepreneurship education models, the StartupBus format is unique. What do you see as the advantages and disadvantages of their approach to teaching and learning? What about their unique model adds value to the learning process? Alternatively, what do you think might get in the way of learning?

2. How does the StartupBus help riders develop entrepreneurial skills? Specifically, how is this accomplished? What factors contribute to entrepreneurial skill development?

Application Questions: Doing

1. In your opinion, does the StartupBus embrace the notion of creative play? If so, identify and describe the ways in which it does so; if not, use your imagination to think up some alternative ways it could do a better job of weaving creative play into its entrepreneurial boot camp experience.

2. What role does creativity play in your life? When does it occur? What instigates it? Who else is involved? Would you rather there be more or less? Why?

Thinking Ahead: Being

1. Can you see yourself ever applying to ride the bus? Imagine you are interested in riding. What would you include on your application? How might you help the organizers determine that you'd be a good candidate?

2. Can you imagine yourself ever starting a company? If so, how do you see yourself developing the entrepreneurial skills necessary to take on the unique challenges of launching your own venture?

3. What stops creative play from unfolding more often in your work? If your goal was to increase creative play in your environment, how might you create the conditions for increased play so that it occurs more often?

2

How to Survive and Thrive in an Era of Innovation and Change

Knowing—The Forces for and Against Creative Thinking

Creativity Lessons From the Chicken

What can a chicken teach us about creativity? If metaphorical thinking is applied, then there is much that can be learned about creativity from a chicken. It has been demonstrated repeatedly throughout history how creative breakthroughs can be sparked through the use of metaphors and analogies. Let's look at an example. Before the middle of the 1400s, book publishing consisted of either individuals copying manuscripts by hand or the labor-intensive process of carving a single block of wood for each page. Johannes Gutenberg used analogical thinking, borrowing ideas from at least two technologies (i.e., coin making, which suggested separate metal letters, and the wine press, which suggested the pressing mechanism) to create the printing press.[1] Dalí was a master at making metaphorical links.

Applying our creative thinking like Gutenberg and Dalí, let's see what parallels might be created between the story of the chicken and creativity. We begin by examining your associations with a chicken. When you think of a chicken, what comes to mind? Immediate reactions are likely to revolve around four categories. Undoubtedly one such category of association is chicken as a meat product; this is no surprise, for in the early 1990s chicken surpassed beef as the most widely consumed meat in America. Some will think of the eggs produced by chickens. They can be scrambled, poached, boiled, and mixed into a great variety of recipes. The third category that might come to mind is the physical characteristics of this bird, that is, its size, color,

Learning Goals

After reading this chapter, you will be able to do the following:

- Describe how socialization and educational practices undermine creative thinking
- Explain the upsides and the downsides of conformity
- Define creativity and describe why creative thinking is included among the most important skills in today's workplace
- Assess your responses to activities and tasks associated with your comfort zone, learning zone, and panic zone with the goal of improving performance through deliberate practice
- Devise a more positive and open-minded response to a creative idea through the use of Yes-And thinking

sound, and even smell. Finally, some may associate chicken with the slang expressions associated with the word, such as a reference to someone who is cowardly.

Many may not realize that humans did not initially seek out chickens for culinary reasons.[2] Rather, the docile creature known to us today is believed to originally have been used for cockfighting, which some refer to as the oldest sport in the world. The Greeks, Romans, and many other cultures paid great homage to the fighting prowess of chickens. However, once the culinary benefits were discovered, chickens went through the process of domestication, yielding a docile ground bird with seriously limited flying capabilities. The following passage from Darwin underscores the physical and mental changes in the chicken brought about by its domestication.

> But this instinct [Darwin is referring to flight] retained by our chickens has become useless under domestication, for the mother-hen has almost lost by disuse the power of flight. Hence, we may conclude, that under domestication instincts have been acquired, and natural instincts have been lost, partly by habit, and partly by man selecting and accumulating during successive generations, peculiar mental habits and actions. . . . In some cases compulsory habit alone has sufficed to produce inherited mental changes.[3]

Darwin's observations can be used to extract from the chicken our first creativity lesson. In the first chapter we suggested that all humans are born to be creative, that our evolution has wired us to innovate and to be creative problem solvers. Unfortunately, what evolution has created society can undo. As Carruthers observed, all human offspring—children, that is—engage in pretend play.[4] However, your observations of most adults, perhaps yourself included, may indicate that somewhere along the line many people lost their instinctual ability to play. Thinking metaphorically, chickens no longer fly, and adult humans often find it difficult to engage in pretend play.

We do not offer only pure speculation—and a chicken metaphor—to make the case that creativity, especially pretend play and imaginative thought, atrophies with age. Extensive empirical evidence supports this view, though most people's own life experiences are likely to bear this out as well. Perhaps the most recent and most expansive study to examine changes in creativity over time was carried out by Kyun Hee Kim.[5] This study, published in 2008, examined changes in creative thinking over a 40-year period. Kim analyzed the creative-thinking abilities of nearly 300,000 students and adults. The student sample spanned all grade levels, from kindergarten through 12th grade. Using one of the most popular measures of creative thinking, the Torrance Tests of Creative Thinking (TTCT), data were collected and compared from 1968 to 2008.

Before looking at the results, let's briefly examine what the TTCT measures. As the name suggests, the TTCT measures creative-thinking abilities, specifically divergent-thinking skills. Divergent thinking is a form of thinking unique to humans. As we discussed in the previous chapter, through evolution humans have developed a capacity to defocus their minds in a manner that allows for a broad search for new alternatives and possibilities, to imagine concepts that do not exist yet.

The main skills measured by the TTCT are fluency, the ability to generate many responses to open-ended tasks; flexibility, the ability to generate different kinds of responses; originality, the ability to produce rare and novel responses; and elaboration, the ability to expand on one's responses. The TTCT has been demonstrated to be a good predictor of real-life creative achievement. High scorers on the TTCT are much more likely to become entrepreneurs, inventors, software developers, and authors. In fact, the TTCT is a much better predictor of adult creativity, and engagement in occupations that involve creative thinking, than the standard IQ test.[6]

Numerous research studies have investigated the positive benefits of divergent thinking. Through these studies we know that divergent thinking predicts a number of important achievements, among others leadership effectiveness,[7]

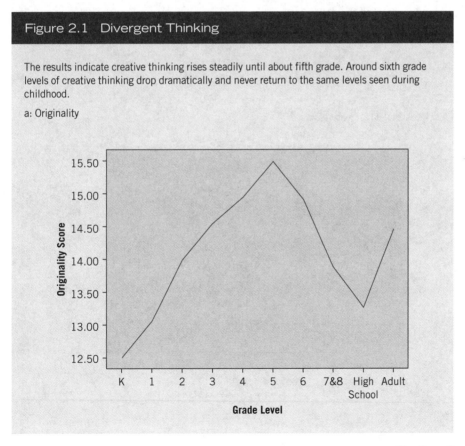

Figure 2.1   Divergent Thinking

The results indicate creative thinking rises steadily until about fifth grade. Around sixth grade levels of creative thinking drop dramatically and never return to the same levels seen during childhood.

a: Originality

(Continued)

Figure 2.1 (Continued)

b: Fluency

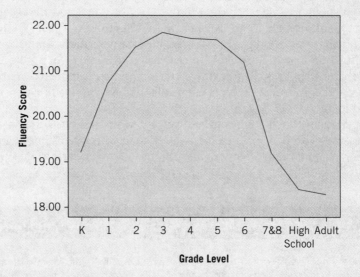

c: Resistance to Premature Closure

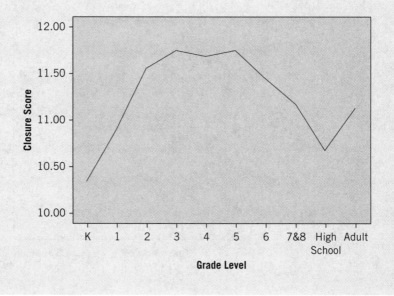

future professional success,[8] entrepreneurship,[9] inventiveness,[10] resolution of social dilemmas,[11] and happiness.[12] We hope you recognize the important role divergent thinking plays in problem solving, success, and life in general. Here is the unfortunate news: Kim's longitudinal study demonstrated that divergent thinking rose steadily until about sixth grade, then dropped dramatically.[13] Specifically, both fluency and originality in thought dropped significantly starting in sixth grade. Originality made a slight rebound, though not statistically significant, in adulthood (see Figure 2.1a), whereas fluency continuously declined into adulthood (see Figure 2.1b). Resistance to premature closure, an attitude necessary to support divergent thinking, followed a similar pattern as originality; that is, scores dropped significantly after sixth grade and bounced back for adults (see Figure 2.1c), although not to a level equal to the high points seen in third, fourth, and fifth grades.

So what does Kim's research tell us? The results of this extensive study highlight what most of us probably already recognize, that the ability to think creatively is present in early childhood but drops over time. In fact, Kim's study gives us some insight into an age and year in school that seems to be the critical nexus point for creative thinking. Up until about sixth grade, roughly ages 11 and 12, divergent-thinking skills grow steadily but then afterward drop drastically. In what ways, then, are humans like chickens? Does the domestication of human beings erode our ability to think creatively? In the same way chickens have lost the power of flight, do humans lose the power to let their imaginations soar? In the next section we explore possible reasons for the decline in creative thinking. The good news—and the research is clear—is that it is possible for us to reignite our creative-thinking skills.

Thought Starter
The 6th-Grade Drop

The Domestication of the Human Being: The Positive Side to Conformity

Whereas a number of factors may undermine creativity in humans, we suggest there are at least two culprits responsible for the slump in creative-thinking abilities around the sixth grade. The first reason relates to the domestication of humans, that is, the socialization process, and the second has to do with how humans are trained to think, that is, our educational experiences. Let's begin by examining how enculturation impacts individuals' creative thinking.

Imagine you are invited to participate in a research study. You are ushered into a room and presented with four lines as seen in Figure 2.2. You are seated at a table with several other individuals, and the researcher asks which line is the shortest. Look at Figure 2.2. Which of the four lines is the shortest? Is your answer C? Look again. Are you certain the shortest line is C?

Returning to the scene of the research study, the researcher goes around the room and asks each person to report out loud the line he or she believes is the shortest. Unbeknownst to you, the other participants in the study are actually working with the experimenter. Each person before you says Line A is the shortest. You can plainly see that Line C is the shortest. So now it's your turn. What do you say?

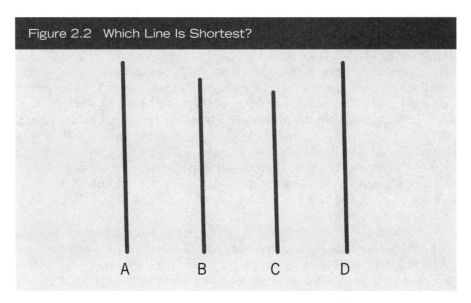

Figure 2.2   Which Line Is Shortest?

A   B   C   D

If you are like most participants in this study, roughly 75%, you will go along with the crowd and give an incorrect answer.[14] You might disagree, vehemently holding the belief that you would not cave in and go along with others who are so obviously wrong, but evolution, which has made you creative, so too has built in a bias for conformity. And this is for good reason, because there are many benefits to conformity. Here are a few:

- *Promotes collaboration.* Conformity makes it much easier for humans to work together, thus promoting group problem solving. It is easy to imagine how banding together enabled our ancestors to survive. Need to protect yourself from threats in the environment? Work together. Need to take down some large animal to feed yourself and your family? Combine forces with others. In other words, conformity, like creativity, enhances survival, and it certainly helps things run much more smoothly in teams and organizations.

- *Forms culture.* Conformity is the underpinning of culture. Through conformity humans develop accepted norms, practices, morals, and rituals. And these agreed-on elements, over time, lead to the formation of a cultural identity. A kind of circularity emerges; that is, conformity helps to form culture and then communicates to individuals the norms to which they must conform to fit into the collective. There are many benefits to adopting a shared culture. A few of these benefits include finding a mate, knowing how to raise children, and experiencing a sense of belonging.

- *Aids learning and spreads creativity.* Conformity enables us to quickly adopt the successful behaviors we see in others. This saves us huge amounts of time and helps us to be efficient by imitating what those before us found to be highly useful.

In this way individuals do not have to invent or discover everything for themselves. Simply learning to imitate others would seem to fly in the face of creativity, and it can, but it also promotes creativity. Without conformity, creative ideas would not get passed along. Evolutionary psychologists Dunbar, Barrett, and Lycett provide an excellent summary of the interplay between conformity and creativity:

> True imitation means that, if you notice that the particular technique someone is using is better than yours, you can adopt his or her technique and improve the quality of your own work. If you then modify the technique and further improve it, others will imitate your technique and take advantage of your innovation.[15]

Of course, conformity has its disadvantages. As a polarity, a concept that has both pros and cons, the previous bullet points underscore the positive side of conformity, but when taken to an extreme, there is a downside to conformity. Strict imitation without experimentation limits the development of new possibilities. Sticking with the tried and true simply because it is familiar can blind us to new opportunities. We suggest that all humans are born with an internal struggle between their conformity bias and their penchant for creativity. To be successful, individuals need to balance conformity and creativity; unfortunately, it could be argued that our society puts a higher premium on conformity than creativity, thus reinforcing our internal conformity bias. Perhaps this explains why Kim found the precipitous drop in creative thinking in the sixth grade. It could be that when students reach sixth grade, they become hypersensitive to others and their opinions, thus turning up the internal conformity meter and downplaying their creativity to get along with others. For further thoughts on the relationship between creativity and conformity, see Gerard Puccio's popular TEDx talk on this topic.

The current state of affairs in our educational system may further compromise the natural tendency humans have to be creative. A 2012 study of 5,000 individuals in five countries showed that 52% of people surveyed believed that their educational experiences undermined their creativity. In the United States this figure was even higher at 70%.[16] Surveys of current students reveal a similarly dismal outlook on the interplay between creative thinking and contemporary educational practices. For example, 71% of teenagers in the United Kingdom said they don't get to be creative enough at school. In the same study, 69% of students ages 12 to 18 said that pressure to pass exams stifled their creativity.[17] And here's what one of the greatest entrepreneurs of our time said about his early years in school: "I encountered authority of a different kind than I had ever encountered before, and I did not like it. And they really almost got me. They came close to really beating any curiosity out of me."[18]

That quote came from Steve Jobs. Although Jobs dropped out of college, he did hang around college friends, sometimes sleeping on their floors and sofas, and he sat in on college classes. And it may have been the content of one such class that was so profound that the lessons learned from this course helped to revolutionize computing. What was this course you ask? It was a college-level class on calligraphy. Jobs reported that the mix of beauty, history, and artistry of typography fascinated him. Later Jobs indicated that everything he learned in that course came back to him when he was designing the first Mac.

William Damon, a professor of education at Stanford University, believes that many entrepreneurs, like Steve Jobs, are unable to satisfy their curiosity in today's classrooms.[19] Damon argues that the focus on improving test scores, with attention primarily given to developing basic and remedial skills, leads to dreary memorization and often pushes out the kinds of courses that these students would find much more stimulating, such as art, music, theater, and emerging media technologies. Moreover, Mark Runco, a current creativity scholar, has suggested that schools put much greater focus on convergent thinking, the ability to get the right answer, to the detriment of promoting divergent thinking.[20] Schools today seem to focus on teaching students to think like everyone else, rather than learning to think for themselves.

The strange irony in the prevailing approach to education today is that rather than helping students develop the highest form of human thinking, creativity, there is a much greater focus on rudimentary thinking skills. Sadly, standardized tests do very little to prepare students for professional careers and lives in which there will be few multiple-choice problems. In her book *The Death and Life of the Great American School System: How Testing and Choice Are Undermining Education*, Diane Ravitch offers a retrospective look at the consequences of standardization. Comments such as the following underscore how standardized testing forces a lid on higher-order thinking skills:

> In Texas, which was the model for No Child Left Behind, students became better and better at answering multiple-choice questions on the Texas Assessment of Knowledge and Skills, known as TAKS; the passing rates on ninth-, tenth-, and eleventh-grade tests steadily increased. But when eleventh-grade students were asked to write a short answer about a text they were given to read, half of them were stumped. . . . They had mastered the art of filling in the bubbles on multiple-choice tests, but they could not express themselves, particularly when a question required them to think about and explain what they had just read.[21]

We will be completely frank. As creativity teachers and scholars, it seems clear to us that the focus on making education more rigorous has caused rigor mortis in students' creative-thinking skills. Of course, rigor is important, and so is critical thinking, but we would also argue that education should promote, not undermine, imagination. As Judy Estrin concludes in her book *Closing the Innovation Gap*, the focus on using test data to evaluate schools has resulted in promoting educational practices that undermine the development of the innovative mind.[22]

Overcome Your Inner Chicken:
Getting Out of Your Comfort Zone

Whereas it is true that society and education shape individuals, it is ultimately up to each person to decide what shape he or she wants to take. Our external conditions, social pressures, and educational practices do not absolve us of individual responsibility for growth and development. Awareness now empowers you to put a stop to the slow erosion of your creativity, to take steps to repel the potentially deleterious effects found in your specific life circumstance. In doing so, it may be helpful to begin by looking at factors most in your control—your own attitudes, behavior, and thinking.

Ackoff and Vergara define creativity as the ability to modify self-imposed constraints.[23] Continuing to take creativity lessons from the chicken, as a slang term, *chicken* refers to being scared, acting in a cowardly way, being unwilling to venture into new territory or to take risks. In his book *Talent Is Overrated*, Geoff Colvin suggests that effective human development can be viewed in terms of three concentric circles (see Figure 2.3).[24] The smallest circle is our comfort zone. The comfort zone refers to behavior, practices, and tasks that we engage in without much thought. They are automatic and feel natural. When engaged in such acts, there is a sense of complete comfort, safety, and confidence. This is where the "chicken" resides, and if you stay in your comfort zone, there is no growth.

The next-largest circle is the learning zone. By venturing into the learning zone, individuals begin to experiment with new attitudes, behaviors, and skills. And because these are new, at first they will feel slightly uncomfortable. Engaging

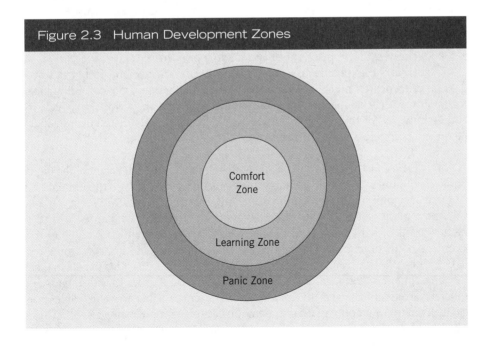

Figure 2.3   Human Development Zones

Comfort Zone

Learning Zone

Panic Zone

in something new can feel awkward; there is a high probability of failure, and self-confidence is likely to waver. The trick is not to retreat into the safety of the comfort zone but to persist so that over time you develop an expanded level of comfort and confidence—resulting in a wider comfort zone. As Michael Jordan, one of the greatest basketball players of all time, said, "I can accept failure, everyone fails at something. But I can't accept not trying."

The third circle is the panic zone. This circle represents new activities and behaviors that stretch us too far. These are activities and behaviors for which individuals are completely ill-prepared and find themselves thrust into with little instruction and limited prior experience. Imagine someone who has never spoken in public before and suddenly finds himself or herself in a position to speak in front of thousands. When in the panic zone, there can be a strong physical reaction, the kind of response indicative of anxiety. Steve Jobs was hailed as a great public speaker. In the latter part of his career, he delivered what many considered to be some of the greatest business speeches ever; however, what seemed to be a natural comfort on stage was not always the case. In what is reported to be his first television interview, in 1978, Steve Jobs was visibly anxious to the point of feeling ill.[25] He was in the panic zone. Over time, with practice and experience, Jobs was able to expand his comfort zone in regard to public speaking.

So how do you expand your comfort zone? The answer is deliberate practice. Consider how people—how you yourself—develop proficiency in some task, such as playing a musical instrument, writing, drawing, or pursuing a hobby or sport. The research shows that mastery is much less dependent on innate talent than on deliberate practice. A wide range of studies, across diverse domains of human endeavor, show consistent results—deliberate practice generally trumps innate talent. As Ericsson, Prietula, and Cokely conclude from their review of factors that contribute to the making of an expert, "Consistently and overwhelmingly, the evidence showed that experts are always made, not born."[26]

Note that we explicitly use the term *deliberate practice* and not just some generic reference to practice. When engaged in deliberate practice, individuals focus on precisely defined elements of performance and then work very hard to successfully master these skills. The following characteristics distinguish deliberate practice from less rigorous forms of practice.

- *It takes time and is highly repetitious.* Research on those who achieve the highest levels of human performance shows that practice, even more so than initial raw talent, is a significant indicator of mastery and expertise. When you see a rap artist, writer, public speaker, athlete, artist, lawyer, or electrician who appears to be a natural at his or her chosen field of endeavor, it only looks natural because of the countless hours of practice. During this extensive training period, those committed to deliberate practice push themselves to repeat again and again skills that lie in their learning zone. For instance, a study that looked at the factors that distinguished different levels of achievement among violinists showed that the chief difference came down to the amount of time student musicians spent practicing alone.[27] Those identified as the top tier, that is, destined for international careers, spent twice as much time practicing alone compared to those considered good violinists. This kind of repetition, the kind of practice that makes body parts ache and brains numb, isn't much fun. It takes great resolve and dedication.

- *As you develop, so must your teachers and mentors.* Although hours must be dedicated to individual practice, it is equally important to balance alone time with the input of teachers and mentors. Learning and development need to be guided by someone who has more expertise than you. Without the watchful eye and guidance of a coach or mentor it becomes too easy to develop poor habits, to stay within one's comfort zone and to limit the scope of one's performance to the skills acquired through random experimentation. Performance is greatly accelerated by exposing oneself to someone who is experienced in the domain. And it is crucial to move through ever more experienced and proficient coaches and mentors as one's skill level improves. Even world-class performers, musicians, and athletes retain coaches and mentors.

- *Effective feedback is continuously available.* According to Colvin, "You can work on technique all you like, but if you can't see the effects, two things will happen: You won't get any better, and you'll stop caring."[28] One of the great advantages of working with effective coaches or mentors is receiving their immediate and accurate feedback. Individuals are rarely the best judges of their own performance. Have you ever had an experience in which you felt your performance was stellar, perfect, beyond improvement, only to walk off the stage, the court, or out of the classroom to be met with surprising, yet admittedly accurate, feedback about your deficiencies? Distance and expertise are necessary for objective and effective feedback. To develop mastery, your opinion of your own performance can only take you so far; it is crucial to receive objective observations of both the things that are working and the things that need to be improved. The teacher, coach, or mentor who knows exactly how to dole out the right dosage of feedback will nurture the performer's growth by providing continuous stretch goals. Performers will stop developing when there is too little or too much feedback.

Through deliberate practice, creative thinking can be improved; the research is clear on this point. An innovative and entrepreneurial mind can be developed. This book is designed to take you on a personal journey that aims to elevate your creative-thinking skills to the next level. However, reading alone will not get you there. Only if you choose to deliberately practice the skills shared in this book will you enhance your creative mindset. Why should you care? Why might this be important to you? Simply put, your professional and personal success may depend on it. Next we explore why creative thinking is considered a 21st-century survival skill.

The Impending Perfect Storm

A "perfect storm" is a scenario in which an exceptionally rare set of circumstances come together to dramatically, and negatively, impact a situation. We believe such conditions exist today, and you run the risk of being swept up in this perfect storm. Here are the forces that are coming together. The first force is human evolution.

As we have argued, evolution has wired and built humans to be innately creative. The combination of thinking skills, attitude, language acquisition, and physical dexterity allows humans to create. However, there is a countervailing force. As highlighted in this chapter, even though humans are innately creative, the combination of societal pressures for conformity, educational systems that focus on lower-order thinking skills and knowledge acquisition, and personally imposed constraints slowly but surely erode individuals' natural creative tendencies (Chapter 10 explores further barriers that undermine our creativity). What makes this a perfect storm is the fact that, perhaps like no other time in modern history, humans are called on to use their creative talents. Change has never come more quickly, and it will only continue to escalate. Consider the following:

- In the 20th century it was estimated that accumulated knowledge doubled roughly every 25 years. In the early 21st century an IBM study put the estimate at every 11 hours.[29]

- In the 20th century most workers were likely to work their entire career in one organization or one field. In the 21st century the U.S. Bureau of Labor Statistics projects that workers are likely to change jobs more than 11 times before they even reach the prime of their careers at age 42.[30]

- Those employed 100 years ago were not only likely to work in the same organization but also on the same product or service for a good portion of their entire career. Today manufactured products go through fundamental redesign every 5 to 10 years, and technological products undergo significant change every 3 to 6 months. How long will it be before that mobile phone in your pocket is considered obsolete?

- Given the pace of change, it is hard to predict the kinds of jobs that will be available in the future. In fact, some sources suggest that as many as 65% of future jobs have not yet been invented.[31] One thing that seems to be certain is the clear trend away from routine physical work.[32] For example, it is anticipated that in 25 years people will no longer drive vehicles; as a consequence, today's 4 million driving jobs will be lost. These lost jobs will join the ranks of numerous other disappearing jobs in manufacturing and other forms of labor, swept away by technological changes.

- In the face of advances in technology, most notably robotics and computers, it is projected that over the next several decades approximately 47% of jobs will become automated. Jobs least likely to be overtaken by machines are those that require creative problem solving, creative thinking, and social intelligence.[33] Some of the jobs with the highest probability of becoming computerized, with a probability of 0.90 or greater, include telemarketers, library technicians, loan officers, bank tellers, credit analysts, insurance appraisers, umpires and referees, tax preparers, budget analysts, waiters and waitresses, and accountants and auditors.

Given the winds of change, the need for creative thinking as a competence to survive and thrive is widely recognized. By *widely recognized* we mean that numerous lists touting the skills necessary for success in today's workplace, and in the near future, include creativity and creativity-related skills. Here are a few examples. According to the authors of the book *Tough Choices or Tough Times*, "What it will take to hold on to our standard of living [is] high skills combined with creativity and a hunger for education." These same authors suggest that "the best employers the world over will be looking for the most competent, most creative, and most innovative people on the face of the earth and will be willing to pay them top dollar for their services."[34] In the book *The Global Achievement Gap*, Wagner lists as his seventh survival skill "Curiosity and Imagination." He argues:

It's not enough to just be trained in the techniques of how to ask questions— as lawyers and MBAs often are, for example. Employees must also know how to use analytical skills in such ways that are often more "out-of-the-box" than in the past, come up with creative solutions to problems, and be able to design products and services that stand out from the competition.[35]

Although we could go on with many more examples and quotes attesting to the urgent need for creativity-related skills, we will go to the marketplace to see what hiring managers say about the skills necessary for professional success in the 21st century. The findings here are drawn from a 2014 study of more than 1,000 hiring managers.[36]

- Seventy-eight percent indicated creativity is required for economic growth.

- Since the Great Recession, salaries have been stagnant, with the exception of employees who possess higher-order thinking skills. Problem solving (51%) and creativity (47%) showed the greatest relationship to driving salary increases.

- According to hiring managers, the top three work skills were tech savvy (88%), communication through digital and visual media (82%), and creativity (76%).

- By a ratio of 5 to 1, hiring managers preferred job candidates with creative skills over conventional skills.

- Eighty-two percent of hiring managers reported seeking well-rounded candidates who are able to apply their creativity skills to a range of business and technical problems.

- Recent graduates who set themselves apart did so by developing a broad range of skills (60%), focusing on increasing their creative skills (47%), understanding that innovation and creativity can be learned (35%), and recognizing that creative thinking would take them further than technical know-how (35%).

Further evidence of this perfect storm of a changing marketplace and unprepared workforce is highlighted in a recent *Bloomberg Businessweek* study of job recruiters. In this study creative problem solving was identified as one of the top five most important employment skills, yet these same recruiters indicated that it was the second most difficult skill to find among job applicants.[37] In fact, a national report on workplace readiness found that more than half of job applicants did not possess the necessary creativity skills desired by prospective employers. And to make matters worse, when asked about the kinds of training provided to employees, nearly 70% of those organizations surveyed provided no skill development in creativity (it actually topped the list of most-needed skills, yet no relevant training was offered).[38]

Here, then, is the perfect storm. Whereas numerous experts, educational leaders, business professionals, and futurists suggest that workplace success depends on an individual's ability to think creatively, society in general and educational practices in particular are incredibly ineffective at promoting this essential life and workplace skill. Organizations desire it but don't know how to develop it themselves. The economy needs it, but society crushes it. Individuals become more valuable and attractive to prospective employers when they know how to think creatively, yet as a workforce we often resemble the flightless chicken in our state of adapted conformity and loss of divergent thinking.

Thought Starter
Perfect Storm

Although we have stated our case in strong terms, we do not believe the point has been exaggerated. To be successful in the 21st century, personally and professionally, one needs to be an effective creative thinker. The purpose of this book is to help the reader reclaim and develop his or her creativity. Yes, creativity is a skill that can be developed. Earlier we described deliberate practice. Like all other skills, creativity can be enhanced through deliberate practice. In the next section you will learn a simple yet highly effective tool for improving creative thinking. The goal is to help you survive and even thrive in an era of rampant change and to become a creative asset to your organization or to use your creativity skills to enhance your entrepreneurial success.

Learning Activity
Comfort Zone, Learning Zone, Panic Zone

Geoff Colvin breaks down human development into three concentric circles: our comfort zone, our learning zone, and our panic zone. Review the meaning of each zone and identify at least two personal examples for each zone. To deepen your understanding, write a sentence or two for each example. Compare and contrast the emotions you experienced in regard to your personal examples across the three zones. Assessing your examples, what cues help you to know when you are experiencing each of the respective zones? Take one of the examples you placed in the panic zone and identify a moment when you pulled yourself out of the panic zone in a way that led to a successful outcome. What happened? How did you do it? What helped?

Doing—Removing the *But* in Your Thinking

Many would say that Ernest Hemingway was highly creative; indeed, he received the Pulitzer Prize in recognition of his literary excellence. We would suggest that he is an excellent example not only of a highly creative person but also of an individual who worked hard to develop and practice his creativity skills. Ernest Hemingway, when at home, would begin writing at six o'clock in the morning. He always began at his standing desk. Starting with a pencil and working furiously to capture his ideas, to keep his pace up he ignored grammar and wrote in incomplete sentences. He avoided overscrutinizing his work, and to that end, the pencils he used had no erasers. When he had a sufficient flow of ideas he would then sit at his typewriter. He generally finished writing by noon, and he always stopped when he knew where he would pick up again. At the end of his writing day he would count the number of words written and chart them. Afterward he would go for his daily half-mile swim. Hemingway, like many other great creators, did not leave his creativity to chance. Great creators find ways to practice their creativity. They make creativity a habit, if you will.

For many great creators it was persistence, experimentation, and mentoring relationships that helped form their creativity routines and procedures. Today, those interested in deliberately developing their creativity have a significant advantage—the more than 60 years of accumulated practice and knowledge in the field of creativity education and training. The research from this field is clear. Analysis of 70 empirical studies on the effectiveness of creativity training programs shows that creative-thinking skills can be enhanced by learning strategies.[39] And this research highlights the fact that the most impactful programs provide learners with cognitive strategies, that is, tools that guide their thinking as they tackle open-ended challenges. Moreover, such training works for people of all intellectual abilities. The evidence is in: Everyone's creative thinking can be enhanced through training and practice.

Here's a simple, easy-to-implement tool that has been used for well over three decades to improve creative thinking. It's called Yes-And.[40] When people respond to a novel idea, the reflexive retort is often "yes . . . but," or sometimes just "but." When someone says "yes, but," there is a strong suggestion something is terminally wrong with the idea and thus it would be foolish to go forward with that idea. Perhaps this tendency to leap to negative judgment is the result of the combination of the domestication of humans and the emphasis on thinking critically in schools. Premature negative judgment of a novel idea generally results in stopping the idea in its tracks and undermining future creative ideas. Yes-But thinking can be applied to ourselves, in our own thoughts, or to others in a verbal exchange. No matter how it is used, it generally results in the same outcome—creative ideas are snuffed out.

The Yes-And response to new ideas has the opposite effect. This tool suggests that the idea has potential merit and that there are ways to improve it. College sports, especially Division I football and basketball, are big business. In the 2011–2012 academic year the University of Texas football team netted a tidy profit of $77.9 million. College athletes at this level receive scholarships, but some now argue that they should receive pay.[41] So imagine if colleges and universities began to pay their players. The automatic reply by many would be, "Yes, but they are amateurs and they receive full scholarships." Let's shift the thinking from Yes-But to Yes-And. The *Yes* part of Yes-And is used to identify points that support the idea, whereas the *And* is used to highlight areas that if addressed successfully would improve the idea. For example, the Yes-And tool could lead to the following statement: "YES, it seems unfair that Division I football and basketball coaches make six-figure salaries, with some earning more than $1 million a year, when the players receive no compensation. AND the idea could be improved if there were ways to be sure that student-athletes do not lose their focus on education and ultimately earning a college degree."

There are two ways to use Yes-And. One approach is to pair every *Yes* statement with an *And* statement, as just shown. This approach might be used in a conversation when responding to a novel idea. The second approach is to create a Yes-And Chart. In this more systematic method, separate lists of *Yes* statements and *And* statements are created (see Figure 2.4). Under each *And* statement, a box labeled "How to avoid?" is inserted. This question forces the mind to think of answers to the objection or limitation identified in each respective *And* statement. The next step is to generate thoughts that will help improve the original idea by addressing each objection or limitation. Finally, suggestions for improving the idea are reviewed to see what might be incorporated into the original idea and decide whether the new and improved idea should be pursued. For example, based on the Yes-And analysis in Figure 2.4, it might be decided to go forward with paying college athletes in good academic standing a limited salary, allowing them to earn extra money through endorsements, and providing financial rewards to players on teams that cannot afford a payroll when they defeat better-resourced teams.

Thought Starter
Yes-And Paid
Athletes

Did the Yes-And Chart begin to shift your thinking toward the idea of paying college athletes? Try it out on others. Share the idea with them and see how they initially react. Then walk them through the Yes-And Chart to see if this analysis opens their minds to the potential in the idea. Compare initial reactions to the idea of paid college athletes to the perceptions after applying the Yes-And tool. Hopefully, in cases where the first impulse was negative, the individual moved toward a more open-minded perspective. The goal of the Yes-And tool is to hold off premature judgment, creating sufficient space to allow the idea to be examined for possible improvements. Afterward, an informed decision is taken as to whether the new and improved idea is strong enough to carry forward.

Figure 2.4   Yes-And Example

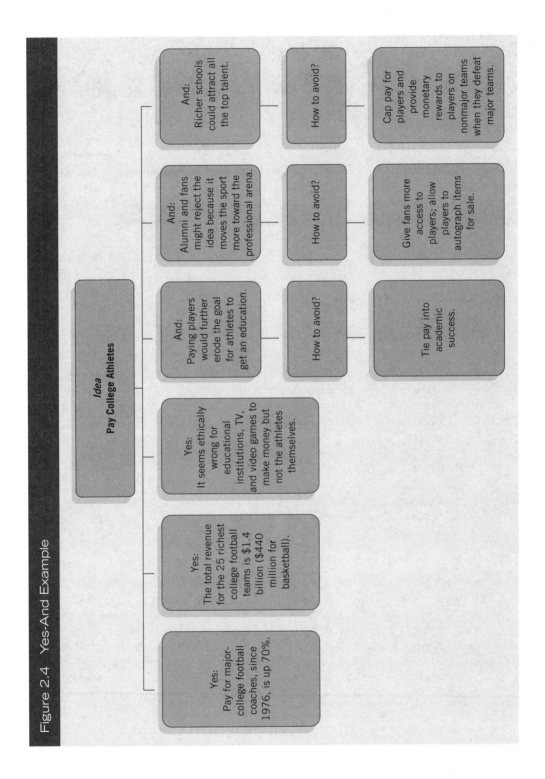

Idea
Pay College Athletes

Yes:
Pay for major-college football coaches, since 1976, is up 70%.

Yes:
The total revenue for the 25 richest college football teams is $1.4 billion ($440 million for basketball).

Yes:
It seems ethically wrong for educational institutions, TV, and video games to make money but not the athletes themselves.

And:
Paying players would further erode the goal for athletes to get an education.

How to avoid?

Tie pay into academic success.

And:
Alumni and fans might reject the idea because it moves the sport more toward the professional arena.

How to avoid?

Give fans more access to players; allow players to autograph items for sale.

And:
Richer schools could attract all the top talent.

How to avoid?

Cap pay for players and provide monetary rewards to players on nonmajor teams when they defeat major teams.

We described how to use Yes-And thinking through the systematic creation of a Yes-And Chart. Practice this process by using Yes-And thinking to analyze and develop any of the following proposed ideas: legalization of marijuana, widespread use of driverless cars, automated waiters and waitresses, Uber's use of independent contractors (versus hiring drivers as employees), the adoption of drones to deliver packages to homes, or your own controversial start-up idea. After completing the Yes-And Chart, analyze and describe the benefits of this tool. It is easy to go back to the old habit of using Yes-But thinking; how might you make Yes-And more habitual?

Being—Reflecting and Redirecting Yes-But Thinking

Tudor Rickards, a longtime business school professor and creativity scholar from the University of Manchester, United Kingdom, felt strongly that Yes-And thinking was central to a successful creative problem-solving attitude. He felt this so strongly that in his own book he instructed readers not to go on until they embraced the Yes-And philosophy. Borrowing from Rickards, we will make the same suggestion. As he put it,

> If the technique has raised doubts in your own mind, stop at this point. Practice the "yes and" approach to explore those concerns until you are satisfied you are ready for the next section, which is otherwise likely to reinforce the feelings that all of this creativity stuff is not for you after all.[42]

Remember that years of socialization and education were likely to build a strong *but* into your thinking. When this simple word *but* is inserted into one's thinking, it has the effect of killing or at least diminishing all forward creative momentum, undermining change in the process. Socialization and education teach us the value of conformity and judgment, and they support analysis. For instance, when a teacher assigns a case or an essay for students to critically analyze, he or she usually has an idea of the answers that provide evidence of good critical analysis. Effective critical thinking enables us to think like everyone else or, at least like other effective critical thinkers, to arrive at the same conclusions or insights. In contrast, it is much more difficult to predict the precise outcome of a task that requires creative thinking. In a world that is less predictable, individuals are expected to come up with their own new and continuously evolving answers. Critical thinking is reactive; creative thinking is proactive. Together they are strong partners. In a fast-changing world, a creative attitude paired with creative thinking enables us to more readily flow with changing circumstances in our personal lives, allows imagination geared toward opportunity finding, and positions us for professional success. Creative thinking creates value and distinction.

Living in a flat world means the competition increasingly possesses the same knowledge and skills as you. Therefore, it will take a life of continuous creativity to survive, that is, to generate novel responses and ideas that effectively solve problems, to produce new ideas to which others are attracted, to flexibly adapt to change, and to thrive by becoming a creative change leader. Mastering Yes-And thinking encourages continuous creativity by looking at the world in a way that spots opportunities as opposed to maintaining the status quo through Yes-But thinking. It is one thing to be effective at using the Yes-And tool on occasion when necessary but another matter to make this a part of your mindset.

To make this kind of thinking a habit, it will be necessary to do two things: reflect and redirect. Reflection allows you to be more aware of how you react to ideas in the moment. Do you find yourself to be an idea killer, of your own ideas or others', or are you an idea promoter? Once you become more aware of your mental habits, you can then catch those times when you are putting the brakes on an idea by focusing only on its drawbacks and redirect your thinking by asking yourself, *What's good about the idea, and how might it be improved?* When you begin to see your surroundings as a world of possibilities rather than just a series of issues, problems, and inconveniences, that's when you are more fully embracing an innovative and entrepreneurial mindset.

Learning Activity
Escaping Your Comfort Zone

As most of us know, it is exceedingly easy to stay within our comfort zone, and the longer we stay within our comfort zone, the easier it is to remain there. Within the next 24 to 48 hours, engage in a new activity or experience—something that is novel and challenging to you. Capture in your journal how this experience went for you. How did it feel? In what ways was it beneficial?

The Challenge

Medical education in the United States takes too long, doesn't instruct the right things, and is biased against admitting the best candidates in the first place. At least that is the thinking driving one medical innovator to lead a national charge to reimagine the process by which the next generation of medical doctors will be trained.

The current path to becoming a medical doctor in the United States consists of 4 years at a college or university to earn a BS or BA degree, often with a scientific focus. From there, interested parties must take the Medical College Admission Test (MCAT), where a strong score is needed to apply to a Liaison Committee on Medical Education (LCME). If accepted, students must complete 4 more years of preclinical and clinical education, thereby earning their doctor of medicine degree (MD).

The journey does not end there, however. Newly graduated MDs who want to specialize in an area of medicine must enter into a supervised residency program that can range anywhere from 3 to 7 years. From there, subspecialty training (a medical fellowship) is an option for some doctors who wish to become highly specialized in a particular field.

After completing undergraduate, medical school, and graduate medical education (GME), physicians—often in their early to mid-30s and carrying more than $200,000 in student loan debt—must still obtain a license to practice medicine from a state or jurisdiction of the United States in which they are planning to practice. They apply for the permanent licensure after completing a series of exams and completing a minimum number of years of GME. Additionally, physicians may choose to become board certified. This certification ensures that the doctor has been tested to assess his or her knowledge, skills, and experience in a specialty and is deemed qualified to provide quality patient care in that specialty.[43]

Indeed, this model of physician education has produced a reliable and knowledgeable pipeline of medical doctors in the United States, yet there are leaders in the field such as Dr. Stephen Klasko, president and CEO of Thomas Jefferson University and Thomas Jefferson Health—an 11-hospital network with annual revenue exceeding $4.8 billion and more than 28,000 employees, 7,800 students, 6,000 physicians/practitioners, and 4,000 faculty—who believe this approach to physician training has reached its expiration date. Furthermore, Dr. Klasko believes that current MD training programs will not be adequate to meet the needs of what he describes as the *physician of the future*.[44]

The Physician of the Future

Health care communications strategist and executive editor of the *Healthcare Transformation* journal Michael Hoad argues: "We cannot continue to select physicians based on their organic chemistry GPA and their scores on a multiple-choice exam (MCAT), and if we do, we shouldn't be shocked when we find that students who excel at memorizing information in textbooks aren't prepared to be empathetic, creative, and communicative when helping patients address their health challenges."[45]

"Physicians join a cult," says Dr. Klasko, and in this cult are baked-in biases toward hierarchy and against risk taking, and an adaptive bias toward accepting full responsibility for patient outcomes and therefore a bias *against* teamwork and collaboration.

This is problematic because, according to Klasko and Hoad, the next generation of physicians will need to work more collaboratively to deliver team-based care. Specifically, they envision a world where an app on a mobile device offers you access to an instant, streamlined health care team consisting of physicians, nurses, clinical pharmacists, physician assistants, and even contributors whose jobs don't formally exist in the health care space (yet): probability experts, electronic health care ambassadors, and telehealth professionals.[46]

Additionally, argues Klasko, the physician of the future must be skilled in the "art of attending"— a program he initiated with colleagues across several partner organizations that focuses on training students to become skilled observers. Instead of training their minds to run through a diagnostic checklist—a task much better suited for a supercomputer such as IBM's WATSON— these students are trained in critically analyzing artwork and developing narrative explanations of the artistic content. In their pilot program, participants who experienced this art-driven curriculum made more observations in physical diagnosis than participants who didn't, they documented more and took more detailed notes, and

they communicated more effectively. In short, they were better physicians.

Another interesting insight emerged from the pilot program: As participants from other academic programs were allowed into the class, an observable distinction emerged in the way that physicians were interpreting an image versus the way that public health students were interpreting the same image.

For example, when public health students looked at the artwork, they were more likely to have looked "outside" the frame to explore factors about the lives of the characters in the artwork (e.g., poverty, nutrition, culture), whereas the prospective medical doctors immediately looked inside the frame—on the hunt for perceptible details present in the painting.

This is important, suggests Hoad, because in a world of augmented diagnosis, where supercomputers handle the diagnostic duties of doctoring, patients will need a different kind of support from physicians—more life-planning and conversational support to help patients understand what life will be like after their diagnosis and their prescribed plan of care. Doctors skilled in the art of attending are the ones who will add more value to these patients' lives.[47]

Dr. Klasko breaks down the future-focused physician skill set further: In a world where the scientific component of medicine is outsourced to computers, the customer-facing physician of the future must be "emotionally intelligent, self-aware, self-managing, with an ability to adapt, and who has social awareness, empathy, and relationship management skills, and who excels at teamwork and embracing change versus fighting it."[48]

(Continued)

The Academic Medical Center of the Future

For admissions criteria to change, and for pedagogical approaches to be updated to reflect the evolving skill sets required of tomorrow's physicians, the core operations and culture of academic medical centers must also evolve.

For Dr. Klasko and Jefferson University, this meant admitting a new class of student into their program and having those students compete not based solely on who had the highest GPA but also on who demonstrated the greatest emotional intelligence and leadership.

In addition to updating curricula with innovative programming such as "the art of attending," the Jefferson team also redesigned their curriculum to ensure that all students had access to mentorship, and that teaching and learning followed a mentorship-driven style (versus traditional lecturing).

The benefits associated with this new approach became immediately apparent. Specifically, as a result of the reworked admissions process, a more diverse group of participants were represented in the cohort. Additionally, students began seeing themselves as contributors to conversations as opposed to recipients of one-directional information. They also began to see self-expression and articulation as valuable competencies, particularly in contrast to the more practiced process of memorization. Furthermore, medical students became more verbal and developed the ability to describe scenarios with a mature narrative style. Finally, participants openly took on cause-oriented positions in discussions and readily identified leadership positions in ethical debates.[49]

It wasn't all positive, however. As you might expect with any new program, potential watch-outs were also present in the inaugural cohort. For example, tension with other medical students occurred, with some nonparticipants expressing uncertainty and resentment for not being included. Another complication arose when considering the upcoming challenges the students would face upon exiting their programs. The United States requires new medical doctors to pass three standardized tests for licensure known as the boards. For some students, there was uncertainty about deviating from the traditional approach of educating physicians, choosing instead to focus on empathy, observation, communication, and bedside manner, knowing that they would have to then turn around and be measured by standardized board exams that would not take into consideration their unique educational experiences and refined 21st-century skill sets.

The Future at Jefferson

In addition to revising admissions standards and updating curricula, Dr. Klasko and the team at Jefferson have begun outlining and implementing a variety of bleeding-edge programs and initiatives to shift the culture of the institution toward becoming the nation's first "academic medical center of the future."

They began building a compelling narrative to help communicate their vision of change to the system. They also hired a senior

VP of innovation—a position carrying with it legitimate influence and power, operating at the level of provost or a senior vice president of academic affairs. Importantly, they also changed faculty tenure criteria to ensure that innovation is valued (versus the more traditional formula that relies almost exclusively on the amount of federal funding received for their research). These moves not only helped set the tone and mission of innovation but also established a practical challenge for everyone to participate. Next, they amplified the message so it was directed not only internally to existing students, administrators, and faculty but also externally to ensure that the entire medical community knew Jefferson is the place to be if you want to be innovative and entrepreneurial.

Hand-in-hand with innovation comes failure. In recognition of this, Jefferson reframed the way it perceived high-risk, high-reward projects and decided it would ultimately recategorize risk as an essential ingredient of innovation leadership. In practice, this means creating a way to forgive people for losing money if their projects do not unfold as designed.

To help showcase new and innovative efforts, the Jefferson Jazz Tank (an internal spin-off of the popular television program *Shark Tank*) was launched. As an additional boost to the innovation engine, health-oriented hackathons were designed and supported in partnership with internal and external organizations such as MIT. These tactics played a key role in recruitment, and, as a result, Jefferson was able to acquire talented individuals in health and the emerging field of telehealth from other areas of the country and the world to join their team.

Again, the message was clear: Jefferson is the place where you can be creative; Jefferson is a home for innovators.

Closing

Hoad describes the transition to next-generation medical services with the following question: Who would choose to schedule an appointment days, weeks, or even months in advance; to then drive to a big, expensive, maze-like building; to deal with the hassles of parking and navigating look-alike corridors; when they could just see a physician instantly by phone? This is not some futuristic view of the medical field; it's already here! Through technologies such as the Jefferson Connect app (JeffConnect[50]), people have a choice between spending $1,500, on average, for a 6-hour emergency room visit during which they actually receive 7 minutes of face time with an actual doctor, or they could spend just $49 for 15 minutes with a doctor on-demand, via their smartphone, tablet, or computer.

The consumer revolution hasn't yet impacted the health care industry the way it has affected others; however, it may just be a matter of time, and physicians such as Dr. Klasko and the team at Jefferson believe that much of the care that average patients need can (and will) be delivered at a retail level—for example, Walmart, Target, Walgreens—and secondary care will be provided via smart device. If history is a guide, consumers will likely reward increased access, convenience, and reasonable (and understandable) costs. How academic institutions will shift their structures and programs to train the physicians of the future who must thrive in this new reality is yet to be seen.

(Continued)

(Continued)

Discussion Questions: Knowing

1. What practices in this case study are pushing up against the comfort zone associated with the field of medicine?

2. How do past and present selection criteria for medical school, as well as practices in the medical profession, limit creative thinking?

Application Questions: Doing

1. Using the Yes-And tool, create a Yes-And graphic associated with this case. Refer to your responses to Question 1 above to assist you with this tool; this might illuminate some of the "buts" people might express relative to future changes in medical practice.

Thinking Ahead: Being

1. In your opinion, how might patients resist future technology and health care experiences described in this case? If you were leading an initiative to help society adapt to these future changes, what would you do? How would you accelerate the degree to which patients might conform to these new practices?

2. What are your reactions to the future of medical practice as described in this case? What are you comfortable with, and what makes you somewhat anxious?

What We Know About Creativity

Knowing—Sorting Creativity Fact From Fiction

Misconceptions and Mysterious Things That Go Bump in the Night

Wolfgang Amadeus Mozart might be considered the poster child for individuals born as great creative geniuses. Let's closely examine his creative process and sort fact from fiction. A letter attributed to Mozart is said to give great insight into his creative process. Mozart begins this famous letter by saying that when he is relaxed and in a good mood, say, walking after an enjoyable meal, compositions seemingly popped into his mind. To directly quote from this letter, "Whence and how they come, I know not; nor can I force them. Those ideas that please me I retain in memory."[1] Mozart's creative process seemed to be straightforward and apparently beyond his control. Creative ideas came easily to Mozart, so much so it was as if they emerged fully formed and out of thin air. As he states later in the letter, "For this reason the committing to paper is done quickly enough for everything is, as I said before, already finished; and it rarely differs on paper from what it was in my imagination."[2]

In the past, this letter has been held up as exhibit A of Mozart's creative genius. Recalling from Chapter 1 how we dispelled the commonly held belief that Mozart came into the world with his creative genius complete and fully formed, statements like those in Mozart's letter perpetuate the misconception that the creative process of great creators is free and easy. To the contrary, it is clear from analysis of Mozart's manuscripts that he worked very hard at creating his compositions, constantly revising his music. And in the case of this famous letter, it would appear someone else had an interest in cultivating Mozart's creative persona in the public's eye, for scholars now agree that the letter was almost certainly a forgery.

Learning Goals

After reading this chapter, you will be able to do the following:

- Contrast popular misconceptions of creativity against evidence-based facts
- Appraise the degree to which you and your present situation fit the means, motive, and opportunity model of organizational creativity
- Assess your internal climate for creativity
- Judge the degree to which your locus of control is more externally or internally oriented

The content of this letter helps to reveal one of the main misconceptions about creativity—the perception that the creative process is magical. By *magical* we mean a process that seems to happen with some element of surprise, like a rabbit being pulled out of a hat. However, magic is an illusion, and the more practiced the magician, the greater the illusion. Similar statements can be made about creativity; great creators can give the illusion that it is a magical process, with ideas seeming to appear from nowhere.

The study of human evolution, creative cognition, and neuroscience has increasingly revealed how our creative minds work, thus removing the illusion of magic. Let's briefly see if we can reveal some of the operations in our minds that specifically support the creative act. As many of us know, only a small percentage of an iceberg is visible above the waterline. Likewise, we see only a small percentage of the creative act, the most visible being the eventual creative outcome or product. However, there is much processing that goes on below the surface. Through this chapter, and especially the process chapters, we reveal the hidden creative processes, thereby demonstrating that rather than being magical and unpredictable, the creative process is actually predictable and repeatable.

The human brain has evolved to engage in two distinct forms of thinking that, when properly balanced, are central to the creative process. On one hand is the ability to generate novelty, using imagination to produce original thoughts and alternatives. On the other hand is the ability to explore the value of novelty, focusing our minds in such a way as to select and develop the most promising novel options.[3] Unique to humans is the ability to shift and direct our thinking; to defocus our minds in a way that facilitates a search for original thoughts, ideas, and solutions; and then to focus our minds to select and refine the most promising option from a set of competing choices.

These two fundamental mental operations may occur in different parts of the brain. Mounting research evidence indicates that greater activity in the right hemisphere facilitates higher levels of divergent thinking—the broad search for nonobvious alternatives.[4] It may be tempting to assume then that such neurobiological research supports the popular misconception that "right-brained" people are more creative. However, creative thinking is complex, and true creative cognition is the balance between the generation of novel ideas in combination with the selection and development of the most promising ideas. The left hemisphere, associated with knowledge acquisition and analytical thinking, then has an important role to play in the creative process as well.[5] Creative breakthroughs come about through the successful integration of both hemispheres of the brain. In Part II of this book, you will learn strategies that build on, and make even more effective, the creative cognition you already possess. Like magicians, who rehearse and perfect their tricks so it appears that they are performing magic, you can practice using cognitive tools that will enable you to generate creative breakthroughs on a more consistent basis. To others not familiar with such practices, you may appear to possess the same creative magic as Mozart.

Through this discussion we have attempted to dispel the misconception that creativity is magical. There are, however, other misunderstandings that can get in the way of taking full advantage of one's personal creativity. Next we present other common misconceptions and their counterpoints. As you read about these misconceptions, consider to what degree you have been susceptible to each one.

Creativity Is All About Having Fun and Letting Loose

There are those who believe that a call for creativity is permission to do anything you wish, that creativity is a license to be free and simply have fun. Engaging in creative acts can certainly be fun and highly stimulating, but at the same time it is generally hard work. The essence of the word creativity is "to create." That is, when one is engaged in creative thinking, the goal is to produce something new and valuable. Along this line of thinking, creativity scholar Reg Talbot provides a succinct definition of creativity as the ability to make a change that sticks—at least for a while.[6] Maya Angelou, Pablo Picasso, Steve Jobs, Dean Kamen, Bill Gates, Frank Gehry, Mark Zuckerberg, the Beatles, and other great creators all worked very hard to produce their breakthrough ideas. Picasso, for example, generated eight full notebooks of sketches before producing his groundbreaking masterpiece *Les Demoiselles d'Avignon*, the painting that launched cubism. Similarly, Apple's iPad was released commercially in 2010, but only after 8 years and numerous prototypes. To be sure, creativity is stimulating and satisfying and can be fun, but as most people recognize, the making of something, especially something that has not been done before, takes a great deal of effort.

Most creativity scholars agree that creativity is the manifestation of something rare, novel, and original and at the same time valuable, useful, or appropriate. When you hear someone utter the statement, "Hey, I'm just being creative," it would seem creativity is being used as an excuse to be different or outrageous. In such cases, the behavior being displayed by the individual may certainly be novel, but the question becomes to what degree it is truly creative—both novel and valuable.

Creativity Is All About Having Ideas

When the word *creativity* is tossed about in conversation, it is often used narrowly to refer to the process of coming up with ideas. Yet being creative is not limited to the production of ideas. If creativity is a process that leads to original and valuable propositions, then our conception of creative thinking needs to be broadened to encompass a fuller and more complete process. Simply put, thinking of creativity as strictly coming up with ideas is like saying all you need for a good hamburger is raw meat.

Although the field of creativity possesses many models of the creative process, none of these models positions idea generation as the sole step necessary to create. In fact, at best, idea generation can be thought of as one fourth of the creative process. Before ideas can be generated, it is extremely helpful to have knowledge about the context or the situation in which a person desires to produce a creative breakthrough (Step 1). This upfront stage of the creative process is all about clarifying, which involves gathering information, identifying important facts, asking good questions, considering what has already been attempted, and framing the most pressing challenges that need to be addressed. To be effective, ideas generally must respond to some issue or challenge. To paraphrase a statement credited to John Dewey, American educator and philosopher, a problem that is properly stated is already half solved.

The clarification step of the creative process sets up the individual or team for effective idea generation. This enables innovators and entrepreneurs to take a more targeted approach to producing ideas by providing a goal for idea production. What challenge do you need to address? What kind of product are you attempting to produce? What type of business model best fits your new enterprise? In what specific ways are you attempting to improve your organization? Only after the situation is clarified can productive idea generation occur (Step 2).

Once generated, the most promising ideas need to move into another step of the process, an area of thought in which good ideas are transformed into great solutions (Step 3). This is where much of the hard work of creativity occurs. And Mozart, the boy genius, offers a good example of how deliberation and development pay off. Despite the claims of the forged letter, Mozart's compositions did not occur to him fully formed. Rather, his manuscripts reveal that he tinkered with, revised, and tested modifications to his compositions as he worked toward the end product. Finally, the new proposition needs to go into action or be put into use, either for the individual or for some group. This is the implementation step of the creative process (Step 4). It is the successful implementation of novel and valuable ideas, on a consistent basis, that earns individuals the badge of innovator or entrepreneur. Without implementation, our new ideas are nothing but idle daydreams and fantasies.

In this brief description of the creative process we hope to have highlighted the fact that creativity is more than idea generation. In Part II of this book, the Doing chapters, we use a version of this four-step creative process to help you, the reader, generate creative ideas more consistently and put them into practice.

Creativity Is About the Arts

Some believe that to be creative means to be a dancer, musician, painter, or some other kind of artist and that creativity is about applying imagination. Whereas imagination certainly plays an important role in the arts, creativity is not limited to the arts. Imagination knows no boundaries and is crucial in all human endeavors. The ability to imagine alternatives and to see new opportunities is equally applicable to business, science, architecture, engineering, medicine, and any other field in which problems need to be addressed and new discoveries hold the promise of building new knowledge—which pretty much means all fields. So, if you can't draw or sing, that doesn't mean you are not creative. Can you use your imagination to solve problems in your field of choice or to add new discoveries? Do you use your imagination in your daily life? It's the application of your imagination that is the indicator of creativity. After all, if an individual has learned to sing a song written and performed by someone else, is he or she really being creative? Such a scenario is likely to be a better representation of talent than creativity.

Creativity Is Associated With Madness and Mental Illness

There are those who quickly associate creativity with mental illness. For some, the thought of a creative person immediately conjures up images of the mad scientist or the depressed artist. Popular culture and a few iconic creators feed these images; think of Virginia Woolf, Ernest Hemingway, and Vincent van Gogh, each of whom committed suicide. People seem to be drawn to offbeat or unusual stories, and as a consequence, there may be a tendency to sensationalize the unusual behavior exhibited by some legendary creators. But what does the research tell us about the link between psychopathologies and creativity? Well, the results are mixed. Some studies[7] have shown a link between schizotypy, traits that enhance the probability of psychotic illness, and creativity, whereas others have shown that high creative achievers score lower on measures of psychopathology.[8] And at least one eminent creativity scholar, Albert Rothenberg, has suggested that the literature that links creativity and mental illness has serious shortcomings.[9]

The fact that research results are inconclusive doesn't really matter, because the prevailing misconception holds that one must be mentally ill to be creative. Even if research shows a correlation between schizotypy and creativity, it must be remembered that this does not demonstrate cause and effect, that is, mental illness is a necessary condition for someone to be creative. There are certainly plenty of examples of people who suffer from mental illness who are not creative high achievers, as well as highly creative individuals who are mentally healthy. A strong case can be made that the stereotypical view of the "mad genius" is simply not true.[10] To the contrary, recent research on the brain shows that consistent creative activity facilitates a longer life, reduces dementia, and promotes more fulfilling relationships and happiness.[11]

Thought Starter

Creativity Misconceptions

There are, of course, other misconceptions of creativity.[12] Our goal is to debunk some of the more common ones. For the remainder of this chapter, we turn our attention to some things we know about creativity.

A Model for Understanding Creativity: Like a Crime

The field of creativity has grown from humble beginnings in the middle of the 20th century to an active academic field with more than 11 journals, countless books, numerous conferences, and a special division in the American Psychological Association. This growing interest in creativity has led to a broad body of knowledge, much too large to attempt to cover in one book. Instead we highlight some of what is known about the nature and nurture of creativity using a model that looks at the conditions necessary for individuals to express their creativity within the organizational context, whether an existing or a newly started enterprise. As such, this model gives us a useful framework for the study and application of creativity in keeping with the purpose of this book—to assist readers in positioning themselves as creative assets, resulting in enhanced entrepreneurial and intrapreneurial activities.

This model, initially developed by Reg Talbot, likens creativity in organizations to the perpetration of a crime.[13] To do either requires three things: the means, the motive, and the opportunity. Detectives in books and movies can zero in on suspects by determining which individuals possess the capability of committing the crime (the means). Here the concern is the degree to which the suspect had the strength, mindset, and tools to commit the crime. The suspect might have had the means to commit the crime, but did he or she have a motive? To what extent did the person have a compelling reason, a driving force, that gives a clear indication as to why the crime was committed? Finally, the detective needs to determine whether the person had the opportunity to commit the crime. Can that person be located at the crime scene, or did he or she have the chance to carry out the crime?

When all three elements intersect (i.e., means, motive, and opportunity), the probability that a person committed the crime is much greater. The same is true for creativity. Creative outcomes are much more likely to occur in organizations when individuals have the means, motivation, and opportunity to be creative. We use this framework as a structure to review some specific components of each.

The Means to Create

We start with the means. We begin here because means focuses on the person, and this is where the scientific study of creativity began. It is also where creativity begins, for without the person there is no organizational creativity. Much of the early work in the field looked at the personality traits that distinguished individuals who demonstrated higher levels of creativity versus traits of those who did not. We do not present a comprehensive list; rather, we share some of the dispositions most often cited in the literature. Because these personality traits are so fundamental to creativity, you will see some of them revisited and further described in additional chapters. To personalize this list, we encourage you to assess the degree to which you possess these personality traits; to bring them to life, we link each trait to an icon of creativity—Steve Jobs.

- *Risk taking.* Individuals engaging in higher levels of risk taking show independence in thought, are often nonconforming, defy the crowd, question assumptions and norms, do not demand guarantees, and move forward even when failure is a possibility. Steve Jobs was a classic risk taker. His penchant for taking risks was evident even from an early age. When he was 12, he dared to call Bill Hewlett, cofounder of Hewlett-Packard, to ask for spare parts to feed his fascination with computers. As Jobs said, "You've got to be willing to crash and burn. If you're afraid of failing, you won't get very far."[14]

- *Open-mindedness.* Highly creative individuals suspend their evaluation, remain open to possibilities, show a high tolerance for ambiguity, show patience in the face of uncertainty, and demonstrate flexibility in considering different perspectives and opinions. They also display a willingness to shift to another approach when the previous strategies are shown to be ineffective. In his 2005 commencement speech at Stanford, Jobs captured the value he placed on being open-minded: "So when a good idea comes, you know, part of my job is to move it around, just see what different people think, get people talking about it, argue with people about it, get ideas moving among that group of 100 people, get different people together to explore different aspects of it quietly, and, you know—just explore things."[15]

- *Curiosity and playfulness.* Those inclined to engage in creative behavior and to produce creative breakthroughs often show relentless interest in discovery and experimentation. They actively explore the world and themselves. They approach concepts, possibilities, and ideas in a playful manner. When Apple was founded, and for a long time afterward, Steve Jobs liked to think of the company as a group of swashbuckling pirates—a small band of mavericks who were going to shake up the computer industry. In fact, Jobs flew the Jolly Roger flag outside of Apple headquarters.

- *High energy level.* Highly creative people throw themselves into their work. They maintain their energy over long periods of time, both on specific projects and across their careers. Steve Jobs was well known for his high energy level, a seemingly endless reserve that allowed him to relentlessly pursue the next big idea. Without such drive, it would have been impossible for Jobs to bounce back from his dismissal at Apple to then serve as cofounder of Pixar Animation Studios. As one professor of entrepreneurship and *Wall Street Journal* blogger said of Jobs, "He didn't flinch from the unrelenting reality of the situation, charted a clear strategy going forward, and was willing to commit to huge amounts of energy to reach the goal."[16]

- *Embodiment of contradictions.* The creative personality possesses traits and attitudes that seemingly contradict each other. MacKinnon's famous study of some of America's most creative architects, for example, revealed such opposing qualities as daring yet also "planful," unconventional and at the same time organized, spontaneous but adaptable, and a mix of both forgiving and egotistical.[17] Csíkszentmihályi made a similar observation of creative people, adding such opposing traits as smart yet naive, high energy but often quiet, a mix of playfulness and discipline, an ability to move from imagination to a rooted sense of reality, both extroverted and introverted, and a mix of masculine and feminine.[18] So, creative people seem to possess a complex personality in which they are able to adopt and merge different personal traits. When Walter Isaacson, author of the biography on Steve Jobs, was asked about his main insight into the real Steve Jobs, he said,

He had a lot of contradictions in his personality. Connecting a countercul-
ture, rebel, misfit sensibility with a business-like, engineering sensibility
is part of what made him contradictory, but what also made him amazing.
He approached all aspects of his life with these contradictions: his cancer,
the products he made, his personal life.[19]

Beyond possessing personality traits that predispose someone to act and think
more creatively, an individual must also possess the necessary knowledge in his
or her chosen field. A scientist, teacher, chef, manager, entrepreneur, or artist who
does not possess the basic knowledge of his or her domain is at a serious disadvantage. Basic knowledge provides the building blocks to creative breakthroughs.
However, to make creative contributions or to stand out as distinctive, one must
avoid being trapped by the limits of current knowledge. This is where the personality traits described earlier contribute to creative success. It is the curious,
open-minded risk taker who is most likely to take knowledge and apply it in
new ways, thus making valuable contributions as an innovator or entrepreneur.
Organizations do not start up and evolve on their own; they do so only through
the imagination of individual members. So having basic knowledge allows you
to acquire the same raw material as everyone else, but the person with a creative
disposition can take that raw material and make something new.

Personality, then, is one part of the means necessary for someone to be
creative. Personality creates the right mindset or attitude that allows the creative mind to roam more freely, but it takes effective creative-thinking skills to
maximize the creative spirit. Attitude creates the space for possibilities, whereas
thinking creates the possibilities themselves. Earlier, when we debunked the
misconception that creativity is some magical process, we indicated that our
minds evolved in such a way that enables us to engage in a number of thinking
skills that promote creativity. Again, a way of thinking that is central to creativity
is divergent thinking. Divergent thinking is the ability to generate many different and original responses to a challenge, and this skill is a strong predictor of
lifetime creative achievements. In the previous chapter, we described the four
main thinking skills associated with divergent thinking: fluency, flexibility, originality, and elaboration. Next we list a few more skills associated with effective
creative thinking.[20]

- *Problem finding and formulation.* Highly creative individuals have been
described as problem finders. They sense gaps and see opportunities where others
do not. They point out problems when others ignore them. They spot difficulties
and deficiencies in things, people, and themselves. Individuals who come up with
new innovations are rarely presented with a nice, neat, and tidy problem. Rather,
they discover interesting problems that need to be solved. And research shows that
the time spent on clarifying the problem translates into more creative outcomes.
Innovators and entrepreneurs cannot generate breakthroughs if they do not know
what problem they are solving.

- *Conceptual combination.* Highly creative individuals are able to integrate previously separate concepts and ideas. They borrow and transpose concepts from one field to another. For instance, George Lucas borrowed from mythology, Nazi ideology, and American Western lore to create the epic film series *Star Wars*.[21] Among all American presidents, perhaps no other has been more written about than Abraham Lincoln. Seth Grahame-Smith's recent fictional book, *Abraham Lincoln: Vampire Hunter*, provides a good example of how a novel combination could shed new light on this well-known historical figure.[22] His novel cleverly weaves vampires into the story in such a way as to offer an entirely new alternative explanation for the cause of the Civil War and portrays this great president as a devout, and immortal, vampire killer.

- *Analogy.* Whereas conceptual combination brings together two, or more, previously unrelated concepts to produce a new outcome, analogical thinking is focused on finding similar situations from which to borrow ideas in order to solve a problem. Charles Darwin, for example, borrowed ideas from geology and the slow development of the physical characteristics of land formations, like river valleys and mountains, to gain insights into biological evolution. Mark Zuckerberg borrowed ideas from the college yearbook to create Facebook. The creators of Google, comparing finding a page on the World Wide Web to locating a single page in an entire library, used this analogy to guide the development of their ubiquitous search engine.[23]

The Motivation to Create

Imagine two people in the same field who essentially possess the same knowledge, personality traits, and creative-thinking skills, such as those skills just described, yet one is primarily driven by an interest in rewards and acclaim, whereas the other is driven by passion for the work itself. Who would you predict is more likely to produce more creative outcomes? It is one thing to possess the means to be creative, but means without motivation is likely to produce very little. And, it turns out, a particular kind of motivation is best at unlocking creative potential—intrinsic motivation. This is the kind of motivation that comes from within; it's engaging in an activity for the pure joy and satisfaction inherent in the activity itself. In contrast, extrinsic motivation has an external focus, an interest in rewards such as fame and fortune. Extrinsic motivators can also take the form of other people, such as competitors or those who will evaluate the performance. In such cases, individuals may become more concerned about the competition or the observer, shifting creative energy away from the task at hand.

Teresa Amabile, Harvard Business School professor, has carried out a great body of research on motivation and creativity, clearly demonstrating the overwhelmingly positive effects of intrinsic motivation and the deleterious effects of extrinsic motivation on creativity.[24] Dr. Amabile uses a wonderful metaphor to contrast the effects of intrinsic and extrinsic motivation. There are two mice whose task it is to move through a maze. The mouse that gets through the maze first gets the food, whereas the other goes hungry. With food as a reward, and given the fact that competition means there will be only one winner, this situation is heavily tipped toward extrinsic motivation. Therefore, our racers will be focused on finding the quickest way through the maze. And if the race is conducted time and time again in the same maze, the mice will simply learn to run faster and faster through the maze, taking the same route, the most direct, over and over again. *So what's the problem?* you say. To the victor go the spoils. Let's say one mouse is curious and wants to spend more time in the maze exploring. This mouse isn't interested in finding the quickest route through the maze but wants to find alternative ways through the maze. The extrinsic dynamics here are likely to undermine this mouse's intrinsic curiosity. After all, being curious and exploring is a big risk, a risk that the mouse will go hungry.

Writers, scientists, entrepreneurs, inventors, and others engaged in creative pursuits are often more like our second mouse; they are curious and wish to spend time exploring interesting alternatives. They report that they are less concerned about money and other rewards than they are about producing interesting work. This is not to say that extrinsic rewards are completely ignored, of course; some level of reward is required to sustain us. And when the extrinsic rewards align with intrinsic motivation, this can become a winning combination, especially as the extrinsic rewards help to reinforce the intrinsic value the person derives from his or her work. Steve Jobs provides a perfect example of this winning combination, but most importantly, he exemplifies the importance of intrinsic motivation and how it feeds creative work. Here are a few quotes from Jobs that underscore how intrinsic motivation fueled his creative power.

> I was worth over $1,000,000 when I was 23, and over $10,000,000 when I was 24, and over $100,000,000 when I was 25, and it wasn't that important because I never did it for the money.

> Being the richest man in the cemetery doesn't matter to me. Going to bed at night saying we've done something wonderful, that's what matters to me.

> Remembering that I'll be dead soon is the most important tool I've ever encountered to help me make the big choices in life. Because almost everything—all external expectations, all pride, all fear of embarrassment or failure—these things just fall away in the face of death, leaving only what is truly important. Remembering that you are going to die is the best way I know to avoid the trap of thinking you have something to lose. You are already naked. There is no reason not to follow your heart.[25]

Doing something for the love of it is what sustains motivation and energy over the long haul. In 1990 J. K. Rowling stood on a train platform in Manchester, England, waiting for a train to London; perhaps fortunately for the world, the train was delayed. As someone who had been writing since she was a little girl, naturally her imagination was not idle during this hour-long delay. A story began to form in her mind, the story of a school for wizards, a character named Harry

Potter, and a train referred to as the Hogwarts Express. Once onboard, she discovered she had no pen or pencil to jot down her ideas, so she spent the next 3 hours elaborating on this story in her mind. When she arrived in London, she dashed home and lost herself as she captured the story that originated on the train platform in Manchester. She experienced the state of flow—that peak experience in which the creator becomes so lost in the creation experience that he or she loses all track of time.[26]

The story doesn't end, however, with this aha moment and state of flow; it took 7 years before the first Harry Potter book appeared in bookstores. And these were not easy years. J. K. Rowling experienced many setbacks and challenges in her personal life. She went through divorce, lost her mother, and lived off government support for a time. Furthermore, as a single mother, it was difficult to find blocks of time to write. In fact, while living in Edinburgh, she would take her daughter out for a stroll in her baby carriage, waiting for her to fall asleep. J. K. Rowling would then stroll her sleeping daughter into a café or coffee shop and write until her daughter awoke.

What allowed J. K. Rowling to persist through these challenging times? We would suggest it was her intrinsic drive to write this story. As Rowling said, she simply knew she had to write the story. So despite the fact that things were so bad that J. K. Rowling referred to herself as the biggest loser she knew, she persisted over those 7 years to see her book finally published. The Harry Potter series is one of the bestselling sets of books in history, with more than $400 million in worldwide sales.

J. K. Rowling found writing intrinsically motivating. If you don't already know what intrinsically drives you, how do you find out? Harvard University education professor Tony Wagner suggests that three characteristics signal activities that are intrinsically motivating for someone.[27] They are play, passion, and purpose, the 3 *Ps* of creativity presented in Chapter 1. If the activity feels like play to you, if you are passionate about it, and if it feels like the activity fulfills, in part, your life's purpose, then you may well be engaged in an intrinsically satisfying effort. People who find their work intrinsically satisfying report greater creative outcomes, joy, and engagement at work.[28] And employees who are intrinsically engaged are significantly more innovative. Where do you experience play, passion, and purpose? It's crucially important to figure this out. Steve Jobs said:

> Our work is going to fill a large part of your life, and the only way to be truly satisfied is to do what you believe is great work. And the only way to do great work is to love what you do. If you haven't found it yet, keep looking. Don't settle. As with all matters of the heart, you'll know when you find it.[29]

Whereas the means to be creative and the motivation to be creative make massive contributions to individual creativity, one more factor is necessary, and this is especially true in organizational contexts—people need the opportunity to be creative.

The Opportunity to Create

About four decades ago, a Swedish professor by the name of Göran Ekvall was studying employee suggestion systems in a large European-based car company.[30] As Ekvall examined how well these employee suggestion systems were working, he discovered something peculiar. Despite the fact that he was studying various manufacturing plants within the same company, he observed that in some locations there was great success, lots of employee involvement, and many ideas being adopted, whereas in other sites the suggestion systems were hardly used. This made Professor Ekvall curious, and he embarked on a program of research to discover what caused such noticeable differences.

Early research in the field of creativity focused on characteristics of the person. More recently, scholars like Ekvall have turned their attention to the environment for creativity. Just because a person has the requisite knowledge, coupled with the right set of personality traits and thinking skills, there is still no guarantee that creative results will follow. Place an individual with the means and motivation to be creative in an unsupportive environment, and you are likely to find very little of this potential realized.

The environment for creativity can be thought of in a number of ways. It refers to physical space and how the structure of the surroundings facilitates or undermines creative thinking. Closely associated with physical environment is the availability of resources to support creativity. Scientists need their labs. Designers need access to material and technology. Artists need their studios. Environment also refers to culture, the deeply held values and norms in society or an organization. It has been argued, for example, that America's cultural values related to individualism, hard work, and self-made success have favored our creativity as a nation. Another concept related to the creative environment is psychological climate. This is the factor Ekvall found to be a significant predictor of successful employee suggestion systems, and he subsequently demonstrated that climate has a profound impact on the level of innovation found in an organization.

Climate refers to the attitudes, feelings, and behaviors that permeate an organization or a work team.[31] Where there is a positive climate, the opportunity for individuals to be creative is much greater. Ekvall identified 10 climate dimensions that promote organizational creativity; to provide a sampling of these dimensions, we describe five of Ekvall's factors. In our discussions with corporate groups, these are the five dimensions most often cited as crucial for employee creativity. When looking for an opportunity to be innovative, we strongly suggest that you examine the degree to which these five qualities are present in your place of employment (or prospective employment). And for those with an entrepreneurial bent, to sustain innovation in your organization, it will be important to imbue your start-up with these qualities. For the other five dimensions, see Ekvall[32] or Puccio et al.[33]

- *Freedom.* A work environment with a high level of freedom means that employees have some degree of autonomy; that is, they can explore different ways of carrying out work. In an environment low in freedom, everything is prescribed; there is no scope for exploration or deviation.

- *Idea support.* This dimension has to do with how ideas are received. In a climate high in idea support, new ideas are treated with great care and actively sought after. Conversely, new ideas are met with immediate skepticism and critique in an environment low in idea support.

- *Risk taking.* A workplace that accepts failure and is comfortable with uncertainty is indicative of a climate where risk taking is encouraged. In contrast, a low risk-tolerant environment is marked by hesitation, fear, and cautiousness. In such environments, employees work hard to avoid making mistakes and therefore rarely experiment or try new ideas.

- *Idea time.* Idea time refers to a climate in which there is time to reflect, time to think, and time to puzzle through complex problems. Without idea time, employees feel a great deal of pressure to meet deadlines. They focus on just getting the job done and pay little attention to more innovative practices and opportunities. Certainly deadlines are necessary, but the most innovative companies, such as Google, Gore, and 3M, adopt organizational practices that allow individuals time to explore interesting ideas.

- *Debate.* In a climate that allows for debate, people are able to disagree and to challenge others' views and positions. High levels of debate encourage an exchange of different viewpoints and greater diversity of opinions. Low-debate environments are likely to suffer from groupthink because people are unwilling to question each other.

It takes the means, the motive, and the opportunity for individuals to be creative. Whereas all three are essential, the opportunity to be creative, especially in the workplace, can often be the crucial deciding factor as to whether an individual is creatively productive and happy at work. This fact is highlighted in the powerful stories and research outcomes associated with Amabile and Kramer's analysis of nearly 12,000 daily diaries generated by 238 employees from seven different organizations.[34] Their analysis of these employees' work experiences showed that more positive work experience translated into more successful and innovative outcomes for their organizations. Of course, the opposite was true as well; employees suffered when creative opportunities were not available, as did the success of the organization. In a dramatic example, Amabile and Kramer describe how in just 4 years a new management team took a consumer products company recognized as one of the 10 most innovative companies in America and drove it out of business. This is not an exaggeration: The company closed down, people were out of work, and a small town lost an important economic engine. In short order, the new management team replaced a vibrant and dynamic corporate climate with an oppressive one that led to what many employees described as an intolerable work experience. Here is a brief list of some of the steps and practices the new management team took that ultimately led to the demise of this innovative industry leader.

- Product design teams lost their freedom to choose their own directions because the new management team exclusively set priority projects.

- Employees' ideas became unwelcome. For example, in examining ways to reduce costs, employees' ideas were rejected in favor of simply sticking with existing cost-cutting measures. And when a project team leader offered new ideas to improve a product concept, an executive told him that his head must have been up his ass (yes, this crude criticism was actually used and apparently was not unusual).

- Upper management showed little tolerance for failure, which led to an atmosphere of fear and blame.

- The new management team installed a confusing organizational matrix in which employees worked under different bosses, with often competing goals, leading to a breakdown in communication and a resistance to sharing ideas.

Those individuals looking to exert their creativity in the workplace would be wise to find organizations with environments that explicitly promote opportunities to create (and to remain innovative, organizations would be wise to create such opportunities). As Amabile and Kramer observed from the analysis of workers' daily diaries,

> People were more creative when they saw their organizations and its leaders in a positive light—as collaborative, cooperative, open to new ideas, able to develop and evaluate new ideas fairly, focused on an innovative vision, and willing to reward creative work. In other words, when people saw that a new idea was treated as a precious commodity—even if it eventually turned out to be infeasible—they were more likely to contribute suggestions.[35]

The need to find opportunities to create seems to be of utmost importance for those who are more entrepreneurially minded. Stanislav Dobrev examined the career paths of more than 2,000 graduates of Stanford's MBA program.[36] The analysis showed a clear pattern among those who founded their own organizations. Such entrepreneurs were likely to leave the organizations they established when their role in these organizations transitioned from founder to manager, which was the case as their organizations moved from the start-up to the growth phase. Dobrev observed that for these entrepreneurs this transition represented a move away from the more satisfying creative components of work they so dearly enjoyed. As organizations mature, and certainly among well-established organizations, the formal structures—reporting relationships, work manuals, procedural guidelines, specific job responsibilities, established procedures—significantly reduce the opportunities for employees to engage in entrepreneurial behavior. Like great creators, entrepreneurially minded individuals require the means, motive, and opportunity to realize their innovative dreams. When they are able to exercise their creativity within an organization, they are more likely to experience what Amabile and Kramer refer to as a positive inner work life. However, when the opportunity to create is not there, such entrepreneurial thinkers are likely to leave and establish their own opportunity to create.

Organizational structures can create a polarity or compressed conflict—two forces that coexist yet pull in opposing directions. On the one hand, organizational structures promote efficiency and thoroughness and create security. On the other, formal structures can limit opportunities to create, to evolve, and to find better or different ways of carrying out work. Like the creative personality, successful organizations must find ways to marry apparently contradictory forces—structure and creativity. Creative employees, those with the means and motivation to add value through their creativity, are essential to the ongoing success of organizations, but when employees are not able to find opportunities to exercise their creative talents, they will become frustrated and withdraw their creative talents. In a flat world, in which change and complexity are on the rise, organizations that do not find a way to leverage the benefits of both structure and creativity run the risk of stagnating and therefore are more likely to become extinct.

Thought Starter
Motive Means
Opportunity

Learning Activity
Myths of Creativity: True/False Test

Answer true or false to the following statements; include an explanation that defends your answer.

1. Creativity applies to any college major.

2. If a person thinks of an idea, that act can be considered creative, even if the person does not implement the idea.

3. Mental illness is a necessity for creativity.

4. Engaging in creativity is not a good use of company time.

Now that you can recognize the myths of creativity, explain the negative consequences of these myths (those in the previous list and in the chapter).

Doing—Creating Your Own Mood

At the beginning of this chapter we referred to a letter attributed to Mozart. Although many scholars now agree that this letter was a forgery, there was one aspect of the letter that was accurate in terms of the creative process. Both neuroscience and research in organizations have clearly and convincingly demonstrated that a good mood promotes creative thinking. When our ideas are under threat, as when we are being self-critical or others are prematurely judging our ideas, our creative output is likely to take a nosedive. The anterior cingulate cortex in our brain, which facilitates the generation of original thoughts, is not activated when we believe we are under attack or are anxious.[37] As a result, we experience tunnel vision, alternatives do not present themselves, and nonobvious answers remain totally elusive. Conversely, when the anterior cingulate cortex is activated, a physiological sign that we are in a good mood, we are much more likely to strike on a breakthrough. Amabile and Kramer's research, described earlier, showed that good mood led to higher employee creativity. To be specific, when employees were in a good mood, there was a "50 percent increase in the odds of having a creative idea."[38] So one way to insert the magic back into your creative process is to learn to put yourself in a good mood.

Andy VanGundy, an expert in organizational creativity, suggested that to be creative, individuals should begin by creating their own internal climate for creativity.[39] Why start with internal climate? First, people are in control of their own attitudes and mindset. If the environment provides opportunities for creativity and an individual does not possess the right mindset, then such opportunities will go unfulfilled even when they are made available to that person. Second, VanGundy argued that a positive internal climate could combat a negative external climate. A strong internal climate for creativity can go a long way in helping an individual to be more resilient in the face of a stifling environment. According to VanGundy, attitudes that create a positive internal climate for creativity included the following:

- *Persistence.* Creativity produces change, and change is not always warmly embraced. In the face of resistance, creative individuals press on. They do not give up in the face of adversity.

- *Openness to new ideas.* Highly creative individuals seek out new ideas, for they recognize that exposure to other people's thinking stimulates their own creative breakthroughs. They acknowledge that being closed off to others' ideas diminishes their own creativity.

- *Independence.* Creative thinkers are not easily influenced by others. They maintain a strong sense of their own identity and therefore resist conformity pressures. They are not bothered when their ideas, insights, and views differ from those of others.

- *Tolerance for ambiguity.* People with a positive internal climate for creativity see the world in shades of gray. The opposite attitude is one in which complex situations are oversimplified into a narrow range of categories or stereotypes or a superficial understanding. Tolerance for ambiguity enables individuals to embrace unstructured problems. A low tolerance for ambiguity can result in a sense of anxiousness, especially as one faces a difficult task, a complex problem, or change.

VanGundy argued that when you embrace these attitudes, you are more likely to see problems in a different way, to generate many novel ideas, and to be a more flexible thinker. Assess your own internal climate for creativity. Ask yourself to what degree you embody the attitudes just described. Self-awareness is crucial in developing a creative mindset.

Learning Activity
Conceptual Combination

Highly creative individuals combine seemingly unrelated concepts to generate new ideas. The following is a list of seemingly unrelated objects and concepts. Combine two at a time to come up with a new concept or idea. Although it may take a few minutes to warm up to this exercise, stick with it. Soon you will find that this simple practice of combining two or more unrelated concepts or ideas is a quick route to original thinking.

- Water bottle, wave, mousetrap, tree, sleep, cook, dream, sunshine, cleanliness, money, plunger, clown, iPad, remote, eyeglasses

- Example: Sleep and cook

- Idea: A new cookbook idea—recipes that cook in the perfect amount of time to take a nap. Make the recipe. Throw it in the oven. Set a timer. Take a nap. Wake up and it's done!

Do any of your combinations respond to a need or present an opportunity? Are any marketable? What's the benefit of knowing how to combine ideas, concepts, and thoughts?

Being—Developing an Internal Locus of Control

You just received poor marks on a big exam, or maybe you just experienced something positive, such as a promotion at work. Whether the situation is positive or negative, your view of the factors that caused the outcome has a lot to do with your likeliness of engaging in creative behavior at work. Do you believe you received low marks on the exam because you were ill prepared, or was your poor performance due to a test that you believe was unfair? How about that promotion at work? Did that come about because of your efforts, or do you attribute your success to a boss who must have liked you?

There is a well-established psychological construct called locus of control that is useful in helping us understand how people interpret situations like those just described. This concept was originated by psychologist Julian B. Rotter and explains how different people attribute the outcomes and events in their lives, such as success or failure, to forces within or outside of their control.[40] People who believe events are wholly within their control are said to have an internal locus of control—called internals for short. Internals believe their actions, abilities, and hard work are the primary force behind the realization of positive outcomes. In contrast, individuals who associate success or failure with environmental factors that are impossible to control are said to have an external locus of control—referred to as externals. Externals, for example, are much more likely to attribute life situations to chance; fate; and powerful others such as bosses, professors, and politicians. The student who sees a poor grade as the fault of the exam, or the employee who believes a promotion was simply due to the good fortune of having a boss who liked him or her, could be said to display an external locus of control.

Locus of control is a personality orientation, a way that someone characteristically views the world along a continuum of internal to external orientation. As a continuum, it is believed people will vary in terms of how strong their orientation is toward one end of this psychological construct. With respect to creativity, perhaps the key link to locus of control relates to individuals' expectations about the future. Specifically, internals believe that future outcomes will be a direct result of their actions, whereas externals are much more likely to believe the future is largely determined by the surrounding environment.

In this chapter, we shared the means, motive, and opportunity model of creativity at work, and with respect to the opportunity aspect of this model, we described how the work environment can facilitate or undermine an individual's creativity. To prevent individuals from playing victim to their work circumstances, we highlighted VanGundy's argument that an individual's internal climate can be useful in combating a poor external environment. To further this point, we suggest

Learning Activity
Evaluate Your Creative Mindset

Extensive research has identified characteristics common among creative people.[43] Check the traits you believe you possess. Which characteristics do you not possess and wish to develop? What action steps might you take to develop these qualities? Ask a few trusted friends or colleagues to do the same for you. Compare their responses to your own. What did you learn by looking at others' perceptions of you?

Thorough	High energy	Risk taking	Spontaneous
Need alone time	Curious	Resourceful	Precise
Courageous	Open-minded	Flexible	Forgiving
Ethical	Sense of humor	Adaptable	Assertive

that our readers explore their orientation toward control. Whereas locus of control may underscore an important individual *means* that contributes to greater levels of creative output, this personal asset may also serve an important role in countering situations that limit the *opportunity* to behave in a creative manner. Indeed, research shows that those with internal locus of control produce more creative outcomes in an unfavorable work environment than those with an external locus of control.[41] Furthermore, studies have shown a link between internal locus of control and entrepreneurship. As Estay, Durrieu, and Akhter indicated in their review of the current research, "Persons with a high level of perceived control (internals) have been associated with entrepreneurial behavior and a preference for innovative strategies."[42] For those who wish to influence others through their creativity, either as entrepreneurs or as intrapreneurs, it would seem beneficial to cultivate a personal mindset with an internal locus of control. If you find yourself giving too much of your creative power over to external forces, how might you modify your own mindset to seize control rather than seeing yourself as a victim of circumstance?

Thought Starter
Locus of Control

Case Study
Hacking Creativity in Taiwan

For decades, the phrase *Made in Taiwan* represented the notion that the intellectual property—the creative ideas for new products—had been imagined elsewhere yet manufactured in Taiwan because of export-oriented trade policies and favorable labor costs. There are some in Taiwan who wish to shed this manufacturing-only label, and they are instigating a shift from *Made in Taiwan* to *Created in Taiwan* in the process.

Indeed, large manufacturers have traditionally sought to increase production volume (making more stuff) to achieve growth, yet it is believed they may also be well positioned to grow by shifting their focus toward value-added activities such as design, brand development, and the integration of their well-established manufacturing prowess with a layer of services companies.[44]

Large companies are not the only ones facilitating Taiwanese creativity. It is also being evidenced in small, local, open-source community membership organizations focused on creativity and innovation called hackerspaces.

Taipei Hackerspace

One of the first hackerspaces in Taiwan, Taipei Hackerspace, was opened in 2012 in the capital city by a Hungarian-born, Cambridge-educated physicist and software engineer named Gergely Imreh.

Anyone can join Taipei Hackerspace and, in so doing, gain access to a wide range of tools, knowledge sharing, and human capital that may not necessarily be available to them otherwise.

(Continued)

(Continued)

For example, electrical power, web servers and high-speed Internet, fabrication equipment (e.g., laser cutters and 3-D printers), software, hardware, electrical components, game consoles, and mobile devices may be available for participants to use as raw ingredients for their imaginations.[45]

The hackerspace has a core group of members but is also open to the community for anyone interested in dropping in, thinking up solutions to problems, and hacking together new inventions. Imreh started Taipei Hackerspace for this very reason: "In addition to wanting it for myself, I thought it would be great if others had access to tools they couldn't afford, nor had the room to keep in a small apartment. Also, the ability to connect and engage with other smart, creative people with similar interests was a big motivating factor for us."[46]

The hackerspace serves as a center of gravity and a support network for anyone with an idea. This means that someone who may be flirting on the edge of creative uncertainty is welcome to come in and give it a go. "Whether it is a new talk you want to give, a project you want to launch, a software hack, a new mobile app, invent a new musical instrument, or perhaps even start your own company, Taipei Hackerspace is a safe haven for this type of thinking," says Imreh.

"This works well in Taiwan because it is relatively easy to start. Sure, you need space and some donated tools and supplies, etc., but there isn't as much entrepreneurial pressure in Taiwan as there is in other places in the world such as Silicon Valley and Shanghai. In those places, there is more pressure to immediately and singularly point your creativity toward launching a tech start-up. In Taiwan, it's okay to explore with less business pressure." At the same time, according to Imreh, creativity may face additional cultural barriers.

Challenges

In Taiwan, parents have a tremendous amount of influence on the educational and professional decisions their children make. According to Imreh, it's an interesting dynamic where the outcomes and results of creativity are rewarded; however, the processes by which someone becomes skilled in creative industries are frowned upon. For example, freelancing on creative projects (e.g., film, photography, web design) while figuring out what you really want to do next is perceived as risky, certainly in comparison to growing up and becoming a lawyer.

This cultural emphasis on safety impacts the creative process in a significant way, says Imreh. "The culture does not encourage confrontation and debate, which I believe is a healthy and important factor for creative expression."

Funding

Sustainable funding is another challenge facing community hackerspaces such as the one in Taipei. Options include obtaining not-for-profit status (which Imreh attempted and moved away from due to administrative complications), fund-raising, or membership dues (the latter can be difficult to maintain because membership ebbs and flows; it also requires a donations coordinator). Government funding is another option, but this puts a hackerspace in competition with already-funded government-operated laboratories. Finally, corporate sponsorship of the space is another route and is the model Imreh and his team have chosen. In this scenario, a corporation or group of corporations is solicited to sponsor the space for an agreed-upon amount of time. "It's not an ideal solution, but it's a good enough solution while we continue to explore sustainable funding opportunities," says Imreh.

Conflict

When facilitating open programming to the community, many types of hackers and creative personalities are often present in the space at any given time, and conflict can arise. For this, a community management strategy is needed. Imreh acknowledges that they don't have this solved 100% yet; however, he suggests the following three guiding principles for those interested in launching a hackerspace:

- As a philosophical guideline, "Do excellent things, and be excellent to each other."

- As an operating guideline, "Take it easy, trust people's common sense, and if not, try to talk sense into them."

- And, finally, a guideline borrowed from a fellow hackerspace operating in Ireland: "There's only one rule to start: Don't do anything that would force us to create a new rule."

Closing

Measuring success in a hackerspace can be challenging, especially because it is such an important factor when reaching out to potential sponsors. Should the goal be to drive membership numbers? If so, how do you value and evaluate active membership versus people who paid dues and didn't actually create anything interesting that month or year? How about the number of active projects in the space? Is there a difference between a successful project and an unsuccessful one? Who measures? Who decides? How about the number of companies started? Again, how are these companies evaluated? Employees hired? Revenue generated? Venture capital raised? How about number of patents filed? Or perhaps "softer" metrics are more germane, such as community momentum and learning? There are many angles to consider, but Imreh ranks one above all others: growth.

Specifically, he cites teamwork and the number of growth-oriented network connections made between people. "People come together and hack away on something and make connections with each other in the community, and it doesn't matter as much whether or not that particular hack worked or not, because the next things they hack on together might—and likely has a higher chance of doing so as a result of their previous effort. Taipei Hackerspace, for us, is a place where people can be creative, and a place where people can challenge themselves and each other; it's a fast track to talent cultivation."

(Continued)

(Continued)

Discussion Questions: Knowing

1. How does the Taipei Hackerspace bring together the motive, means, and opportunity for individuals to be creative?

2. In this chapter you were introduced to five of Ekvall's dimensions of a creative work climate. Describe how any or all of these dimensions come alive in the Taipei Hackerspace.

Application Questions: Doing

1. From what you read about Gergely Imreh, how does he reflect the internal creative climate described by creativity scholar Andy VanGundy?

2. If you were responsible for a hackerspace, how would you measure success?

Thinking Ahead: Being

1. If you were to launch your own hackerspace, what rules would you establish to maximize its mission and success?

2. Do you think the role of hackerspaces will grow or diminish in the future? Why?

The Practical Benefits of Creativity

Becoming an Innovation Asset

Knowing—Top Reasons for Studying and Developing Your Creativity

Chapter 4 closes Part I of this book. In Chapter 1 we made a case that you were born to be creative, suggesting that all humans with normally functioning brains have been hard-wired with the thinking skills and attitudes to engage in creativity. Chapter 2 explored ways in which these naturally occurring creativity skills diminish over time, specifically examining how educational practices and societal pressures can rob individuals of their creativity. In the last chapter we dove into some of the knowledge accumulated about the nature and nurture of creativity. So, we hope by now you know that you were born creative, that over time it is likely that powerful forces have constrained your creativity, and that you have a better sense of the true nature of creativity (as opposed to some of the popular misconceptions). In this final chapter of Part I, we build on this foundational information and explore the benefits of studying and developing your creativity.

Creativity is a transdisciplinary area of study—it cuts across all areas of intellectual pursuit and human endeavor. The ability to think creatively is beneficial, and necessary, in all jobs and in many aspects of life. We explore what we consider to be the top benefits associated with mastering your own creativity. Whereas there are many benefits to studying and developing creativity and creative thinking, we focus on those most pertinent to individuals who wish to position themselves as organizational innovators or entrepreneurs.

Learning Goals

After reading this chapter, you will be able to do the following:

- Describe, in specific terms, why creativity and creative thinking are personally and professionally valuable
- Explain the reasons why creativity and creative thinking are considered 21st-century workplace skills
- Assess, through force field analysis, the sources of assistance and resistance to an innovative idea
- Devise a habitual routine that facilitates greater levels of creativity

Reason #1. Sustains and Fuels Prosperity in the Innovation Era

Welcome to the age of innovation. It is inescapable; organizations and the economy are driven more and more by innovation (defined as the successful introduction of new technologies, the discovery of new applications for existing products and services, the creation of entirely new markets, and the development of new organizational forms).[1] As Felix Janszen, a professor in management of technology, observes, "After the age of efficiency in the 1950s and 1960s, quality in the 1970s and 1980s, and flexibility in the 1980s and 1990s, we now live in the age of innovation."[2] If it feels like *innovation* has reached buzzword status, that's because it has. We examine some data points that highlight the widespread concern for innovation.

Just before the great recession, January 2008 to be exact, McKinsey & Company provided a report on a worldwide survey of senior executives; results showed that more than 70% believed innovation would be among the top three drivers for their companies' growth through the year 2013.[3] In 2010, after the global economic meltdown, McKinsey & Company carried out a similar survey. Results indicated a strong recognition that innovation would continue to be a major driver of growth. More than 84% of the more than 2,000 leaders surveyed indicated that innovation was either "extremely" or "very important" to the growth of their organizations.[4] As with business leaders from around the world, those in the United States have a strong focus on innovation as well. A *Businessweek* survey found that 54% of U.S. executives placed innovation among their top three priorities, and nearly 90% ranked innovation in their top 10 organizational priorities.[5] Mission statements, those public expressions organizations create to communicate their purpose, provide yet another strong indicator of the extent to which organizations have embraced innovation. According to one report, approximately 88% of companies in the United States include either the word *innovation* or *creative* in their mission statement.[6] It would seem that almost every organization wishes to be recognized as the most innovative in its industry.

Governmental leaders also tout the importance of innovation for a thriving economy. For example, in his 2013 State of the Union address, President Obama stressed the importance of innovation as a way to bring jobs back to America. He cited the need for innovation across many sectors, including manufacturing, science, health care, and energy. In fact, he argued that America needed to exceed the high levels of research and development seen during the space race: "If we want to make the best products, we have to find the best ideas."[7] Why so much focus on innovation? In the words of the 2008 McKinsey & Company global report,

> As globalization tears down the geographical boundaries and market barriers that once kept businesses from achieving their potential, a company's ability to innovate—to tap the fresh value-creating ideas of its employees and those of its partners, customers, and suppliers, and other parties beyond its own boundaries—is anything but faddish. In fact, innovation has become a core driver of growth, performance, and valuation.[8]

To remain competitive, organizations have no choice but to innovate. Here is a short but powerful story of an organization that failed to engage in continuous innovation:

Motorola—heroic and innovative pioneer of the cell phone at first, then scorned failure when it didn't jump fast enough to digital phones, then reborn champion when it created the sleek RAZR, then goat once again when it couldn't produce a successor, and finally a casualty of competition with its decision to unload its cell phone business completely. Motorola achieved lots of great cell phone innovations—just not enough of them.[9]

Blockbuster, the onetime giant of video rentals, provides yet another example of a company that went under mainly because it did not engage in continuous innovation. Blockbuster established itself in the 1980s because of its innovative database and distribution system. Blockbuster was a sensational success; in 2004 this company peaked with more than 60,000 employees and 9,000 stores. Only 6 years later Blockbuster, too wedded to its brick-and-mortar business model to see new opportunities, filed for bankruptcy. The competition from companies that brought new innovations to the video rental business, such as Netflix (i.e., video rental delivery that evolved from shipping to streaming videos directly to the customer's home) and Redbox (i.e., video rental machines located at other companies' stores), drove Blockbuster out of business. This paradigm shift meant people no longer needed to go to a particular store to rent videos for in-home use. Ironically, Blockbuster was so blinded by its own business paradigm that it passed on the opportunity to purchase the 1-year-old Netflix for $50 million in 2000.[10]

These are tragic stories, at least as far as Motorola and Blockbuster are concerned, but does innovation truly result in profitability and success? According to Janszen, "Innovation is the golden route to building a growing and prosperous company," but is there evidence for this claim?[11] A team of researchers tested whether innovation translated into bottom-line value for organizations. When they compared the more than 300 firms in their study, Soo, Devinney, Midgley, and Deering found that the most innovative firms enjoyed more than 30% greater market share when compared to the least innovative companies.[12] Apple provides a concrete example of an organization's return on innovation. Within 4 years of its introduction of the iPod, Apple sold 42 million units after an initial investment of $10 million. Combining iPod sales with purchases from Apple's iTunes store produced over $7 billion in revenue from 2000 to 2004.[13] Yet another example of the positive return yielded by innovative research can be found in President Obama's State of the Union speech cited earlier. According to Obama, every dollar invested in mapping the human genome has yielded $140, a very impressive return rate of 140%.

Innovation provides other benefits to organizations beyond financial return. Successful innovation can build confidence in an organization, leading to a willingness to take greater risks and to experiment more in the future. Innovative organizations make themselves more attractive to prospective employees interested in generating and pursuing creative ideas. When organizations innovate, they are much more likely to set new industry standards and to enhance their brands. Business consultants Andrew and Sirkin capture the many advantages of innovation:

If a company does generate cash through innovation, it can create new ideas and products and services and processes, and achieve organic growth for itself. In turn, it can stimulate growth in the global economy and increase the quality of everyday life for its employees, customers, and people around the world. Innovation can create new markets and help economies adapt to changing environments—by developing whole new approaches to such pressing concerns as energy, health care, education, and poverty.[14]

To be sure, there are many benefits to innovation; however, innovation does not happen simply because an organization claims to be innovative in its mission statement or because innovation can be found among its strategic priorities. There is a close relationship between creativity and innovation. Creative thinking is necessary for innovation. When they examined the factors that stimulated innovation, Soo et al. found that the most innovative firms in their study were the most active in applying creativity to develop new knowledge. Specifically, these researchers concluded that "creativity in problem-solving is the main driver of new knowledge creation and innovation."[15]

Reason #2. Necessary for Success in Today's Workplace

Many organizations recognize that their ability to innovate depends largely on the creative talents of their employees. Therefore, creative thinking and problem solving are widely recognized and touted as some of the most desirable workplace skills. Employers are looking for individuals with these skills, and government leaders see that such skills are needed to keep the economy vibrant and healthy. Table 4.1 provides a sampling of seven government, business, and education reports (there are many more reports that reflect the same sorts of skills) describing crucial skills for success in today's workplace.[16] Every list includes one or more skills specifically related to creativity (for ease of reference these skills appear in bold print). What is interesting about these lists is that they show great consistency over time; from 1990 to 2016, every expression of the skills necessary for success in the workplace includes creativity and creativity-related skills.

The important role creativity plays in the workplace is no fad! As long as we find ourselves in an age driven by innovation, skills related to creativity will remain among those deemed most crucial for job readiness. The year 1991 represents a crucial transition point for the U.S. economy. This was the first year that expenditures related to knowledge exceeded industrial expenditures. Since that time, countries around the world have been investing more and more into creating and managing knowledge versus manipulating material goods.

We believe it is reasonable to expect that creativity will continue to be a highly sought-after workplace skill. Specifically, the Institute for the Future, working with a set of business experts, used a forecasting methodology to predict skills

Table 4.1   Skills Necessary for Success in the Workplace

Workplace Basics (1990)	Partnership for 21st-Century Skills (2009)	Future Work Skills 2020 (2011)	Characteristics for Employee Success, Student Results (2012a)	Characteristics for Employee Success, CEO Results (2012b)	Bloomberg Businessweek (2015)	World Economic Forum (2016)
The foundation—knowing how to learn	Learning and innovation skills—critical thinking and **problem solving**, communication and collaboration, **creativity and innovation**	**Sense making**	Communicative (79%)	Communicative (67%)	Communication	(in order of most importance)
Competence—listening and oral communication		Social intelligence	Collaborative (68%)	Collaborative (75%)	Analytical thinking	• **Complex problem solving**
Adaptability—creative thinking and problem solving		**Novel and adaptive thinking**	**Flexible** (67%)	**Flexible** (61%)	Collaboration	• Critical thinking
Personal management—self-esteem, goal setting	Digital literacy skills—information, media, information and communication technology	Cross-cultural competency	**Creative** (66%)	**Creative** (61%)	**Strategic thinking**	• **Creativity**
Group effectiveness—interpersonal skills, negotiations, teamwork		Computational thinking	Analytical/quantitative (49%)	Analytical/quantitative (50%)	Leadership	• People management
Influence—organizational effectiveness and leadership	Career and life skills—**flexibility and adaptability**, social and cross-cultural interactions, productivity and accountability, leadership and responsibility	New media literacy	**Opportunity seeking** (45%)	**Opportunity seeking** (54%)	**Creative problem solving**	• Coordinating with others
		Transdisciplinarity	Globally oriented (45%)	Globally oriented (41%)	Motivation/drive	• Emotional intelligence
		Design mindset	Technology savvy (41%)	Technology savvy (41%)	**Adaptability**	• **Judgment and decision making**
		Cognitive load management	Assertive (28%)	Assertive (25%)	Quantitative	• Service orientation
		Virtual collaboration	Disruptive (11%)	Disruptive (16%)	**Initiative/risk taking**	• Negotiation
					Decision making	• **Cognitive flexibility**
					Industry-related work experience	
					Global mindset	
					Entrepreneurship	

necessary for success in the workplace in 2020. The 10 skills identified in this report (see Table 4.1) featured three specific creativity skills—novel and adaptive thinking (i.e., coming up with solutions beyond those that are rote or rule based), design mindset (i.e., developing work processes that lead to desired outcomes), and sense making (i.e., ability to derive deeper meaning from what is being observed). According to the authors of this report, the combined effect of increased automation and global offshoring has caused a bifurcation in the job market—middle-skill blue-collar and white-collar jobs are down, and the opportunities for high-skill jobs (e.g., technical and management occupations) and low-skill jobs (e.g., food service and personal care) are up. The curious commonality between jobs at either end of this spectrum is that they both require an ability to apply imagination in responding to unexpected and novel situations. As this report indicates, "Tasks as different as writing a convincing legal argument, or creating a new dish out of set ingredients both require novel thinking and adaptability."[17]

Table 4.1 shows the results of a 2012 global IBM survey of both students and CEOs. There is a striking consistency between what students and CEOs see as the top personal characteristics for success in the workplace; standing head and shoulders above all other characteristics were communicative, collaborative, flexible, and creative. In describing the necessity of this skill set in today's workplace, the authors of the study noted that these four personal characteristics "help the employees and leaders of tomorrow become 'future-proof'—they will be able to continuously adapt by acquiring skills and capabilities that may not exist today."[18]

Thought Starter
Creativity in the
Workplace

Creativity is a high-demand skill in established organizations, and it is a vital skill for those who wish to create new business ventures. The very description of an entrepreneur is akin to that of the creative person. For example, one study of entrepreneurs described them as opportunity focused, open to change, innovative, flexible, unafraid of failure, resourceful in an environment of constraints, fluent idea generators, curious, and intuitive.[19] As with all successful creative people, across a variety of fields, they focus on the identification of novel ideas that create value for themselves and others. They are creative thinkers who envision new futures and creative problem solvers who produce workable solutions to intractable problems. The entrepreneurial process is imbued with creativity.[20] Entrepreneurs allow their minds to freely explore new opportunities, possess a risk-taking attitude that fortifies them as they launch new enterprises based on their novel ideas, create a vision and plan for sustained growth, and remain persistent in the face of setbacks.[21] Finally, at the end of the day, entrepreneurial success would seem to depend a great deal on one's creative prowess.[22] Not all creative people are entrepreneurs, but it would certainly seem that all successful entrepreneurs are creative people.

Reason #3. Contributes to Effective Leadership

What it means to be an effective leader is largely determined by the context in which one leads. In a world experiencing increased levels of change, traditional approaches to leadership no longer work. IBM conducted a survey of more than 1,500 business leaders around the world; these leaders reported that the business environment was more complex than they had ever seen it, and they were confident that it would continue to become more and more complex.[23] Where their confidence waned was regarding their ability to lead in such quickly changing times. Given this leadership challenge, most of these top leaders felt creativity was the most important leadership quality going forward.

In times of change, leaders need to be flexible so they can adapt quickly to new situations. Leaders must not only be equipped to respond productively to change but also be effective at driving change. Management is an organizational practice that promotes the status quo. Leadership, by contrast, is a practice that brings about change. In an era defined by innovation and change, we need creative leaders effective at spotting new opportunities. Industry research shows that among various qualities, such as years of experience, cultural intelligence, and personality, creative leadership practices made the strongest contribution to driving organizational innovation (i.e., challenging the status quo, creating a shared vision, fostering intrinsic motivation).[24]

Whether you are an executive, a school principal, a director of a not-for-profit organization, an owner of a start-up company, a shift manager at a restaurant, or someone who wants to bring about community change, the common denominator among leaders at all levels, and in all arenas, is the ability to facilitate the movement of a group toward the attainment of meaningful goals. As leaders guide groups toward goal attainment, there undoubtedly will be challenges along the way, and this will be especially true for those who lead their start-ups into uncharted territory. Leaders, therefore, need to be effective problem solvers, and because many of the problems they face do not have clear solutions, they need to be creative problem solvers. Indeed, Michael Mumford of the University of Oklahoma has found clear evidence that the more successful leaders are effective creative problem solvers.[25]

One of the authors of this book, Gerard Puccio, and his colleagues have argued that the 21st century has ushered in a new kind of leadership—creative leadership.[26] Creative leaders are individuals who embrace their own and others' creativity so they can inspire and guide teams, organizations, communities, and even countries in new and productive directions. The Dalí sketch on the next page illustrates a leader and followers who were unwilling to explore a new direction, like the organizational examples of Kodak, Motorola, and Blockbuster. Unless you are willing to use imagination and flexibility to redirect your destiny, eventual changes in the environment are likely to disrupt your business model, thereby threatening the survival of your organization. As creativity has become an essential skill in the workplace, so too have creative thinking and creative problem solving become core leadership skills.

Reason #4. Improves Problem-Solving Skills

You face a problem anytime there is a gap between what you have and what you want. And you need to use creative thinking to solve that problem when you do not have a solution in mind for how you will close that gap. Problems differ in

Salvador Dalí,
Tour cycliste de la mort
(Death's Cycling Tour), 1937
pen and ink on paper, image:
12 in × 8½ in

© Salvador Dalí,
Fundació Gala-Salvador Dalí, Artists Rights Society (ARS), New York 2017

© Salvador Dalí Museum, Inc.

their nature. For example, a simple distinction is to differentiate algorithmic from heuristic problems.[27] There is a known method for solving an algorithmic problem, and the application of this method typically leads to a single correct solution. The field of mathematics provides classic examples of what we mean by algorithmic problems, but our daily lives also provide useful examples of algorithmic problems. You wake up in the morning, and there's no milk for your cereal. Do you need to apply your imagination to solve that problem? Probably not. The issue is whether you have time to get to the closest grocery store and back before you have to set off on your day. Wi-Fi stops operating in your home. What do you do? Brainstorm possible solutions? Probably not. Experience has taught you that rebooting the router solves the problem 99 out of 100 times.

In contrast to solving these closed-ended and straightforward problems, sometimes you have no predetermined response in mind or formula you can follow to produce that arguably correct answer. These are referred to as heuristic problems. This is when you need to employ creative thinking in your life. As J. P. Guilford, a pioneering scholar in the field of creativity, said, "To live is to have problems, and to solve problems creatively is growth."[28] Perhaps your company needs that breakthrough idea to survive. Maybe you just got laid off from the only company you've ever worked for and now you need a new life plan. Or you need an alternative plan because you've just discovered that you are missing a crucial ingredient for a meal and you don't have time to get to the store. Your team needs a new game plan as they prepare to compete against an opponent with much greater talent. In all these examples, creative thinking is required to discover or invent an imaginative solution—one that closes the gap between where you are now and where you wish to be. Without creative thinking, you are forced to accept situations as they are presented to you. Using imagination deliberately enables individuals to generate novel and useful responses to problems.

Everyone faces problems; it's inescapable. Children give their parents plenty of practice at problem solving. Artists and writers solve problems when they create. Scientists by nature are problem solvers. And entrepreneurs endeavor to create commercially viable solutions to consumers' problems. Problem solving is a key aspect to successful relationships. And as we argued earlier, creative problem solving is essential to effective leadership. Learning to be a more creative thinker, and to use imagination on demand, enables people to be more effective in all aspects of their lives.

Reason #5. Enhances Resilience, Coping Skills, and Psychological Well-Being

An ability to solve problems creatively is closely connected to resilience, coping, and psychological well-being. Improve your ability to solve problems creatively, and you make yourself more powerful in the face of life's ups and downs. Effective creative problem solving builds resilience, without which people run the risk of not fulfilling their potential.

Psychologist Mihály Csíkszentmihályi, known for his work on the concept of flow, argues that seeing alternatives improves coping skills. Csíkszentmihályi makes the case that people can choose how to respond to stressful situations.[29] Where one person might see himself or herself as a victim of the circumstances, such as the 40-year-old who loses a well-paying job and becomes a drunkard, another person could suffer the same fate but responds by undergoing retraining and then successfully embarking on a new career. Csíkszentmihályi describes the latter case as an example of transformational coping. We would argue that transformational coping goes up considerably when individuals are able to engage in creative thinking. You are at the greatest risk when you see no alternatives. Creative thinking is about seeing, and generating, many possibilities, and the more alternatives available to you, the more likely you are to find a productive way forward. When there are no, or limited, alternatives, the situation feels out of control; creating many alternatives places you in control, thereby reducing stress and increasing probability of success.

Creativity goes beyond being able to cope with stress; engaging in a creative lifestyle is likely to contribute to a much more positive sense of well-being. Before positive psychology, there was humanistic psychology, and many of the leaders in this field argued that creativity and self-actualization were closely related. Carl Rogers, for example, believed that creative people are able to realize their full potential; these are people able to expand, develop, and express their fullest capacities.[30] Self-actualized people are fully functioning, mentally healthy individuals who have embraced a creative approach to life and employ this positive attitude to develop themselves to their greatest capabilities. Psychology professor Gary Davis eloquently summarizes the intersection of self-actualization and creativity: "Living creatively is developing your talents, learning to use your abilities, and becoming what you are capable of becoming."[31] Today the main aim of positive psychology is to help individuals find greater fulfillment in their day-to-day lives by helping them to be more happy, adaptive, and creative.[32]

In a world that moves quickly, where stability and predictability are short-lived, creativity can go a long way in helping you to be more resilient and adaptable when it comes to life's inevitable changes. Even more, some medical doctors now report that keeping your brain young, by remaining curious and creative, promotes a longer life, more satisfying relationships, and greater happiness and reduces the risk of dementia.[33]

This chapter presents five reasons for studying and developing your creativity (see following list). Add your own reasons (personal, professional, general), generating five more to bring the list to a robust set of 10.

1. Sustains and fuels prosperity in the innovation era

2. Necessary for success in today's workplace

3. Contributes to effective leadership

4. Improves problem-solving skills

5. Enhances resilience, coping skills, and psychological well-being

What does this list tell you about the state of the world today, both in terms of professional and personal challenges? What might be some future trends that will reinforce the importance of creativity?

Doing—Selling Creativity

The top five most prolific inventors of all time each hold more than 1,000 patents. Further down that list, with 186 patents to his credit, is an inventor whose creative imagination helped to transform the auto industry in the first half of the 20th century. Today his name is perhaps more widely recognized for its association with cancer research, for he was one of the two philanthropists who helped establish the Sloan Kettering Institute. Charles Kettering was passionate about building cars consumers wanted, cars that were safer and more powerful, offered greater comfort, and were more reliable. To a large degree, it was his drive and inventiveness that enabled General Motors to surpass Ford as the number-one car manufacturer in America.

As founder of Delco, and later as head of research at General Motors, Kettering was involved with many inventions that revolutionized automobiles, such as the self-starter and unleaded gasoline, but we highlight one of his lesser-known but nonetheless transformative innovations (one we believe you will appreciate). When Kettering became head of research for General Motors in the early 1920s, the first project he dedicated himself to was the painting process. At that time, it took 37 days to paint a car. In those days the painting process was still very much influenced by the old approaches used for stagecoaches and furniture— hand application of layer upon layer that had to dry in between coats. This was a huge bottleneck in the manufacturing process and made it impractical to produce cars in a range of colors—in the early days of the auto industry, cars were mainly painted black because it was more economical to limit the options to one color, and black paint dried the fastest. Kettering challenged the paint team to speed up the process, and after close analysis, the team reported that they could reduce the time from 37 to 30 days. Kettering was unimpressed and in frustration snapped, "An hour would be more like it."[34]

Shortly after this meeting, Kettering found himself window-shopping along Fifth Avenue in New York City, where he noticed a pin tray finished in a beautiful lacquer he had never seen before. He purchased the tray and then through some detective work located the producer of the lacquer in a backyard in New Jersey, where he acquired a sample. Working with DuPont, Kettering was able to homogenize the lacquer with paint so that it was thin enough to apply through a spraying process. This new type of paint could be applied efficiently and dried quickly. Furthermore, it was weather resistant and when dry had a glossy finish. Kettering now had his solution to the cumbersome auto-painting process. He returned to General Motors and shared his solution with the paint team, who warmly received it and quickly adopted it. Right? Wrong!

Recall that generating creative ideas often places one at odds with prevailing practices, sometimes pitting one against the crowd. Selling a novel idea can be a difficult proposition even when you are the boss, which was the case for Kettering, whose nickname, by the way, was "Boss" Kettering. His idea of converting the painting process from the slow brush application to the spray-on lacquer paint that dried quickly was met with great resistance. Kurt Lewin, a social psychologist, indicates that any time change is introduced, forces will either support the proposed change or resist it.[35]

Kettering, known for his persistence and his bent toward practical jokes, was not about to give up on this creative idea and went to unusual lengths to woo his doubters. He took one of the most vocal naysayers to lunch. During their meal they talked about paint, and Kettering rehashed the merits of his proposed new painting process. The paint man remained unconvinced, and Kettering kindly escorted him to the man's car in the parking lot. When they reached his car, the man looked confused and explained that it looked like his car but that his car wasn't that color. Kettering replied, "It is now!" During their lunch, Kettering had a team paint his guest's car a different color to prove the effectiveness of his creative idea. And Kettering was successful. This practical joke was crucial in turning this doubter around, and soon after General Motors was selling cars in different colors. With the economic boom of the roaring 1920s, demand for cars increased; with the increased appetite for cars, consumers were growing tired of the only color option on the road—black. The ability to personalize one's car helped to undermine the sales of the Model T and eventually pushed this car into extinction. In the competitive world of business, one company's innovation often leads to another's demise.

Thought Starter
Selling Creativity

Kettering is an excellent example of someone who brought his creativity into the workplace and drove innovation at General Motors. The moral of the story we just shared is that Kettering was a successful innovator because he used his imagination to overcome resistance to his proposed change. Happily, there is a tool you can use to think like Kettering. It's called force field analysis. Kurt Lewin developed this tool in which you capture the forces that support or oppose your proposed change, whether that be a new product, service, policy, or procedure. In its simplest form, you create two columns (see Figure 4.1). In the left column, you list the forces that will support your change, and in the right column you list the sources you believe will oppose your creative idea. Forces can be individuals, groups, facts, and reasons that will stand in support of your idea or against it. After listing these forces, you can then assign a number to gauge the strength of each force. For example, you might use a scale from 1 (low) to 5 (high). Once numbers are assigned, columns can be totaled to subjectively assess the relative strength of the factors for and against your proposed change. This analysis can be used to determine whether you go forward and, if so, how you might leverage forces that will support you and devise plans to address those factors likely to stand in your way. Sometimes the most important place for imagination in the creative process is in overcoming the forces that resist your new idea. Therefore, when using force field analysis, we strongly advise you to not simply create lists of the sources of assistance and resistance but to actively think about how to leverage the sources of assistance and overcome the sources of resistance.

Figure 4.1 Force Field Analysis Worksheet

Proposed Change, Idea, or Venture

Supporting Forces	Score (1–5)	Score (1–5)	Opposing Forces
	Total:	Total:	

Possible Action Steps
(Ways to Leverage Supporting Forces and Address Opposing Forces)

You work for an advertising agency. You have been approached to create a public service announcement on the value of creativity for society and business. Script a 30-second commercial for the Internet, radio, or television. What was your major selling proposition relative to promoting the importance of creativity? How would you use this proposition to pitch a course or workshop on creativity to an organization (your own if you are currently working)?

Being—Making Creativity a Habit

As we close the first part of this book, we wish to encourage you to explore ways in which you might make creative thinking a habitual part of your life. Whether you work inside an organization or are interested in your own start-up, the reality is that you become a greater organizational asset, like Charles Kettering was for General Motors, when you enhance your creative prowess. And creativity, like all other abilities, is improved through repetition and practice.

Despite the popular misconceptions of great creators who receive great ideas in a lightning-bolt flash of inspiration, the reality is that creativity is hard work. And great creators work hard at their creativity. As Steve Jobs noted, the secret is that there is nothing separating you from other great creators. It is simply a matter of finding your passion and practicing your creative imagination—along with developing a vision, determination, and willingness to defy the crowd. This is the recipe for creative success in both your professional and personal life.

Stephen King's work has frightened millions of people. This imaginative writer has produced more than 50 novels that have sold well over 300 million copies. Writing in the genres of horror, suspense, supernatural fiction, and science fiction, King's success depends on an active imagination, and his longevity highlights a kind of creativity that has been sustained over time. Stephen King, like other successful creators, does not leave his imagination to chance. Instead he, like other writers, artists, scientists, and entrepreneurs, has created a daily work routine that feeds his creativity. He writes every day of the year, generally at the same time and in the same place. He produces at least 2,000 words each and every time—good, bad, brilliant, or mediocre—2,000 words every single time. As King notes in his memoir, his work routine is a signal to his mind that it is time to dream and to create.[36]

Mason Currey's book *Daily Rituals: How Artists Work* reviews the habitual routines established by 161 writers, artists, scientists, composers, entrepreneurs, and other creative types.[37] Not surprisingly, there is no single winning formula—there are early risers and late-night creators; there are those who create in bed, whereas others need to be seated at a desk; some eat and drink, yet others avoid food; some require a neat and organized work space, whereas others prefer to be surrounded by clutter—but what seems to be consistent is the regularity of these creators' routines. And some found that their creativity did not flow until they discovered their own creativity rhythm. As a young writer, Henry Miller would work from midnight until dawn, but he soon realized that he was really a morning person. When he switched his writing time so that he worked between breakfast and lunch, his creative productivity soared.

Of course, there is no common work routine among great creators; they vary, and thus you will need to find your own habits that will serve as cues to create and innovate. You may not be a writer, but the same creative practice is equally applicable to you. Like Stephen King, you might wish to dedicate some time every day—and if not every day, at least on a regular basis—to allow yourself to deliberately dream about opportunities, modified practices, challenges that might be overcome, or new operations. In other words, just as you may set aside time for physical exercise, use this creative time to exercise your imagination. This practice will truly make you an innovative organizational asset.

To some it may seem contradictory for the authors of a creativity book to recommend establishing a routine to be more creative. But behavioral psychologists have shown us that humans can be conditioned to respond in predictable ways, so why not use operant conditioning to stimulate creativity? What is important is that you find, through experimentation, the kind of routine or habits that enable you to think more creatively. Does the buzz of a coffee shop help you to think, or do you need utter quiet? Perhaps background music stimulates your creative thoughts. Do you find that creative ideas come to you more readily when you work under bright lights or in a room that is dimly lit? Do you require frequent breaks, or do you prefer long periods of sustained focus? The goal is to find what works for you and then repeat that practice when you need to facilitate your own creative thinking. By doing so you will put yourself into a mood to create.

Learning Activity
Creativity Ritual

Identify someone you consider to be a creative success and interview that person to see what rituals he or she has adopted. Consider questions like these: Identify the steps in your creative process. Can you list the attributes that make you a creative person? Where are you when you are most creative? What kinds of creative behaviors do you demonstrate on a daily basis? What conditions have the biggest impact on your creativity? What are you doing when you are most creative? What are the sources for your most creative ideas? Use this interview to identify rituals that you might add to your own routine, and begin to introduce these rituals into your daily life.

When Kyle Wild was 11 years old, he decided that he didn't believe in God—a problematic insight for a young man in the middle of a Catholic school education in a part of the United States commonly referred to as the Bible Belt. At 13, he submitted a paper on Pascal's Wager, adopting a critical stance on what he was being taught at school and fueling a strong desire to find an alternative school.

This conflict between what the learner was seeking and what the institution was professing led Wild to drop out and enroll in the Illinois Math and Science Academy (IMSA). Unlike the Catholic school model, the IMSA approach embraced the following beliefs that resonated with Kyle:

- All people have equal intrinsic worth.
- All people have choices and are responsible for their actions.
- Belonging to a community requires commitment to the common good.
- Diverse perspectives enrich understanding and inspire discovery and creativity.
- Honesty, trust, and respect are vital for any relationship to thrive.
- Learning never ends.
- Meaning is constructed by the learner.
- No one's path in life is predetermined. The ability to discern and create connections is the essence of understanding.
- We are all stewards of our planet.[38]

These academic guiding principles not only attracted Kyle Wild, but they were also attractive to a group of young men and women who would go on to become his best friends and future start-up cofounders. During high school and in college, this group would go on to start many projects, including failed companies, a think tank, and even a Burning Man camp(!)—most of which didn't work out the way they'd imagined.

After college Wild took a job at Google. He describes the experience as being told to turn a wrench exactly the same way, 100 times per week. In response, he devised a method to achieve this wrench-turning quota before the end of the day on Monday evening! With Tuesday through Friday available to him, he began to experiment on his own; however, he was singled out for this unconventional strategy and reprimanded for appearing lazy. "I understand why you would want to organize yourself that way if you were a manufacturing company, but if you're a software company, why would you want that?" asks Wild.[39]

The experience was profound enough for Kyle to leave the Internet search giant. In hindsight, it was a fortuitous decision, for he would reconvene with his friends from high school and go on to cofound Keen IO, a fast-growing data analytics company.

With 3,000 paying enterprise customers, approximately 50,000 software developers using their platform, and more than 50 employees, and flush with a recent infusion of Series B venture capital ($14.7 million raised in June 2016), Keen IO is poised for continued growth.[40] Their success, however, presents a

(Continued)

(Continued)

challenge: how to grow and also maintain the identity and values that helped the company thrive in the first place?

In response, the Keen IO team has evolved into a "deliberately developmental organization."[41]

The Nature of a Deliberately Developmental Organization

A deliberately developmental organization (DDO) is one that strives to weave the personal growth of employees into the nature of the work itself. It's a layer of effort and planning and investment in people, with the goal being not just the growth and development of the business but also of the people within it. The argument, according to advocates of DDO theory, is that companies can become more profitable if personal development is treated as a core operating principle of the business.[42]

For Keen IO, this commitment to self-development is evidenced in their prioritization of concepts such as emotional well-being, continuous learning, honesty, empathy, and personal agency. According to CEO Kyle Wild, "We invest in these areas believing that all other types of performance will catch up; introspection is the number one value around here, and if I see week over week performance growth, I'm willing to ignore short term results."[43]

The company website is further evidence of this transparent, people-first approach to organizational design. The Team tab at the Keen IO site, for example, reveals a rotating layout of employee profiles (versus a static, hierarchical pyramid with CEO and executive team always on top), and site visitors are offered links to employee Twitter handles, LinkedIn profiles, and top five Gallup StrengthsFinder[44] values.[45]

To support Keen IO in the execution of this nontraditional, deliberately developmental personnel strategy, the company turns to its VP of People, Lisa Nielsen. Nielsen, an organizational psychologist with graduate degrees in organizational development and psychology, is tasked with the design and implementation of programs to help guide people toward embracing challenges, inviting and internalizing feedback, and relentlessly pursuing opportunities for mastery.

Specifically, at Keen IO, Socratic coaching programs challenge employees to look inward and engage in *self-stretching*. In addition, Keen IO employs a full-time feedback coach and charges other team members to support employees with peer-to-peer coaching. The goal is for employees to spend at least 1 hour every other week identifying opportunities for growth and then, through conversation, surface their own strategies and tactics relative to their most significant growth opportunities.

Furthermore, the Keen IO team invests time and energy into nontraditional workplace programs such as yoga, meditation training, emotional regulation, nonviolent communication strategies, emotional intelligence, and mindfulness and has even begun developing external-facing workshops.

The public Keen IO learning labs not only support employee development, but in opening them up to friends, investors, customers, and the community at large, the team is strategically sharing their appetite for growth and learning with key stakeholder groups, while simultaneously boosting their profile and ability to attract technology talent in a hypercompetitive marketplace.

In addition to talent attraction, there are practical business benefits to being deliberately developmental and learning to self-regulate one's own mood, argues Wild. Emotional awareness plays a huge role in the hiring at Keen IO, and the teams pay close attention to fear and aggression because of how effectively they can kill creativity before new ideas have had a chance to be explored.

Furthermore, Wild considers these programs to be important because of the physical symptoms that manifest in the brain and body when someone feels or experiences an intellectual threat. For example, "If investors push back on a business decision we've made, because of deliberate practice, I can self-monitor, catch it, 'breathe,' and then create space for solutions to present themselves later." Also, Wild believes this skill of self-monitoring has helped him become more effective at evaluating new ideas. Where the temptation may exist to criticize a new idea immediately, says Wild, "I've learned to wait five minutes and consider the idea from multiple perspectives before turning a critical lens to it."[46]

Organizing to Be a DDO

Keen IO is a Montessori-style company, says Wild, and it was designed this way so that it could be capable of systematic serendipity: "If you overplan and overoperationalize everything, then no positive surprises can happen. And at the same time, it's also important to strike a balance, because we've learned that you need to insert controls when you get up to 25+ employees."

For Wild, there is a constant interplay between what he thinks of as "creative thinking" versus "optimization thinking." At any given moment, the Keen IO team is determining how much to invest in *evolution* versus *revolution*. "We must determine whether we are crawling toward a local maximum versus missing out on an entirely new mountain peak to climb." This balance is important, says Wild. "You can't invest too much in creativity, or else you'd never eat!"[47]

Closing

Kyle Wild's early educational experiences not only fostered the important friendships that would develop into future business partnerships, but those experiences also helped him think about the ways in which environments and organizational design influence creativity and problem solving—lessons that would be invaluable to him in his career and life.

"If I had to design an engine to punish kids and destroy their creativity, I'd make sure there was a timing bell and seats that were only allowed to face forward; I'd enhance conformity wherever I could, and I'd make sure that students were all willing to turn the wrench the same way." By contrast, the experience at the Illinois Math and Science Academy reflected more of a Montessori-style educational philosophy: "We sat in circles and the pace was driven by the top performers in the class, versus the pace being set by the slowest in the class; everything was built on collaborative problem solving."[48] These positive and negative experiences allowed Wild and his team to evolve their ideas and company into a fast-growing DDO that unleashes the creativity of all employees.

(Continued)

(Continued)

Discussion Questions: Knowing

1. In what ways is Keen IO designed to promote creativity? How would you predict that this organizational design promotes greater levels of organizational innovation?

2. How do creativity and creative thinking play a role in Kyle Wild's leadership style?

Application Questions: Doing

1. In your opinion, how does Keen IO deliberately make creativity a habit?

2. Emotional intelligence is the ability to be aware of your own emotions, to facilitate your emotions in a way that does not allow them to undermine success, and to be able to read others' emotions. Given this description of emotional intelligence, in what ways do you see Keen IO generally, and Kyle Wild specifically, display high emotional intelligence? Emotional intelligence is covered in a number of chapters, most notably Chapter 10. After reading that chapter you might wish to return to this case to identify ways in which emotional intelligence is exemplified here.

Thinking Ahead: Being

1. If you were a member of a start-up company, how would you convince others to adopt the deliberately developmental organizational strategies seen in the Keen IO case?

Doing

Proven Practices for
21st-Century Innovators

CHAPTER

5

Think

How to Improve Your Fundamental Capacity to Think in Creative Ways

Learning Goals

After reading this chapter, you will be able to do the following:

- Describe the role judgment plays in the creative process and the consequence this has on organizational creativity

- Summarize the four fundamental steps of the universal creative process—creative problem solving and design thinking mash-up

- Discuss how creative behavior results from the interplay among knowledge, imagination, and evaluation, combined with a playful attitude

- Develop a more creative mindset by adopting the principles of divergent thinking

- Generate a broader range of alternatives through the application of divergent thinking

Knowing—Understanding the Creative Mind

A Story About Managing Judgment

We start Chapter 5 with a short story, a story gleaned from Buddhist teachings.[1] Two monks were returning to their monastery. One of the monks was older and much more practiced in Zen philosophy, the other his younger pupil. Due to the heavy rain that had fallen earlier that day, the streets were filled with deep puddles. As they walked along, they came upon a young woman standing on the side of the street. From the forlorn expression on her face, it was obvious that she was greatly concerned about crossing the street for fear of soaking her new dress. Upon witnessing this dilemma, the older monk approached the young woman and, with her permission, carried her across the street, placing her safely on the other side.

The younger monk was aghast, for he had been taught that monks were not supposed to touch women. This obvious indiscretion so plagued his mind he was unable to meditate that evening and had great difficulty sleeping. The next morning he confronted his master by saying, "You know that monks are not allowed to touch women, yet yesterday you carried that young woman across the street." The older monk smiled and replied, "I dropped her on the other side, but you are still carrying her."

In this chapter we explore the basic thinking involved in the creative process, that is, the foundational thinking necessary to leverage your creative mind. Of particular importance is the way in which we manage our judgment. To be sure, judgment and evaluation play an important role in the creative process, but when misapplied, judgment and evaluation place blinders on creative thinking. In the opening story, the older monk was able to set aside his judgment and as a result recognized an opportunity to assist the young woman. In contrast, the younger monk, unable to suspend his judgment, not only missed an opportunity but became overly preoccupied with the situation. When you hold too tightly to a thought or idea, it becomes difficult to entertain other thoughts and ideas. Learning to manage your judgment opens your mind to new possibilities.

You might think that the lessons from this story do not apply to organizations, but organizations are merely a collection of people who may or may not be adept at spotting and leveraging new opportunities. In the business world, this could make the difference between continuous growth and survival versus stagnation and death. This inability to spot new opportunities can easily be witnessed in a few classic examples, and in both cases these ideas originated from the brains inside of the company. Xerox, a U.S.-based company founded in 1906, was a pioneer in the duplication and document management business. As a company with a penchant for innovation, Xerox initially developed and demonstrated computers that featured a graphical user interface in the 1970s. Reports have it that the then board of directors did not see the value in such technology and ordered Xerox engineers to share these inventions with Apple technicians. The upstart computer company hired away some of the Xerox employees, refined the technology, and went on to feature the mouse-driven graphical user interface in one of the first successful personal computers—the Apple Macintosh.[2]

An innovative pioneer in the photography industry, Kodak filed for bankruptcy in January 2012. This former longtime industry leader found itself in financial ruin as a consequence of its very slow transition from film photography to digital photography. The irony in this story is that one of Kodak's very own engineering teams, led by Steve Sasson, is credited with building the first working digital camera in 1975.[3] Unfortunately, due to the long development cycle for this new idea, in conjunction with Kodak's existing business models based on film photography, this once highly innovative company was initially skeptical of this opportunity and then was exceedingly slow in joining the digital world. In 1976 Kodak possessed 90% of film sales in the United States and 85% of camera sales. It has been reported that Kodak's market dominance led to an unimaginative and complacent corporate culture.[4]

Like the young monk in the story, Xerox and Kodak both overlooked the opportunity in front of them. Both companies were unable to relax their judgment, which had become fixated on the past and current business practices. According to Collins and Porras, authors of *Built to Last: Successful Habits of Visionary Companies*, those organizations that are best able to stand the test of time are those that do not get wedded to ideas and actions embedded in their strategic plans.[5] Instead, strategic plans are approached much more flexibly, just like the older monk who was able to deviate from the prescribed teachings of his faith. When opportunities come along, successful organizations are able to manage their judgment to adapt to emerging situations.

Thought Starter
Judgment

Creative Thinking and the Creative Process

An open and flexible mind is better prepared to receive creative opportunities when they present themselves; however, individuals do not have to wait passively for creativity to arrive. Rather, it is possible to coax creativity along. Creativity does not need to be left up to chance; instead, people can be taught to create ideas and resolve challenges in a way that leads to new opportunities. That is to say, creative thinking is a trainable skill. Solid empirical evidence demonstrates that educational and training programs can significantly enhance individuals' creativity.[6] It is definitely possible to learn to be a better creative thinker. In the chapters in Part I of this book we referred several times to a specific set of creative-thinking skills called divergent thinking. As a reminder, divergent thinking is the ability to generate many diverse and original thoughts; the degree to which you can engage in divergent thinking is a strong predictor of the level of creative behavior you are likely to achieve. Earlier we noted that longitudinal research with nearly 300,000 school-age children highlighted the fact that the ability to engage in divergent thinking rises until about sixth grade and then drops sharply, never to regain its former level.[7] We would argue that if divergent thinking can be drummed out of us, the inverse is also true, that divergent thinking can be improved through training and education.

Creativity training programs have proved effective at not only increasing divergent-thinking skills but also improving problem-solving skills, creative performance, and creative attitude. A rigorous selection and analysis of 70 scientific studies of creativity programs shows that creativity training is effective.[8] Let's examine these outcomes more closely. Regarding divergent thinking, creativity training has been shown to significantly increase such skills as fluency (ability to generate many responses), originality (ability to generate novel responses), flexibility (ability to generate a diverse range of responses), and elaboration (ability to expound on a concept or response). Furthermore, creativity training programs have demonstrated a positive effect on improving individuals' ability to produce original solutions to complex problems. Creativity programs have been shown to significantly improve overall creative performance, that is, the ability to generate creative products. Finally, creativity training has been shown to enhance creative attitudes and behaviors, such as modifying how people react to novel ideas. Creativity training does not favor any particular type of learner, for the authors of this meta-analysis of creativity programs concluded that

> creativity training contributed to divergent thinking, problem solving, performance, and attitudes and behavior for younger and older students and for working adults, and for high achieving and more "run of the mill" students. . . . Taken as a whole, these observations lead to a relatively unambiguous conclusion. Creativity training works.[9]

This research team also evaluated key factors contributing to the effectiveness of the most successful creativity training programs. Here the researchers found that programs based on cognitive models, that is, a focus on teaching ways of thinking, were by far the most effective. Programs based on cognitive models explicitly focus on teaching creative-thinking principles and skills that make up the creative process and then engage individuals in learning deliberate strategies that allow creativity to happen on demand. Specifically, this research team's analysis pointed to creative problem solving as the most successful creative process for the purposes of creativity training (one of the main models taught at the International Center for Studies in Creativity at Buffalo State).

In its most basic form, creative problem solving includes four steps. To begin, the mind must first clarify the nature of the problem to be resolved. Once the problem is identified and understood, then the mind can generate ideas to address the problem. These ideas represent tentative solutions, and in the next stage of thinking, the mind develops these initial concepts into workable solutions. In the final step of the creative process, the mind must work out the plan for moving the proposed solution into reality. At this point, the mind must identify the action steps necessary to launch the new creative solution and, to ensure success, must monitor and adjust as needed to guide the fragile fresh concept through to its full realization. For shorthand we refer to these four steps as Clarify, Ideate, Develop, and Implement.[10] Although there is a natural progression through these steps, the mind is able to jump back and forth among them.

These four areas of the creative process are universal; all human minds use these forms of thinking. As noted in Chapter 1, the ability to apply imagination to solve problems gave humans a competitive edge; you evolved to think creatively. No matter your level of intelligence, your gender, or your nationality, because of evolution, you came into the world wired to innovate. And the creative process is universal in that it cuts across all areas of human endeavor. The same thinking process is equally valuable in business, art, science, human service, music, technology, and more.

To this universal creative process we wish to add concepts associated with design thinking. Over the last several decades, design thinking, a deliberate creative process specifically focused on generating products and services with the consumer in mind, has attained great popularity in organizations and business schools.[11] The strength of design thinking is its clear focus on creating solutions that are human centered—making something new that is driven by the person or people for whom the solution is intended. This human-centered approach is central to design thinking; it's not about engineers creating solutions for other engineers but is focused on creating solutions that really work for the user. As Steve Jobs said, "Design is not just what it looks like and feels like. Design is how it works."[12] Not surprisingly, as a deliberate creative process, the stages associated with design thinking closely parallel the universal steps of the creative process outlined earlier (i.e., Clarify, Ideate, Develop, and Implement). Boiling it down to its simplest form, design thinking can be outlined in the following way: first, empathize with users by understanding their needs and issues; second, define the specific opportunities and challenges that emerge through an understanding of users; third, generate solutions that respond to these opportunities and challenges;

and fourth, create prototypes of the best solutions and refine them by soliciting feedback from user groups.

To best promote the creative-thinking skills of our readers, we have created a mash-up of the creative process. That is, we took the best of the cognitive models proven to enhance creative thinking (i.e., Clarify, Ideate, Develop, Implement) and married this to some of the most powerful features of design thinking (i.e., Empathize, Define, Ideate, Prototype). Our creative process mash-up merges the strengths of these two powerful models—creative problem solving's flexible application to a wide range of organizational challenges with design thinking's focus on the development of new product concepts and services. Through this mash-up, our goal is to help you maximize your creative-thinking skills in a way that positions you as an innovative asset to your organization, either as an intra-preneur or entrepreneur. This mash-up is presented in Figure 5.1.

For our purposes, the four steps of the creative process mash-up are Understand, Ideate, Experiment, and Implement. In the first step, the goal is to closely observe a situation to define the most important opportunities and chal-lenges to be addressed. In the second step, Ideate, the insights gained from this understanding are used to visualize and generate a range of creative ideas. These creative ideas must be refined into great solutions. The purpose of the third step, Experiment, is to develop the best ideas and to validate their appropriateness. For innovation to occur, creative ideas must be put into action. The final step, Implement, is aimed at getting buy-in for the proposed solution and making this proposed change stick.

With the goal of helping you to enhance your creative prowess, we use this creative process mash-up as a framework to explore and develop some specific creative-thinking skills. In the next four chapters, we use this model to explore and practice two skills associated with each step. For Understand, we examine the power of observation and how it influences the ability to define interesting problems (see Chapter 6). With Ideate, we discuss the role of visualization, the ability to see ideas in the mind's eye, and ways to generate a wide range of ideas (see Chapter 7). In the Experiment step, we discuss ways to develop good ideas into great solutions and

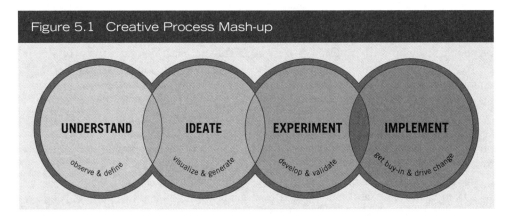

Figure 5.1 Creative Process Mash-up

UNDERSTAND
observe & define

IDEATE
visualize & generate

EXPERIMENT
develop & validate

IMPLEMENT
get buy-in & drive change

then how to validate them (see Chapter 8). Finally, with Implement, we examine approaches for gaining buy-in for a novel solution and then how to manage the change that naturally occurs when a new solution is adopted (see Chapter 9). To be clear, we could explore many other creativity skills, but we feel that highlighting a few crucial skills is likely to maximize learning and application. And both our knowledge and experience tell us these combined eight skills are absolutely fundamental to creativity. Therefore, we are confident that the information (the knowing) and practices (the doing) we present relative to these eight skill areas will do much to enhance your natural creative-thinking skills (the being).

Developing the Mindset for Improved Imagination

The International Center for Studies in Creativity at Buffalo State (the State University of New York) has been studying and teaching creativity for 50 years. One of the founding faculty members and a pioneer in the field of creativity education, Dr. Ruth Noller, devised an elegant description of creative behavior.[13] As a mathematician, she saw creativity as a formula that can be summarized as follows: $C = f_a$ (K, I, E). In this formula, the degree to which an individual will achieve creative outcomes (C) is a direct function of three factors: (1) the amount of knowledge (K) the individual possesses regarding the task, situation, or problem; (2) the extent to which the individual is able to apply imagination (I) to generate novel approaches; and (3) the level of effective critical evaluation (E) the individual can apply to select and develop the most promising creative idea in light of the situation.

This formula has stood the test of time and provides an excellent framework for thinking about how to nurture higher levels of creative behavior. To begin, as many models and theories hold, the foundation to most creative breakthroughs is a sufficient level of knowledge and expertise. If you are going to contribute creative breakthroughs, for example, in business, physics, art, music, cuisine, computer technology, or literature, it is necessary to possess some basic knowledge relative to that domain. Knowledge alone, however, is insufficient to cause a creative insight. To the contrary, knowledge can sometimes get in the way of creative thinking, and thus, imagination is necessary to ensure you are not trapped by your knowledge—the belief that what you now know represents the full range of what is possible. Imagination, the ability to see new possibilities, has always been the springboard to the creation of new knowledge. Finally, imaginative possibilities need to be refined and made real through good critical thinking.

Thought Starter
Creativity Formula

Noller's definition reflects the thinking process that some believe led to the creative explosion in human civilization that we described in Chapter 1. In Noller's formula, knowledge serves as the input into the creative process, and at a broad level the creative process is represented as the balance between imagination and evaluation. Recall that some experts believe that the ability of humans to shift and direct their thinking among defocused thought, imagination, and focused thought (evaluation) contributed to the creative explosion. However, whereas the physiological components, the ability to engage in defocused and focused thinking, were in place approximately 100,000 years ago, it wasn't until *Homo sapiens* learned to suspend judgment—what Carruthers called pretense—that the creative explosion occurred. Returning to Noller's definition, note the small *a* at the beginning of her formula. According to Noller, it is this small *a* that makes all the difference, that is, whether someone fully uses his or her knowledge, imagination, or evaluation. This part of the formula refers to attitude. For *Homo sapiens* to truly take advantage of their creative thinking, they had to adopt a more open-minded attitude toward possibilities. It is one thing to be able to think of imaginative possibilities and quite another to have the right attitude that allows your mind to entertain and play with such possibilities. Remember that the two monks in the story at the beginning of this chapter both had the physical capability of carrying the young woman across the street, but it was the older monk who was able to suspend his judgment and come to her aid.

A crucial component of the creative attitude is an ability to manage judgment, especially the ability to postpone judgment in order to see new and interesting possibilities. For your own creative explosion to occur, you too must learn how to unleash your creative thinking by properly managing your judgment. In the Doing section of this chapter, we describe four principles that, when employed by an individual, have been proven to enhance creative thinking.

Learning Activity
Draw Your Process

Think back to a time when you solved a problem creatively. Once identified, sketch the process you went through to resolve this situation. Use images and icons to make your creative process visible. Upon completion, review your work to identify links between the creative process mash-up presented in this chapter and your own experience. Additionally, examine your drawing for connections to Noller's formula for creativity. In the Experiment step of the process we describe the importance of taking time to explore an idea and improve it. Tools such as sketching can be helpful (more elaboration on this point is found in Chapter 8). What insights do you get for improving your own creative process by looking at your sketch?

Doing—Training the Creative Mind

Improving Imagination by Applying Principles for Divergent Thinking

As discussed, creative thinking balances both imagination and evaluation. Just as some physical abilities are useful across a range of athletic endeavors, such as strength, speed, and agility, imagination and evaluation make positive contributions to each of the four fundamental steps of the creative process. And like physical abilities, thinking skills can be learned and applied, resulting in improved imagination and evaluation. Just as you can learn to be physically flexible, as depicted in the Dalí sketch titled *Hysterical Arch*, so too can you learn to be a flexible and creative thinker. Practice the principles and strategies in this book, and through this mental exercise you can become a more flexible and creative thinker.

In this chapter we indicated that divergent thinking was a skill shown to be directly and positively impacted by training. Divergent thinking fuels imagination as it allows the mind to actively search for novel alternatives. Research into creativity training has highlighted a set of principles that when learned and internalized significantly enhance one's ability to engage in divergent thinking. Next we briefly describe four principles, two of which focus on cognitive strategies for improving divergent thinking and two reflecting attitudes that support divergent thinking. Learn to follow these principles, and you will immediately improve your capacity to engage in divergent thinking and, as a consequence, your ability to generate creative breakthroughs on demand. We begin with the two principles that help to set the right attitude for creative thinking, and then we describe two principles designed to guide good thinking.

Salvador Dalí, *L'Arc Hysterique* (Hysterical Arch), 1937 ink on paper, image: 22 in × 30 in.

Defer Judgment: The Key Attitude to Open the Creative Mind

We began this chapter with a story about two monks. The older one was able to suspend his beliefs in order to assist a stranded young woman. But the younger monk's judgment was so fixed he not only missed the opportunity to help but also became so preoccupied with the older monk's behavior that he was unable to meditate or sleep that evening. This story highlights the key principle to divergent thinking: The extent to which a person is open to new possibilities is directly impacted by a willingness to temporarily withhold evaluation. Judgment focuses the mind. When an individual begins to employ judgment, the range of thought narrows mainly to the item under consideration, and consequently, it becomes difficult to perceive other possibilities. Fixation, then, results in stagnation.

When seeking new possibilities, premature evaluation and the application of judgment block the imagination. This has been demonstrated by research.[14] In one of the earliest investigations into creativity training, two groups of students were compared in their ability to generate ideas. In one case, students were presented with a problem and told to follow the defer judgment principle; that is, they were taught to withhold their judgment and to record all ideas that came to mind. The second group of students was presented with the same problem; however, they were instructed to generate only good ideas. In other words, the researchers prompted these students to apply judgment as they were simultaneously generating ideas. When the ideas generated by students under the two different sets of instructions were compared, the group that withheld judgment was found to have produced nearly twice as many good solutions for the problem.

Why does this happen? When an individual is able to let go of judgment, the mind is encouraged to defocus. The benefit of a defocused mind is that the brain is able to freely search through memory for answers and is likely to be much more open to new stimuli and unique combinations of thought. Gabora and Kaufman, in their description of the evolution of the human brain, provide an eloquent reflection on the neurological mechanisms at play when evaluation is suspended: "When the individual is fixated or stuck, and progress is not forthcoming, defocusing attention enables the individual to enter a more divergent mode of thought, and working memory expands to include peripherally related elements of the situation."[15]

Whereas the defer judgment principle reflects a creative attitude, it seems to have a physiological basis in terms of brain function. When the mind is defocused, activation within the brain's neural net is flat, meaning that thought is more diffuse, intuitive, and associative. In contrast, when humans engage in evaluation, the shape of the activation function is spiky, reflecting analytical thought. Gabora and Kaufman observe that the defocused brain "is conducive to divergent thought; it enables obscure (but potentially relevant) aspects of the situation to come into play."[16]

When you come upon a situation that requires imagination, don't leave a breakthrough up to chance. Instead, use your ability to reflect on your own thinking, a skill called metacognition, to direct your mind in such a way as to relax your judgment. Allow your mind to explore all options and alternatives in an unfettered manner. Do not judge your own or others' thinking while simultaneously searching for imaginative ideas and solutions. Instead, apply evaluation only after you have exhausted the search for possibilities.

Seek Novelty: An Attitude to Ensure Original Thinking

The defer judgment principle opens up the mind, but this does not ensure that imaginative options will be generated. To further bolster a creative mindset, we encourage individuals to intentionally seek out novelty. Creative breakthroughs are both novel and valuable. Whereas the defer judgment principle is designed to create a friendly forum in which individuals entertain all possibilities, it does not necessarily facilitate new thinking. By following the principle of seek novelty you are intentionally generating and examining options that are original. Recall that you engage in divergent thinking when there is a need for imagination; to ensure original thinking, we encourage you to include ideas that at first glance may even seem outlandish.

The well-known design firm IDEO follows these same principles when engaging clients in divergent thinking.[17] (By the way, the person who originated these principles was Alex Osborn, developer of brainstorming.[18]) While working with Air New Zealand to reinvent their customer service experience for long-haul flights, IDEO encouraged the client team to seek novel possibilities. This led to the generation of such outlandish ideas as harnesses that hold people upright while flying, installing hammocks on flights, and using bunk beds. Such wild concepts ensured a forum in which all options were considered, which led to another outlandish idea, or at least one that seemed crazy at first. The idea was a seat that would allow passengers to lie flat in economy class. At first this might seem ridiculous because such seats in first class take up much more room, thus reducing capacity. However, experimentation with the idea led to a workable concept called the Skycouch. The design features a heavily padded section that swings up like a footrest, enabling a couple to lie down together. The Skycouch has been installed in Air New Zealand's international flights, and the company has won industry awards for this new concept.

The defer judgment principle opens the door for possibilities, but by seeking novelty you usher original ideas through the door. The brain is like a muscle; if you want more imaginative responses to problems at work and to life's persistent challenges, practice seeking novelty.

Go for Quantity: A Universal Cognitive Strategy

Whereas the first two principles are aimed at forming a creative mindset, the next two principles describe cognitive strategies that feed divergent thinking. The go-for-quantity strategy is straightforward; perhaps the best way to have breakthrough ideas and thoughts is to have lots of ideas and thoughts. We refer to this as a universal cognitive strategy because it turns out that no matter the field of creative endeavor, those who produce and play with more ideas tend to generate more creative breakthroughs. Steve Jobs, Dean Kamen, Thomas Edison, Pablo Picasso, Ernest Hemingway, Maya Angelou, the Beatles, and other eminent creators didn't simply produce a small number of ideas that eventually became breakthroughs. Rather, great creators tend to generate and examine many ideas, of which a small percentage achieve the status of creative breakthrough. Alex Osborn, originator of these divergent-thinking principles, said it well when he argued that a quantity of ideas tends to breed quality. Think about it—quantity allows you to leverage probability. When you face a challenge, isn't it better to have an array of options instead of just one option? The more options you create for yourself, the more likely you are to find an answer that will work.

James Dyson, inventor and entrepreneur, is a living example of the go-for-quantity principle. For example, he created 5,127 prototypes before striking on his first successful bagless vacuum cleaner. In a recent interview, he was asked to provide advice to those interested in innovation and invention. One of the major points he offered was to try many ideas and to fail often. As Dyson observed, "Failures are interesting . . . if you welcome them and try to understand them and watch them. I think that's the most important thing, . . . actually building and watching your own prototype fail. That's what gives you the idea of how to improve or change it."[19]

The rule of quantity leading to quality works for not only individual success but for organizations as well. According to the research they conducted into companies that have stood the test of time (defined as 100-plus years), Collins and Porras found that the most successful organizations "try a lot of stuff, and keep what works."[20] The go-for-quantity principle means that from many options some will emerge as successful breakthroughs, and as a consequence many options will emerge as failures. Think of it in these terms: Just as experimenting with many variations is fundamental to biological evolution, experimentation with many alternatives is vital to the creative process. As Collins and Porras concluded about successful companies,

> It might be far more satisfactory to look at well-adapted visionary companies not primarily as the result of brilliant foresight and strategic planning, but largely as a consequence of a basic process—namely, try a lot of experiments, seize opportunities, keep those that work well (consistent with the core ideology), and fix and discard those that don't.[21]

Companies are not living things; they do not generate and experiment with new ideas. Rather, it is the people within organizations who generate and experiment with new possibilities. Therefore, to enhance your success and to make yourself an even more attractive asset for your organization, we encourage you to practice the principle of go for quantity. For those mainly interested in entrepreneurial ventures, the go-for-quantity principle will help you generate many start-up ideas, as well as provide you with the mental horsepower to more skillfully respond to the abundant challenges associated with starting a new enterprise.

By training your brain to generate lots of options, you will immediately improve the number of creative breakthroughs you generate both at work and in your personal life.

Thought Starter
Go for Quantity

Make Connections: The Cognitive Ability to Form New Combinations

Creative breakthroughs rarely emerge from a vacuum. They are not gifts from some mysterious muse. Instead, most new ideas evolve from past ideas or emerge from the combination of previous ideas. As Albert Einstein once said, "The secret to creativity is to hide your sources." And research into creativity training has shown that one of the most successful cognitive strategies is conceptual combination, which is the ability to link two or more concepts into a new idea.[22]

For instance, Julie Corbett received her first iPhone in 2007, and she was greatly inspired—not by the phone, but by its packaging. It came nestled in a biodegradable smooth fiber tray. Despite the lack of a design background, Corbett, who worked in investment management, began toying with ideas for new kinds of packaging. Corbett synthesized a number of past ideas into a new form of environmentally friendly packaging that could be used to replace plastic bottles. The exterior of her bottles are made from old cardboard boxes and newspaper, and the interior, inspired by the milk bags she used growing up in Montreal, Canada, is made from thin plastic. The shell provides a sturdy exterior, and the thin plastic interior holds the liquid. In 2008 Corbett filed a patent for this design and started a company called Ecologic Brands. This design uses 70% less plastic than conventional bottles, and it can be broken up for recycling. Ecologic has sold more than 2 million bottles and is building a new factory that is expected to turn out 9 million bottles per year.[23]

Julie Corbett's story is not unusual. Her creative breakthrough was sparked by another idea. In fact, she found a way to synthesize two ideas into one new idea—the iPhone packaging and milk bags led to an eco-friendly bottle. Great creators recognize that others' ideas are a springboard for new thinking. Picasso borrowed and built on many art forms. Hemingway said he got his ideas not only from other writers but from musicians and artists as well. And as we noted earlier in this chapter, Steve Jobs, the poster child for technical innovation, borrowed the idea of the graphical user interface to develop the mouse-driven personal computer from a visit to Xerox.

One of the best ways to stoke your creativity is to use others' ideas as catalysts to your own thinking. Scan your environment, look for analogous situations, and borrow ideas from fields outside of your own. Be alert to the insights you can gain into your own challenges by paying attention to the stimuli in your surroundings. As screenwriter Wilson Mizner once said, "When you take stuff from one writer it's plagiarism, but when you take from many writers it's called research."[24]

Learning Activity
Exercising Your Creative Mind

Pull out your smartphone and set the timer for 5 minutes. On your computer, tablet, or notebook, capture all the good ideas you can think of for alternative uses for a brick. When the timer goes off, stop. Now try it again. This time, review the principles of divergent thinking to be sure you understand these guidelines. Once again, set your timer. Keeping these guidelines in mind, now generate all the alternative uses you can think of for a wire coat hanger. After the timer goes off, compare your two lists. How are they different? Which set has more creative responses? How did the guidelines help you to be more divergent in your thinking? What might you work on to improve your capacity for divergent thinking?

Being—Internalizing the Divergent Thinking Principles

Creativity is an ability. And like all abilities, the best way to improve it is to practice, practice, practice. You now have four principles, two attitudinal and two cognitive, that you need to practice in order to make them second nature. Try the following activities to help you internalize the four divergent-thinking principles. When someone looks like a natural in some activity, it is generally because that person has engaged in many hours of deliberate practice. You can transform your ability to engage in creative thinking by committing to practice these two cognitive abilities and two attitudes. Once they are internalized, you will carry the power of creative thinking wherever you go, applying your imagination in such a way as to render yourself an invaluable organizational asset. As the title of this chapter notes, we believe these skills are fundamental to creative thinking. And as research shows, divergent thinking is a very strong predictor (stronger than IQ) of adult creative achievement, problem-solving performance, and effective leadership. As such, we conclude this section not with a single learning activity but with one for each divergent-thinking principle. Practice fosters mastery, and the goal of these activities is to help you open your mind and to think more flexibly, fluently, and originally.

Learning Activities
Mastering Divergent Thinking

Defer Judgment

For many, this is the hardest principle to internalize. Far too often, the natural reaction to our own and others' thinking is to immediately criticize. Begin by practicing self-awareness; notice your reaction to your own and others' thinking. Do you tend to move quickly to criticism? If so, practice suspending your judgment. For assistance, you can use a tool learned earlier in this book, shifting from Yes-But thinking to Yes-And. When presented with a new idea, avoid the tendency to put it down, and instead begin by saying "Yes, and . . ." Then complete this statement starter by inserting a thought that helps to build the idea up rather than tear it down. The next time you encounter a challenge, begin generating initial solutions by withholding your judgment. Whether alone or with others, first make a list of possible solutions, then go back and evaluate the options generated by selecting those that seem to hold the greatest promise. Perhaps the most difficult aspect of the defer judgment principle is to master the ability to suspend judgment of yourself. Learning to do so will unshackle your thinking, reduce anxiety and self-doubt, and clearly indicate that this principle has been internalized.

Seek Novelty

Make it a goal to try at least three new things over the next several days. These can be small adjustments to your routine or completely new activities. Some examples might include finding a new restaurant (perhaps a cuisine that you have never tried), watching a film from a genre that is new to you, speaking with a stranger, visiting a museum or gallery, reading a magazine that is new to you, taking in an event that you've always wanted to try, or experimenting with a new sport or recreational activity. When you have completed the assignment, ask yourself what new insights, learning, or feelings resulted from your experiment with novelty. These can be insights about yourself or the world. Perhaps you might capture these thoughts in a journal. Continue to challenge yourself to try out new activities in your life.

Go for Quantity

Make a list of your personal and professional strengths. Count the number of strengths you identified and draw a line below the last strength. Now add to this original list by generating at least twice the number of strengths found in your original list. For example, if your original list had a total of nine strengths, now add at least 18 more strengths for a grand total of 27. Use the two attitudes of defer judgment and seek novelty to add to the original list. Do not scrutinize each and every item as it comes to mind; instead, simply add it to your list, focusing on hitting your target number without evaluating the items you add to the new list. As you go, be sure to seek novel strengths, items you feel are unique to you. When you are satisfied with your list, go back and identify the strengths that really capture you. If you had to highlight your strengths to someone else, what would you share with that person? If the principle of go for quantity worked for you, we suspect that there will be some core strengths that came up in the extended list. Had you not

continued to diverge, you might have overlooked these important personal qualities. Next time you have a challenge or an assignment that requires some new thinking, employ the same strategy. Generate your initial list of ideas, then generate a second list, going for twice the quantity and remembering to use the attitudes of deferring judgment and seeking novelty to assist your divergence.

Make Connections

Identify a current challenge you face in your life. Sit down with a magazine, looking through the headlines of the articles, the photographs, and the advertisements. Make a list of ideas that come to mind as you review the content of the magazine. Pose the following question to yourself: What new ideas do I get for solving my challenge by looking at the articles, photos, and advertisements in this magazine? Employ the principles of defer judgment and go for quantity to help you amass a long list of connections. Go completely through the magazine from front cover to back cover. When you are done, go over your list to see if there are any ideas that hold promise; if so, select some to pursue. In your life, continue to feed your ability to make new connections by learning about new subjects, attending courses outside your area of expertise, visiting new places, interacting with a wide range of people, and being trapped by specialization. The more diverse the range of ideas and thoughts you feed your mind, the more likely you are to create interesting new combinations.

With more practice, the more you will be able to internalize the skills of divergent thinking, foundational to an innovative and entrepreneurial mindset. If you have a résumé that includes skills, how might you describe these skills in your résumé?

Introduction

A great deal of fanfare is often attributed to the birth of a new idea—the celebrated aha or *eureka* moment. It's important to remember that creativity is as much a process as it is a singular moment or event. Yes, the creative *process* can be designed and facilitated, deliberately, with the intention to solve a specific problem in a short amount of time (e.g., a half-day or full-day workshop). It may also unfold over time by individuals (and organizations). The following case involving Dr. Dominic D'Agostino and his research lab at the University of South Florida, Morsani College of Medicine, is a compelling example of the latter.[25]

Dominic D'Agostino has a gift. He has developed an ability to be more committed to things than you and me. He doesn't own a television, choosing instead to spend his evenings reading research papers and studying the newest ideas in his field. In addition to staying abreast of the latest research, he is also an accomplished scuba diver, and he has logged hundreds (and perhaps thousands) of hours of dive time. He's an athlete too. In 2010, D'Agostino set the record for most weight squat lifted in 24 hours—crushing the previous record with hours to spare![26]

This ability to both be maniacally focused while also being open to new ideas from his parallel interests would play an important role in a series of breakthroughs that have gone on to save lives and influence the cutting edge of multiple fields of medical and high-performance human physiology research.

Background

Navy Seal divers have a bubbles problem. It stems from a tool they use called an oxygen rebreather. The rebreather is important because it allows divers to go to depth without releasing bubbles (thereby eliminating noise and removing a visual signal of their presence).

The rebreather itself works fine, but a potentially deadly side effect may occur because its usage results in increased oxygenation levels in the diver's blood. This, plus the high-pressure environments experienced by divers as they go deeper and deeper, puts them at an increased risk of a seizure. These seizures come without warning and are untreatable with medication. For a Navy Seal, this represents a life-or-death scenario.

D'Agostino, an avid diver, had recently completed a postdoctoral fellowship (after earning his PhD in neuroscience and physiology) and needed to establish a research lab in his first full-time faculty research position at the University of South Florida. His initial goal: Tackle the Navy Seal rebreather/seizure problem, and to support this investigation he was awarded a research grant from the Office of Naval Research. The grant focused on two questions: Why do these mysterious, untreatable seizures occur? And how might they be prevented?

This research had unique observation and measurement needs. In order to simulate the functioning of a human brain in an undersea environment, D'Agostino had to build a high-powered microscope *inside* of a hyperbaric oxygen chamber. Once the chamber was built and calibrated,

D'Agostino began studying cell behavior in these high-pressure and high-oxygen environments and realized that neurons in the brain were becoming overstimulated when oxygenation levels and pressure were increased—and that these factors were producing a decrease in brain energy metabolism and perhaps triggering the seizure potential.

These insights led him back to the library (recall that he owns no television and spends his evenings immersed in scientific literature), where D'Agostino discovered that these seizures were similar to those experienced by epilepsy patients.

For D'Agostino, a new path had presented itself: If the seizures facing the Navy Seal divers were similar to drug-resistant, epileptic seizures, perhaps some of the tools and strategies developed to address those epileptic seizures might be useful for the divers? This idea led him down an entirely new path—food.

The Ketogenic Diet

D'Agostino discovered that there was a diet-based strategy for mitigating the impact of medication-resistant, epileptic seizures. This diet—known as the ketogenic diet—consists almost entirely of fats and proteins, compared to a traditional Western diet high in carbohydrates and low in fats.

Investigating this food-based strategy, D'Agostino learned that the ketogenic diet was not only effective at reducing seizure rates for epileptics, but it had also been used to treat other types of neurological disorders too. He also learned that the human brain is like a hybrid engine in that it uses glucose (sugar) as the primary fuel, but during periods of limited glucose availability (e.g., fasting, starvation, extreme exercise), the body will enlist the liver to convert fatty acids into ketone bodies, which then serve as an alternative fuel source for the brain.

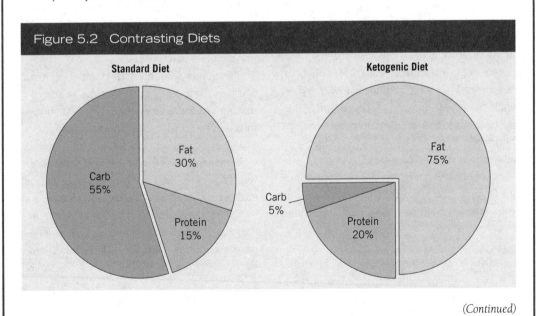

Figure 5.2 Contrasting Diets

Standard Diet

Carb 55%
Fat 30%
Protein 15%

Ketogenic Diet

Fat 75%
Carb 5%
Protein 20%

(Continued)

(Continued)

We are hard-wired for this back-up plan, says D'Agostino, because we didn't always have access to three carbohydrate-based meals per day. It makes sense that the brain would have evolved a mechanism to tap into this secondary fuel; after all, grocery stores and refrigeration are both modern-day luxuries, only available to us during the most recent sliver of human history.

Armed with this new insight, D'Agostino returned to the oxygen rebreather bubbles problem and postulated that Navy Seal divers could consume ketone supplements before diving, thereby tricking their brains into switching from one fuel source to another (from glucose to ketones), and that this metabolic strategy could be an effective tool to reduce the instances of underwater seizures. He was right.

Cancer

During the course of tackling the seizure problem, D'Agostino also learned that a specific kind of cell needs glucose more than the rest: cancerous ones. In fact, they can't live without it. "Cancer cells are a little bit like damaged hybrid engines," says D'Agostino. "They lack the ability to transition to an alternative fuel source." Furthermore, he adds, "We can say that sugar addiction is their Achilles heel."[27]

This insight presented a new opportunity for Dominic and his team. They wondered why such little attention was being paid to nutrition as a mechanism for exploiting this profound weakness of cancer cells.

Diving back into the research literature, D'Agostino discovered that precedent for this approach had already been established via the work of a man named Otto Warburg, who, in 1931, was awarded the Nobel Prize for developing a very important concept: that cancer cells are damaged cells, that these damaged cells require high uptake of sugar (glucose) in order to multiply, and that they can live in low- and no-oxygen environments.[28] In doing so, Warburg hypothesized that cancer is a metabolic problem and that you might be able to kill it if you removed sugar from the equation.

Energized by the pioneering work of Warburg, D'Agostino took to the Internet and discovered that a researcher at Boston College, Dr. Thomas Seyfried, had dedicated his career to extending the thinking of Warburg into the current era of cancer research.[29]

With a new thought partner and a new mission to tackle cancer, D'Agostino and his team began investigating the unique behaviors of cancer cells and their addiction to sugar. Thanks to Warburg and Seyfried, they already knew that cancer cells were glucose dependent and that they were capable of living and thriving in low-oxygen environments.

Equipped with his DIY microscope inside of a hyperbaric oxygen chamber, he wondered if that formula could be reversed. His research team subjected these glucose-dependent cancer cells to a high-pressure, high-oxygenation environment within his microscopy chamber and discovered a shocking result. Referred to as blebbing, the cell membranes of cancer cells starting to bubble and some even began exploding! Even more exciting, the team observed that the same levels of oxygen that were causing the cancer cells to self-destruct were nontoxic for the healthy, normal cells around them. "Because we built the tool, we were in a position to make breakthrough observations with the tool," D'Agostino said. The academic journal

Neuroscience agreed and published their ground-breaking results.[30]

"These observations inspired us to test the combination of the ketogenic diet and hyperbaric oxygen treatment in a mouse-model of metastatic cancer," reported D'Agostino. It worked. Mice with an aggressive form of metastatic cancer were treated with the ketogenic diet and high-oxygen environments, and the results, according to D'Agostino, "demonstrated the therapeutic efficacy of a new, nontoxic approach to cancer management."

D'Agostino believes that nontoxic strategies (such as diet and oxygenation treatment) can be effective at managing cancer—especially for patients with difficult-to-treat brain and metastatic cancers (the ones that move rapidly in the body, jumping from organ to organ) that do not respond well to existing approaches of chemotherapy and radiation.

Closing

The notion that creativity is as much a *process* as it is an *event* is summed up by D'Agostino: "What started out as a Navy Seal project and then led to a promising mitigation strategy for oxygen seizures in the form of ketone supplements, ultimately led us down a path to this unexpected discovery. We now know that oxygen can kill cancer cells and that ketones can a) reduce cancer cell proliferation and b) cause cancer cells to die in a petri dish."[31]

International Center for Studies in Creativity (Buffalo State) instructor Michael Fox often reminds students that good research will generate more questions than answers, and this rings true for D'Agostino and his lab mates. For these pioneering researchers, new questions are always on the horizon, and cancer is just one of the medical nightmares upon which they've set their sights. In the near future they intend to expand their research program from the neuroscience of seizures and cancer to ALS (amyotrophic lateral sclerosis, also known as Lou Gehrig's disease), wound treatment, glucose transporter deficiency syndrome, and other promising areas of treatment opportunity.[32]

Discussion Questions: Knowing

1. Reflecting on the case study featuring Dr. D'Agostino, what factors do you think helped him and his team to unlock such breakthrough ideas? What helped them see what no one else could see? Identify and describe the advantages of their approach. Can you list and describe any potential disadvantages?

2. There are many scientists and researchers attempting to tackle the same health-related challenges as Dr. D'Agostino and his colleagues. Why do you think they have been so successful in a such a short time period relative to their peers?

Application Questions: Doing

1. Consider the chapter and the creative process mash-up model presented.

(Continued)

(Continued)

On a sheet of paper, map the evolution of Dr. D'Agostino's work to the process stages identified in the chapter. Where can you imagine the researchers tapping into their problem-solving skills of understanding (observation and problem definition), ideation (visualization and idea generation), experimentation (solution development and validation), and implementation (getting buy-in and driving change)? Draw connections between the efforts undertaken by the researchers and the creative process stages.

2. Reflecting on the chapter, recall the formula for creativity presented by Dr. Ruth B. Noller, $C = f_a (K, I, E)$, where *creativity* is the result of the interaction among knowledge, imagination, and evaluation—all driven by attitude. Can you make connections between the creative process Dr. D'Agostino went through and the key categories of creativity identified by Noller? Identify as many connections as you can and describe their role or significance.

Thinking Ahead: Being

1. Recall the introduction of the case study, which describes D'Agostino's level of commitment and dedication to his craft. Not only did he read about the ketogenic diet and begin to apply it in his research laboratory, he also subjected himself to it! Dr. D'Agostino changed his personal diet and has been measuring the amount of ketone bodies in his blood levels for almost a decade to ensure that he stays in ketosis (low glucose, high fat). You may wonder what this has done to his body. Consider researching his articles and videos online to observe the impact it has had on him. Hint: He once starved himself (fasting) for 7 days and then executed 10 repetitions of a 500-pound deadlift!

2. Dr. D'Agostino demonstrates an incredible work ethic inspired by the nature of problem solving itself. There are grand challenges facing humanity, and considering this case study, this chapter on the creative process, and the book thus far, what grand challenges can you see yourself getting involved in? What might it take to catalyze your imagination and work ethic in a similar manner to D'Agostino's? What do you care about so much, or love so intensely, that you would be willing to push yourself to the boundaries of your comfort zone (and potentially beyond) in order to achieve breakthrough success? What do you want, and what are you willing to give up for it?

CHAPTER 6

Understand

The Power of Observation and the Importance of Problem Definition

Knowing—Seeing and Questioning What Others Miss

How often have you seen a great new idea, or an innovative business approach, and thought *Now why didn't I think of that?* You could have, and you can. The evidence shows that successful entrepreneurs are serial opportunists in the way they observe seemingly routine situations, see something out of the ordinary in them, ask probing questions, and then reframe problems in the context of solutions waiting to happen. Luckily, this is a learned skill, not a unique talent, as you will see in this chapter.

Jeff Bezos, the founder of Amazon, is a classic example of how the powerful synergy of these two creative capacities—observation and problem definition—can lead to a business breakthrough. In the early 1990s, Bezos, only 28, was senior vice president at the cutting-edge trading firm D. E. Shaw & Co., where he had risen rapidly through the ranks.[1] Like others, David Shaw, the company's founder, thought the Internet showed great promise, although he did not yet understand the technology and its potential. At that time, the U.S. government discouraged companies from using the Internet for commercial purposes, maintaining that the Internet was insecure. To bypass security concerns, businesses required new customers to preregister their credit card numbers on a form and fax or mail it in so they could be set up with an e-mail account for future transactions. In effect, this registration process was simply an upgrade to a telephone ordering system, which was still more competitive because few people had e-mail service. To Shaw's credit, he tagged Bezos with the responsibility of operationalizing the Internet for his company's commercial purposes.

After extensive research, Bezos uncovered an eye-opening fact: Internet usage was growing at 2,300% a year.[2] Two further observations, along with an ability to reframe and redefine an existing business problem, led to an entrepreneurial breakthrough.

Learning Goals

After reading this chapter, you will be able to do the following:

- Describe ways to enhance creativity through mindfulness
- Explain how seeing a problem from many angles and points of view contributes to finding breakthrough solutions
- Identify the subprocesses involved in making effective observations
- List four essential everyday tactics of mastering problem framing
- Contrast two fundamentally different ways to define a challenge
- Practice ways to enhance your own observational and problem-framing skills

105

First, Bezos observed that exponential growth is uncommon, hence, not a situation that many people are adept at understanding. This insight propelled him to ask more in-depth and better questions about the trend or, in other words, to think like an ethnographer, a social scientist who documents and describes new cultural phenomena. Second, based on this singular and holistic understanding of the situation, Bezos saw there was a good chance this intense growth rate was not an anomaly; rather, it could become ubiquitous in the future as Internet service spread around the globe. Applying the present observations to the future, Bezos realized that retailers and customers needed a new retail service that would connect them seamlessly and securely with the products in the purchasing transaction.

Next, when it came to defining the problem, Bezos knew that he could not frame it as an abstraction, so he looked around for a business context that needed this new Internet sales solution in a desperate way. He looked for the top 20 business products that could be sold on the web. To his surprise, books made the top of his list. Although he had no experience with it, he focused on the bookselling industry, which analysis revealed was large and fragmented, with no one company dominating. Bezos investigated the root causes of this fragmentation, learning that physical bookstores were costly to run. Moreover, book publishing and bookselling were highly inefficient because publishers, suppliers, and retailers often worked at cross-purposes. For example, 35% of the 460 million books shipped could be returned to the publisher for credit if they remained unsold. By seeing the problem from many angles and points of view, Bezos was able to question the assumptions of different stakeholders and argued that an online bookstore could significantly reduce the problem of a high rate of return. Interestingly, despite all of Bezos's well-grounded observations and how he framed the online bookselling business, Shaw rejected Bezos's recommendation, perhaps unable to distinguish the problem as he presented it from the one that Bezos more clearly understood. The rest is history.

Observation and Problem Defining: In Our DNA

In fact, this creative capacity to understand what is happening around us—based on meticulously observing and ingeniously defining problems—is wired into our brains. Yet it can atrophy. A look at two examples on the continent of Africa, one ancient and one modern, shows how we must constantly recognize and continually develop our knowledge-building skills. These lessons are important. For once we accept problems as a routine part of our environment, whether in business or in life, we render them nearly impossible to solve. The popular phrase "it is what it is" serves as a good example of an individual who is resigned to accept the problem as given without considering more empowering views. Just because a problem is presented in a particular manner does not mean you must accept it as such.

Homo habilis, an early predecessor to the modern human, lived approximately 2.4 to 1.4 million years ago, as evidenced by bone fossils and purposefully constructed stone tools found in Tanzania and Kenya. These tools included highly efficient and durable instruments to chop, scrape, and pound in the context of everyday survival tasks. The stone flakes may appear primitive next to our Black & Decker chain saws and power drills, but they were advanced for their day. To produce such tools, *Homo habilis* employed both keen observation and astute problem-defining abilities. First, they identified and located hard rock materials that would satisfy the purpose of being fashioned into strong and effective stone tools. Second, they examined the surface carefully to see where and how to strike it without shattering the rock. Anyone who has ever admired a Native American arrowhead knows how difficult it must have been to recognize inherent angles in the rock, then apply good hand-eye coordination to strike in just the right place, in the proper direction and with the proper force. Finally, by understanding the purpose for which the tool was needed, *Homo habilis* matched the right stone with the right tool for the right task. This is no small feat of problem definition for a people surrounded by as many predators as prey.[3]

Let's fast-forward to today, however, and a modern creativity parable in the country of South Africa. Here, in impoverished sections of Johannesburg, women and children walk for miles to fetch safe drinking water. Traditionally, they carried heavy containers of water on their heads for long periods of time, putting themselves at risk for disabling spinal cord and neck injuries. Yet the practice has continued for centuries, almost unconsciously, evolving into what industrial designer Jane Fulton Suri called a "thoughtless act."[4] Someone with empathy who was paying attention to the human factors in this situation might see the people's unstated needs associated with this thoughtless act. In fact, Piet Hendrikse, the coinventor of the Q Drum, did just that.[5] He carefully observed the water carriers in action, thought about the task from a new perspective—that of the carriers' health—and listened to their concerns, like an ethnographer. Based on the power of this observation, he and his brother were able to redefine the problem as not one of carrying, but transporting, water. They then conceived of a cylindrical, durable, inexpensive water container that can be pulled and rolled using a rope threaded through a donut hole in the center of the drum (Figure 6.1). Not surprisingly, the women and children of Johannesburg embraced the Q Drum as a labor- and health-saving tool. Since its invention almost two decades ago, the Q Drum's popularity has spread around the world, and the Hendrikse brothers have won numerous awards and international praise for an invention in service to humanity.

As these examples show, the creative process is *in our DNA*. We face problems and try to solve them every day. What, however, led Bezos, the Hendrikse brothers, and other serial opportunists to see something important that we might have missed? What subprocesses are involved in making a keen observation? By the same token, what kind of intellectual energy goes into defining a problem creatively instead of routinely? How do we distinguish the real problem from the perceived problem? In the next section, we take a closer look at what the evidence

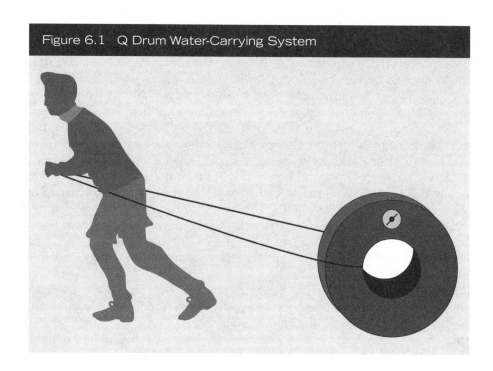

Figure 6.1   Q Drum Water-Carrying System

says about observation and problem definition. For the serial opportunist, these are crucially important skills.

The Power of Observation

"You can't miss it." If you have ever asked someone for directions to a new restaurant and heard these familiar words, you know what a jinx they can be. Yet this should not come as a surprise. Most of us have received little formal training in the art of keen observation. It's no wonder the other person's directions often do not align with what we see—or think we see—when we are driving in unfamiliar surroundings. In fact, unless we are trained social scientists or criminal investigators, most of what we know about observation has probably been learned in an ad hoc and haphazard fashion. For instance, in his book *Seeing What Others Don't: The Remarkable Ways We Gain Insights*, cognitive psychologist Gary Klein shares a story involving two police officers on routine patrol, waiting behind a luxury car for a traffic light to turn green.[6] One officer observed the driver of the luxury car idly flicking his cigarette ashes onto the seat of the car. The cop wondered: Why would the owner behave so carelessly inside a car he had paid an arm and a leg for? You guessed it. By paying attention to the unusual behavior, the officer correctly deduced that the car must have been stolen.

To empower this kind of creative capacity, we must train ourselves to employ three subprocesses: (1) see what others do not see, (2) understand the situation at hand, and (3) think like an ethnographer.

See What Others Do Not See

Human beings are driven to make sense of their world.[7] Research shows that if we see a new situation, we may rely on clues from others we know and trust for an explanation. For example, in one study, 1-year-old children were presented with an unfamiliar object, a type of box; all of them looked to their moms first for a reaction.[8] If the moms reacted in a positive way, the infants felt it was safe to approach the box. If the moms reacted in fear or disgust, the infants froze. Even as adults, we still look for visual clues to inform us of how to best respond to some new situation. In contrast, if we observe a familiar situation, we may seize on a standard explanation based on our prior experiences, and fail to look for new clues or information. This habit, too, is a behavior learned early in life.

For more than two decades, Ellen J. Langer, a Harvard University professor of psychology, has been researching this phenomenon of mindlessness versus mindful noticing to help people see what others miss. The author of the pioneering book *Mindfulness* and, more recently, *Counterclockwise: Mindful Health and the Power of Possibility*, Langer defines mindfulness as a quality of constant and careful scanning for early signs of change, opportunity, or trouble.[9] Langer describes three ways to see what others miss: (1) create new categories for processing experiences rather than limiting yourself to old ones; (2) invite, rather than deflect, new information, even if it is contradictory; and (3) look at situations more than once from more than one viewpoint before fully processing them. In today's increasingly complex, "mindless" world, Langer argues that the ability to see what others miss could positively impact those around you, just as the Hendrikse brothers did with the creation of the Q Drum and Bezos with the formation of Amazon (and an indication of the impact of Amazon can be seen in their formidable growth: sales up $23 billion in 2015, representing 60% of total U.S. online sales growth).[10]

Let's put Langer's advice into practice. Dalí was famous for his hidden images and double meaning. Look at the sketch on the next page titled *The Bather*. At first glance what do you notice? Now look again. What can you see when you take a different perspective? Compare your observations to others'. Did you make any observations that they did not? Take your observations and cluster them based on what they have in common. Were you able to see a variety of categories?

Understand the Situation at Hand

We referenced Benjamin Franklin earlier; we return to him to illustrate how his strong desire to understand a situation drove his creative prowess. Careful analysis

of his letters shows that when confronted with an unfamiliar subject, he possessed an insatiable desire to gain mastery of it.[11] Franklin's scientific triumphs are legendary, such as the time, after steady contemplation of a fire in his chimney, he wrote his brother to describe our modern meteorological understanding of how hot and cold air work to fuel a violent storm. Yet few people know how his keen observational skills played a critical role in his success as a politician and statesman. Instead of involving himself in legislative debates, Franklin took the time to watch the triumphs and humiliations of assemblymen. Highly disciplined in his approach to acquiring knowledge, he discerned that he could be more influential behind the scenes than he could from the bully pulpit.

Joe Navarro, author of *Louder Than Words* and an expert in nonverbal communication and body language, says Franklin became the quintessential diplomat and entrepreneur because he was able to immerse himself completely in another person's situation and respond accordingly.[12] For example, when the fledgling America needed France during the Revolutionary War, Franklin went to that country as our first ambassador and instantly adapted to the niceties and nuances of French culture. "Franklin seeing necessity, reinvented himself for his new calling, and he adjusted very well. He in essence became French, adopting dress, demeanor, hairstyle, and their social ways. He even powdered his wigs," writes Navarro in his blog "Spycatcher" for *Psychology Today*.[13] This great observer, then, "socially engineered" his political success—and America's victory in the war with French military help—by realizing what makes people comfortable and engendering their trust. Franklin used what is commonly known today as emotional intelligence to truly understand the situation at hand.

Fast-forward 200 years to Amazon's Jeff Bezos, who approaches observation in the same rigorous way. The more he uncovers, the more patterns he sees, the more salient his understanding, and the more opportunities emerge. Hence, creative thinkers, from Franklin to Bezos, not only see what others miss, they also do their homework and make sure they fully understand the situation before they act.

Think Like an Ethnographer

Among those professionally trained in observation are ethnographers, or academics who study culture as participant observers; this means they conduct research as insiders, not outsiders. Popular ethnographies range from Margaret Mead's classic *Coming of Age in Samoa*, published in 1928, to Karen Ho's provocative *Liquidated: An Ethnography of Wall Street*, published in 2009. Regardless of the topic, a first-rate ethnography provides a model for seeing in a whole new way and capturing an accurate baseline profile of an unfolding event or culture of concern in our environment. As James P. Spradley explained in his book *Participant Observation*, ethnographers make descriptive observations that involve first looking at a social situation as a member of the group and then recording as much as possible of what they see.[14] Importantly, an ethnographer approaches an unfolding event without any particular question in mind.[15]

In the business world, Jane Fulton Suri, chief creative officer at IDEO, is a good example of an entrepreneur who thinks like an ethnographer. IDEO counts among its award-winning designs the first computer mouse for Apple. Fulton Suri is the author of *Thoughtless Acts: Observations on Intuitive Design*, a fascinating guide to how she uses her background in psychology and architecture to integrate social science strategies and skills to create "people-friendly products." Her observation method centers, always, on people and their everyday activities, from how a mom looks for a place to hang her purse on a grocery cart while she situates a child to how you might hold something between your teeth or under an arm when your hands are full. These acts, which she refers to as "thoughtless," involve workarounds that we create when the product we are using is not designed to meet our current needs. "Empathetic observation," embedding, collaboration, and "experience proto-typing" are just a few of the techniques she uses. When asked in an interview to describe the best kind of observer, she replied, "I find that curiosity, open-mindedness, and imagination are important. It helps to be non-judgmental, able to move easily from noticing detail to thinking about patterns and the big picture, perceptive about (their own and other) people's behavior, motivations, and personally genuinely interested in other people's points of reference."[16]

Consider this. Why did it take car manufacturers so long to design hands-free access to a car trunk, a fairly recent automobile function, when there is no doubt that workarounds have existed for years if not decades? Perhaps managing to open a trunk or hatch when one's arms are full fell into the category of an unobserved thoughtless act. It might be argued that the technology for hands-free access did not emerge until recently. That could be, yet there may have been low-tech solutions or recognition of this thoughtless act might have sped up the development of the solution. You are surrounded by such thoughtless acts, which represent opportunities for innovative solutions and entrepreneurial endeavors.

Thought Starter
Thoughtless Acts

The Importance of Defining the Problem

It is one thing to keenly observe and then another to frame the identified difficulty in a way that leads to a breakthrough. Again, as the pioneering educator John Dewey wrote, "A question well put is half answered; i.e. a difficulty clearly apprehended is likely to suggest its own solution."[17] If, however, a problem is not clearly defined or properly framed, an opportunity to solve it is missed, or the proffered solution doesn't work. Either outcome can prove embarrassing or costly.

Accurate problem defining, then, points the way to a gap in knowledge. Properly done, this act of definition creates a question or series of questions that triggers visualization, experimentation, and implementation (discussed in the chapters that follow). As a result, creative thinkers reshape our lives by successfully framing problems. And they do not shy away from the big ones. Consider, for example, how Bill and Melinda Gates defined philanthropy as global citizenship, how Oprah Winfrey defined television talk as cultural currency, how Sheryl Sandberg defined feminism as "leaning in" to a career, or how Stephen R. Covey defined effectiveness as seven habits anyone could learn. Unfortunately, for most of us, problem defining is often done prematurely or haphazardly, which can lead to cart-before-the-horse solutions or an entirely new set of problems.

The research is clear on the importance of taking the time to define and frame the problem. Getzels and Csíkszentmihályi, for example, observed the process used by art students to produce a still life sketch. They found that those students who spent more time examining the available props before sketching, and who spent more time exploring a greater range of props, produced artwork judged to be superior. Follow-up with the same set of research participants years later also showed that those who exhibited the greatest attention to problem framing during the original still life study later became the most successful professional artists.[18] The value of problem definition was further reinforced by a meta-analytic study of creativity training programs. In perhaps the most thorough analysis of creativity training programs, a research team from the University of Oklahoma found that among the core processes included in creativity training, problem identification had the strongest overall contribution to divergent thinking, problem solving, creative performance, and creative attitudes.[19] In fact, training in problem definition methods had an even greater positive effect on participants than did learning idea generation procedures (though it was second, a distant second). The value of problem identification and definition in the creative process should not come as a surprise. After all, how you see the problem determines all of the thinking that comes later—how you frame the problem determines how you solve the problem. And if you don't recognize the problem at all, there is no creative thinking at all—no creative breakthrough, no innovation, and no new entrepreneurial success story.

Problem definition requires a high level of skill, acquired through knowledge and practice. In the next section, we discuss three essential everyday tactics for mastering problem framing: (1) question assumptions with a growth mindset, (2) have courage in your ideas (positive deviance), and (3) employ jobs-to-be-done theory.

Question Assumptions With a Growth Mindset

The familiar expression "The fish will be the last to discover water" serves as a metaphor for someone who does not challenge assumptions and maintains a fixed view of the world. For decades, Carol S. Dweck, motivational psychology researcher at Stanford University, has studied this phenomenon, which she calls a "fixed mindset" (i.e., a belief that intelligence and talent are static qualities and that success results simply from talent, regardless of effort).[20] It starts in childhood, continues into adulthood, and causes people to move through life in performance mode, rather than learning mode. "As soon as children become able to evaluate themselves, some of them become afraid of challenges. They become afraid of not being smart. I have studied thousands of people from preschoolers on, and it's breathtaking how many reject an opportunity to learn," she writes in *Mindset: The New Psychology of Success*.[21] In a follow-up book, Dweck says that CEOs face this choice every day: whether to take the risks of a learning curve or to create a static business environment where they perform perfectly all the time, or at least the people around them *tell* them they do. She argues that this is the mistake Lee Iacocca made at Chrysler, becoming a "nonlearner" and falling behind developments in the automobile industry. If you have a growth mindset, she writes, "you believe you can develop yourself, then you're open to accurate information about your current abilities, even if it's unflattering. What's more, if you're oriented toward learning, as people with a growth mindset are, you need accurate information about your current abilities in order to learn effectively."[22]

A great example of an executive adopting a growth mindset is Michael Dell, founder of computer company Dell. In a *Harvard Business Review* article, "The Innovator's DNA," business professors Jeffrey Dyer, Hal Gregersen, and Clayton Christensen describe how the idea of the Dell computer emerged through a process of questioning assumptions.[23] Dell revealed that he would take computers apart and question why some of the parts that cost $600, for instance, sold for five to six times the cost. He had perceived the problem simply as a need to build computers independently and then sell them. However, as he explored the problem, challenging his own and the industry's assumptions, he discovered that he could sell computers directly to consumers, sidestepping the middleman and the markups.

This discovery not only shifted his view of the problem but ultimately led him to a growth mindset of exploring exciting opportunities to establish a niche. So what is the key takeaway from this example? Michael Dell learned not to assume the initial problem (how to sell computers) would be the problem as he eventually understood it (how to produce a computer closer to the sum of its parts).[24]

Have Courage in Your Ideas: Positive Deviance

Paul Torrance, one of the first educational psychologists in the field of creativity research, outlines the problem-defining process as beginning with "becoming sensitive to problems, deficiencies, gaps in knowledge, missing elements, disharmonies, and so on; [then] *identifying the difficulty*."[25] But not everyone goes on to frame that difficulty as a problem worth solving, as Torrance and his colleagues have learned in their groundbreaking studies on creativity in U.S. schoolchildren. As described in Chapter 2, Torrance's measure of creativity, the TTCT,[26] has been used for decades to document the gradual drop in creativity scores among American schoolchildren, a situation that magazines like *Newsweek* labeled "the creativity crisis."[27] In his 1995 book *Why Fly? A Philosophy of Creativity*, Torrance describes why creative children and creative teachers might stifle their creativity in a structured, bureaucratic school system.[28] Creative people are not as predictable as conformists (which makes administrators uneasy), they respond to the best ideas (which may not be the ones the bosses espouse), and they have an "independent spirit" (which may cause them to interpret supervision as interference).[29] "The most essential characteristic of the creative person is courage," he posits in a chapter on courage in *Why Fly?* "Whenever a person thinks of an original idea, he or she is usually a minority of one, at least in the beginning."[30] Innovators and entrepreneurs add value by seeing problems in a new way. As Rollo May indicated in his seminal book *The Courage to Create*, "If you do not express your own original ideas, if you do not listen to your own being, you will have betrayed yourself. Also you will have betrayed the community in failing to make your contributions to the whole."[31] We should note that courage is not the same as being reckless or foolhardy. Courage, as described by May, is commitment even in the face of doubt, one's own and others'.

Thought Starter
Courage to Create

When you understand what it takes to define a problem creatively, it is easy to see why creative people are frequently engaged in what sociologists call positive deviance. First identified in global health situations, this phenomenon occurs when the actions of a few people in difficult situations achieve notably better outcomes.[32] Typically, their actions are common sense and prudent, as when a few poor families in a village boil water to purify it or feed children balanced traditional diets in spite of scarcity. As Torrance said, it takes courage to go against the prevailing patterns of neighbors or, in the business world, competitors. One example of a company engaged in this kind of creative problem defining is Merck & Co. In 1978, Merck, one of the world's largest pharmaceutical companies, accidentally discovered a potential cure for river blindness while producing an antiparasitic drug for animals. However, this discovery presented the company with a dilemma.[33] The drug would not make money if marketed to developing countries, where consumers could not afford it. Further, no other pharmaceutical company was manufacturing and distributing its drugs for developing countries at a financial loss. But Merck's corporate mission was "to discover, develop and provide innovative products and services that save and improve lives around the world."[34] Reflecting on positive behaviors that move away from the norm, Merck accepted the financial loss that would accompany offering the drug for free, puzzling competitors and analysts but delighting global health advocates.

Employ Jobs-to-Be-Done Theory

Finally, a third key way that creative people frame problems to innovate reflects a relatively new theory called jobs to be done, as described by Clayton M. Christensen, Scott Cook, and Taddy Hall in an online forum for the Harvard Business School. These authors explain, "The marketer's task is to understand the job the customer wants to get done, and design products and brands that fill that need. [This means] designing products that *do a job rather than fill a product segment*."[35] This theory is best illustrated by a situation most homeowners are familiar with. Several decades ago, consumers who faced home repairs (and who doesn't?) either had to hire an expensive contractor to complete the work or purchase expensive equipment, designed for contractors, and try to do it themselves. Black & Decker, however, spotted an opportunity to offer a quick and affordable solution to this budding do-it-yourself (DIY) movement. Had Black & Decker followed a pathway to serve the traditional expectations of the market sector, the company would have produced tools with improved quality, but still as expensive, or more tools for contractors. The jobs-to-be-done theory suggests that consumers want a product that does the job but because they might not be able to conceive of what that product is, meeting their expectations might not make their lives easier. Black & Decker realized that what homeowners needed were not contractor-grade and -priced tools but tools that were good enough, affordable, and scaled for DIY work. In properly framing the problem for the DIY consumer, Black & Decker saw a solution that would substantially reduce the number of steps to get the job done.[36]

At this point in this chapter, you may be saying "I get it" when it comes to the processes of observing and problem defining. Yet we all know that it's one thing to intellectually understand what you need to do to tap into your creative DNA and another thing entirely to put new principles into effective action. Two simple but essential strategies apply here. First, adopt what Dweck calls a growth mindset and practice these skills every chance you get.[37] Second, find good role models, both people close to you and famous people you read about in the news. The first will coach you, and the second will inspire you.

Learning Activity
Watch Carol Dweck's TED Talk

Search for and watch Carol Dweck's TED talk titled "The Power of Believing That You Can Improve." Answer the following questions: What insights do we get from neuroscience about the growth mindset? How has your education helped or hindered your growth mindset? What recommendations does Dweck give about ways to promote a growth mindset?

Doing—Acting Like a Serial Opportunist

The first part of this chapter focused on what we know about good observation and problem framing; in this section, we suggest ways you might enhance your own observational and problem-framing skills.

Honing Observational Skills

Embedding is an easy "doing" strategy that forces you to stretch almost all your observational skills in an attempt to understand another person's point of view (POV). For example, your organization, say a hospital, desires to be the best caretaker of patients. You are asked to examine what might be done to improve patient care. You decide to begin with observation, but from the perspective of a patient, not as an employee. What's the advantage of embedding yourself as a patient? If you do not literally lie on a hospital bed for hours with nothing else to stare at but the ceiling, are not fitted with a back-exposed garment, do not eat hospital food, are not wheeled on a bed past visitors and staff to another area of the hospital, are not made to stay overnight in a room shared with a groaning patient in lots of pain, and are not accompanied to the bathroom to prevent falling from weakness, then you're missing vital points of view that can help frame problems from many angles.[38] We just mentioned the POV of a patient with one set of demographics. But what about the POV of other patients, such as minorities, immigrants, the elderly, or the terminally ill? What about the POV of a doctor, a nurse, family members, the roommate behind the curtain that divides the room, children, the designer of the hospital room, and the vendors? They, too, provide important angles, which could be addressed by taking a team approach to participant observation.

Admittedly, what you observe can be overwhelming. To help you structure your observations and draw a more complete picture, ethnographer Spradley provides nine major dimensions to consider.[39] Grab a notebook and a digital recorder (if you are at liberty to use one) and try to cover as many of these as possible when making observations.

1. *Space.* Describe all the details of the place, such as purpose, customer type, organization, floor plan, size, materials, objects, colors, light, temperature, mood, and activities.

2. *Actor.* Describe all people who are engaged in the setting or event, who they are, how they place themselves in the space, how they engage in the activities, the emotions they exhibit, and the desired outcomes they seek.

3. *Activity.* Describe the regular actions, behaviors, or performances; whether the activities include feelings; the desired outcomes; how activities vary; and interesting details.

4. *Object.* Describe the objects or artifacts present in the social setting; where they are located; how they are used by actors, times, and conditions; and outcomes or feelings.

5. *Act.* Describe the *single* actions people do, perhaps spontaneously; performance details; and any acts associated with them or perceived outcomes.

6. *Event.* Describe in detail all the important events you see; when they occur; and if they include artifacts, evoke certain feelings, and achieve the desired outcome for people involved.

7. *Time.* Describe the time periods (beginning and ending); what takes place in between (draw a visual timeline of events); what significance you see in objects, interactions, and how events occur; and any emotions triggered.

8. *Goal.* Describe the goal or what people are trying to accomplish, the ways goals involve use of objects, how various goals affect the different actors, and your understanding of the goals.

9. *Feeling.* Describe the feelings you see and how these feelings impact goals, actors, events, and intended outcomes.

Honing Problem-Defining Skills

Now let's take these nine dimensions and connect them to an event that inspired the development of a new product. After many instances of watching moms or dads (actor) struggling (feeling) to simultaneously carry (activity) multiple items (object), keep a child (actor) from wandering off (act) through the airport (space), and reach a boarding lounge on time (event, goal, and time), a flight attendant designed a small fold-up chair—the Ride On Carry On—that can be hooked onto a carry-on bag. A child can now easily sit in the attached fold-down chair and enjoy the ride as the parent rolls the luggage through the airport.[40] In this example, the inventor had noticed how her son would hitch a ride on the carry-on bag as she pulled it through the airport. Reframing the problem, she had wondered, *What if she could make an improvised seat that could then be attached to her bag?*

Another everyday strategy to practice framing involves harnessing the power of language. We offer two easy language tactics for problem defining: (1) open-ended questioning and (2) semantic switching. Language and thinking are intimately connected. How you phrase a problem has a direct impact on how you think about that problem. The statement "I need a vacation" simply expresses a desire, but it doesn't solicit a response or action. Expressing the problem as "I can't afford a vacation" merely points out an obstacle and as such may not be very motivating. In our experience, the most productive way to frame a problem, as in the language that is most likely to stimulate creative thinking, starts with an open-ended invitational statement and includes a specific challenge that requires action. For example, the question "How might I raise the funds for a vacation?" focuses on a specific challenge—raising funds—and the invitation "How might I . . ." encourages you to begin to seek solutions. Rather than problem statements, we refer to these kinds of questions as challenge statements, for they are designed to get you to begin thinking about how you might address an important issue. Besides "How might I/we . . . ," other useful statement starters include "How to . . . ," "In what ways might I . . . ," and "What might be . . ." By the way, being flexible in your thinking and generating alternative challenge statements, such as "In what ways might I devise an affordable vacation?" opens up different solutions and thus ways to achieve your ultimate goal.

Once you learn to use good challenge statement language, you may find it valuable to play with the words found in the challenge statement. The connotative meaning of words may prevent you from seeing the real problem or from developing a breakthrough insight into the best way to tackle the problem. This is where semantic switching may be useful. Beginning with an initial statement of the challenge or opportunity, using the challenge statement language just described, identify the key words and then replace them to see if semantic switching serves to clarify the issue. For example, in the challenge statement "How might I reduce my concerns related to the financial conditions of my counseling clinic?" the key words are *reduce*, *concerns*, and *financial conditions*. On a piece of paper, draw three columns and place each word or phrase at the top of a column. For each word or phrase, think of all the words that might be used to replace the key words from the

Thought Starter

Semantic Switching

original challenge statement. Use a thesaurus to help you. Once completed, you will have a menu of words to help you generate a divergent list of other challenge statements or questions. More importantly, you now have words, with new meanings, that can potentially change your view of the problem. By way of example, after creating alternative words for the key elements of the challenge statement and changing the sequence, the original challenge statement might be rephrased as "How might I lower my stress by consolidating the counseling clinic's expenses?"

Learning Activity
Create an Empathy Map

Filtering and recording observations can be overwhelming, especially when you are not sure what is relevant. IDEO uses a straightforward observation tool called empathy mapping.[41] This tool helps the observer become more mindful of how the customer or user is thinking and acting. Go into a retail shop and observe the checkout process, from beginning to end. While observing, capture field notes and then later organize them into an empathy map as described next (if you need more information on empathy mapping there is plenty on the Internet, but a good source is www.copyblogger.com/empathy-maps):

1. Divide a dry-erase board, flip chart, or computer screen into four sections. Name the upper left-hand quadrant *Say*, the lower left-hand quadrant *Do*, the upper right-hand quadrant *Think*, and the lower right-hand quadrant *Feel*.

2. Record your observations of what people say and do on the left-hand side of the map. Try to capture the most striking observations, rather than every small detail—what seems most important or interesting?

3. After recording your observations, use the skill of inference to record what people are likely thinking or feeling on the right side of the map. Make a note to pay attention to body language, tone of voice, and use of vocabulary.

4. Synthesize. Look at the broader connections and themes of the empathy map. Considering your observations, capture the users' *Pains* (fears and frustrations) and *Gains* (needs and wants).

    Once completed, use the empathy map to identify ways to improve the checkout process. What surprised you? What were you not aware of previously regarding the users' experience? What value did you get from doing the empathy map?

Being—Living Like a Serial Opportunist

You are constantly making observations and defining problems about the things present in your surroundings. The key to capturing this creative potential is turning problem observing and defining into a habit of mind. For example, let's take the "exact change" person in the grocery checkout line. To some impatient few, this person can be a real annoyance. If, however, an observant entrepreneur saw this person as an opportunity to create a simple device for instantly sorting change and making it accessible at the checkout counter, the line could move much faster. Fulton Suri advocates paying attention to these perceptive interpretations, for they do serve as a seedbed for framing problems and producing ideas. As she says, "Thoughtless acts reveal how people behave in a world not perfectly tailored to their needs."[42] Whether you are observing the person in front of you at the checkout line or the engineering attributes of an object, you can train yourself to make observations in an ethnographic way—and intuit new and exciting solutions in the process.

In the end, the key to becoming a serial opportunist, a person who continually sees, questions, and pushes until he or she understands, is to incorporate these activities into your identity, into the very fabric of who you are. It's also important to have the courage to be creative, as we described earlier and can see in the inspiring story of Yelitsa Jean-Charles. Yelitsa turned internalized racism on its head for young black women by nudging them to see themselves in a much different light, free from society's harshly imposed beauty standards that typically steer young girls away from their natural beauty.

Yelitsa is an artist, a social innovation fellow at Brown University, and as you will learn, the founder and creative director of Healthy Roots, an organization that spawned a movement. Her organization produces dolls designed to inform and empower young black women to fight against colorism—a form of discrimination that treats people with lighter skin better than those who have darker skin, which can lead to indelible consequences such as self-hatred and contempt for one's own race.[43]

The reason why some young black women are susceptible to colorism runs deep. Take for instance the time Yelitsa flew down to Florida on vacation. Worried about too much sun exposure, family members questioned why she was permitted to stay out so long at the risk of letting the sun darken her skin. Many scholars link this way of thinking to the residual effects of slavery in the United States where race was socially stratified; black is bad and white is good.[44] For example, relaxing hair so that it's seen as "good hair" used to be a predominant way to reduce social stratification.[45] Good hair meant no kinks and was generally seen by the black community as nicer looking. More unsettling, however, good hair had suggested that it closely resembled the hair of a nonblack individual. Yet converting hair to look nonblack was and continues to be no easy task. It has to be relaxed. And to relax the hair of a black woman requires a powerful chemical called sodium hydroxide. As Chris Rock reported in his satirical documentary, the chemical is so strong it can burn a woman's hair off or, worse, her skin.[46] Now think about this. Children as young as 3 years old are exposed to these relaxers!

Yelitsa paid sharp attention to this phenomenon, questioned it, and with her restless indignation pushed to understand it. And when she observed that toys shaped how children think, how they behave, and how they see themselves, she decided to produce dolls to teach young black girls about their heritage and the record of events associated with the African diaspora.[47] Moreover, the dolls are designed to inform children and mothers about the joy and beauty of natural hair.

Not one to limit herself, Yelitsa also produced the Healthy Roots' *Big Book of Hair* to combat the media's influence. Healthy Roots' *Big Book of Hair* stemmed from an observation that only 8% of books published for children highlighted a child of color. Her book now serves as a manual to inform young women on how to care for their hair, while empowering them to embrace cultural identity and natural beauty. Like a passionate coach, Yelitsa pushes the argument that "when you're ignored by the mainstream media, you have to become a problem solver, and innovator."[48] It is these kinds of entrepreneurial activities that Yelitsa weaves into her identity, into the very fabric of who she is now, and that has helped start a movement.

Learning Activity
Practicing the Growth Mindset

The growth mindset is all about acknowledging the power of *yet*. In other words, instead of saying "I can't ski," say "I can't ski . . . yet." Identify a current struggle. Using the *yet* mindset, complete the statement "I can't . . . yet." Make some notes about how this simple change in your own self-observations changes your attitude. Looking back on your life, what activities and experiences, if any, might have been improved or different had you taken a growth mindset?

Case Study
Innovation by Observation: NanoTouch Technology

Pioneer of the germ theory of disease and inventor of the pasteurization process, French microbiologist Dr. Louis Pasteur famously argued that "chance favors the prepared mind." In a similar spirit, it may be said that innovation favors the observing mind, and an average, run-of-the-mill lunch meeting in 2011 between entrepreneurs Mark Sisson and Dennis Hackemeyer lends credence to this idea.

Seated at their restaurant table, Sisson and Hackemeyer were preparing their stomachs and their minds for what would become an important and lucrative aha moment. The two found themselves engaging in a discussion about the latest research being done in the fields of materials science and nanotechnology when the pair noticed a man approaching the front door of the restaurant and catching a sneeze in his hands. Instinctively, the inbound patron outstretched those germ-laced hands, clutched the door handle, and entered the building.

Sisson and Hackemeyer commented to each other that they'd better not touch that handle on the way out! This observation and half-joking comment then led to an extended visual scan of the restaurant scene. They noticed an employee cleaning table after table with the same dirty rag and a mother cleaning her table and children's toys with her own antibacterial wipes.

These observations sat with the table mates, and they realized that the technologies they had just been discussing could potentially be used to solve these restaurant cleaning problems—and perhaps other similar clean-surface challenges. Soon thereafter, they assembled a team and set out to develop what is referred to as a self-cleaning surface.[49]

Traditional approaches to cleaning a surface involve the application of disinfectant sprays or wipes. Sisson and Hackemeyer set out to turn this traditional approach upside down. Their idea was to create a surface capable of *cleaning itself*, continuously, with no additional effort or disinfectant. "It is not meant to clean your hand or clean objects set in the surface. The surface itself is simply self-cleaning," says Sisson.

Thanks to the help of titanium dioxide—a common ingredient found in toothpaste, milk, and sunscreen—and some clever science and product design, the company's NanoSeptic surface continually oxidizes organic material, germs, bacteria, and dangerous pathogens, which are broken down into their basic molecular components and no longer threating. "The goal of our NanoSeptic surface is to inhibit the transfer of microbes from one contact to the next, as well as provide a safer surface to rest personal items," explains Sisson. "Unlike sanitizers and disinfectants, which provide a one-time cleaning, our surface kills microbes continuously, 24/7."[50]

Not only was the big idea for the product inspired by skillful observation (the sneezed-upon hands in the restaurant), but the company also leveraged its observation skills to explore opportunities to apply its new technology in

the world. On the lookout for market applications, the team sent researchers to explore the ways in which different industries were currently tackling their cleaning challenges, and they witnessed opportunities in a wide range of consumer and industry markets.

Consider the journey of a pair of shoes from the restroom floor of an airport bathroom to the front of the security line. Shoes must be removed and placed in a bin. After scanning, the bins are emptied and returned to the front of the line, without cleaning. The next person may put shoes in that bin, or it may be a backpack, phone, wallet, or personal item of clothing. No matter what the item, a transfer of bacteria has taken place.

Another example—and one with a corresponding NanoTouch product in production—involves the germ transfer between hands that touch a tissue box. More often than not, hands seeking a tissue box belong to someone who is sick, and, for this market need, NanoTouch has developed a self-cleaning tissue box shell. Now, every touch of the tissue box is self-cleaning.

The list goes on: mobile phone covers (think of all the dirty surfaces that your phone touches and how infrequently you disinfect it!), door handles, cruise ships, and keyboards and technology accessories (some schools are now offering self-cleaning computer mouse pads for students).

The goal is not to create a completely sterile world (an oversterilized environment can weaken immune system resiliency), but sterile is a desirable quality in one critical area: hospital operating rooms.

Bacteria transfer in operating rooms can be a matter of life or death, and, in response to this market need, NanoSeptic presents a compelling technological solution that can save lives.

(Continued)

(Continued)

In 2015, the company sent 3,500 self-cleaning surfaces to a hospital in Saudi Arabia to help prevent the spread of Middle East respiratory syndrome.[51]

Closing

Already a growing business with more than 20 employees, a diverse line of products, and an evolving research and development agenda, the company continues to innovate, using creative financing approaches (including a recent $2 million grant courtesy of the Tobacco Commission[52])

to grow the team, engage subject matter experts, and scale product development and distribution from their Virginia-based offices. An entire line of NanoSeptic products has already been developed and distributed to 29 countries, but the company also plans to invest time and capital to conduct additional market research in the health care, education, facility management, commercial janitorial, and food service industries. For founders Sisson and Hackemeyer, their mission remains clear: "A cleaner environment in which we live, work, and play."

Discussion Questions: Knowing

1. Self-awareness of one's comments can serve as a precursor to an idea. From Sisson and Hackemeyer's scan of the restaurant setting, identify the moment that nudged them to extend their visual scan of the restaurant setting.

2. Knowledge plays an important role in producing creative breakthroughs. What knowledge contributed to the aha moment?

3. What skills prompted Sisson and Hackemeyer to extend their scan?

Application Questions: Doing

1. Spradley identifies nine dimensions ethnographers use to structure their observation. Applying these dimensions, what other observations could Sisson and Hackemeyer have made?

2. Do you recall the section on honing problem-defining skills described in this chapter (e.g., open-ended questioning and semantic switching)? What are some of the open-ended questions Sisson and Hackemeyer could have asked to

continue reframing the problem involving sanitation?

Thinking Ahead: Being

1. Using what you learned from the Sisson and Hackemeyer case study, what might be some products, services, or processes in your work or educational context that could be improved?

2. How might you become an ethnographer to find ways to improve your creative confidence in the workplace?

Ideate

Ways to Visualize and Generate Breakthrough Ideas

Knowing—Ideating: The Mind's Capacity to See the Future

Unlike other mammals, humans have the capacity to think deeply about the future, or to see in the mind's eye and envision alternative possibilities. If you have ever said to yourself, *If only I had seen around the corner on that one*, you understand the importance of forward thinking. Entrepreneurs, people who innovate on their own *outside* of a large organization, are well known for this capacity. Intrapreneurs make equally important innovations by creating new business ideas *inside* of an organization. Intrapreneurs do this because they possess an ability to view their organization from the outside in, as well as the inside out, and are constantly on the lookout for what is new, what others are doing, and what works in a dynamic, changing environment. As Meg Wheatley, an American management consultant who studies organizational behavior, puts it, "Innovation is fostered by information gathered from new connections; from insights gained by journeys into other disciplines or places; from active, collegial networks and fluid, open boundaries."[1]

In Dalí's sketch titled *Head of Gala* we see the ability to envision alternative possibilities in action. Dalí not only creates alternative sketches but makes forced connections between seemingly incongruent concepts, such as playing with shoes and hands in place of a traditional hat. By making unusual connections, he was able to envision further alternatives.

Seeing into the future is an essential thinking skill that allows people to form new ideas—an ability to use one's imagination to see new possibilities. Paul Torrance, the aforementioned pioneer in modern creativity research, promoted ideational thinking in the most hierarchical of organizations, the U.S. military. A psychologist and psychiatric social worker, Torrance worked for the U.S. Air Force from 1951 to 1957, in a Survival Research Field Unit at the Advanced Survival School, Stead Air Base in Reno, Nevada. The air force hired Torrance, a noncombat veteran of the U.S. Army, after observing that World War II bomber crews

Learning Goals

After reading this chapter, you will be able to do the following:

- Identify essential behaviors for visualizing new ideas
- Describe strategies for producing many alternative ideas
- Explain how play fuels imagination and an innovative mindset
- Use associative theory to discover how nature solves problems that parallel ones you currently face
- Practice idea production using an idea system

Salvador Dalí,
Head of Gala
(with elephant-
swan apparition),
1937–38 pencil
on paper, image:
9 3/4 in × 13 7/8 in.

© Salvador Dalí,
Fundació Gala-
Salvador Dalí, Artists
Rights Society (ARS),
New York 2017
© Salvador Dalí
Museum, Inc.

survived expulsion from their air-planes (environments they knew well) but frequently died on the ground (in strange and often hostile environments). Torrance's job was to study survival psychology. Focusing on jet aces from the Korean conflict, he underwent rigorous military exercises to experience the conditions the crews encountered behind enemy lines. He found, for example, that an individual's acceptance of something as simple as survival food, such as pemmican, could predict life or death. In his authorized biography, *The Creativity Man*, Torrance identified the skills key to survival in extreme conditions: inventiveness, creativity, imagination, originality, flexibility, decision making, and courage.[2] As Torrance explained,

> Creative solutions to aircrew survival situations required imaginatively gifted recombination of old elements (information about how the American Indians had lived off the land, how the early explorers survived in the Arctic, how men had survived shipwreck, how airmen in World Wars I and II had escaped and evaded, etc.) into a new configuration— what is required now. The elements of a creative solution can be taught, but the creativity itself must be self-discovered and self-disciplined.[3]

The capacity to visualize new ideas, through imagination, flexibility, and originality in thought, not only enhances survival rates among downed airmen but also is equally important to the success of entrepreneurs and intrapreneurs. In today's business world, Woody Norris is a classic example of an ideator, or someone who combines discovery and discipline to create new solutions to old problems. When he was young, Norris worked at a low-level university job so he could take a wide variety of courses for free (although he never earned a degree). A naturally curious person, he freely explored new technologies, including sound. In the early 1960s, applying the principles of FM radio, Norris created a system that could detect and decode movement beneath the skin as ultrasonic sound waves, which led to the modern sonogram. "I enjoyed the process—looking at a problem and identifying a way to solve it," he said in an interview for *Inventors Eye*.[4] Today he is an award-winning inventor and the owner of a variety of patents, including one for a long-range acoustic device (LRAD). For decades, he explained, inventors had wanted to be able to focus sound in the same way laser technology focuses light but had been unable to because of an inability to overcome distortion. Norris saw a way to do so by layering audible sound on top of ultrasound and making a smaller device that needed no receiver. A handheld, nonlethal weapon, the LRAD emits loud, piercing sound in a targeted way and has been used to disrupt attacks by bands of Somali pirates in the Middle East. "I am no genius. I am just 'smart enough.' I still find wonder in the mundane. I like to question the unknown and undone, and I never think that I can quit learning and tinkering," Norris said. "Sometimes it is better not to know something can't be done, and then maybe you'll find a way to do it."[5]

Visualize: Understanding the Behaviors That Lead to Seeing Ahead

To visualize new ideas, you must be able to engage in four essential behaviors that, if practiced daily, lead to the development of possibilities. As you will read, these behaviors—staying motivated through self-actualization, dreaming new possibilities, embodying ideation through personality, and imagining an end state—are all based on established psychological theory. These behaviors are drawn from major theoretical families that have been used to study the creative person.[6] This is not intended to be a comprehensive review of each theoretical family but a glimpse into how these theories inform ideational skills.

Stay Motivated Through Self-Actualization

Abraham Maslow and Carl Rogers suggested that the process of self-actualization, or the quest for personal fulfillment and maximizing one's potential, results in increased production of novel ideas.[7] A perception of fulfillment arises from exposure to personal and professional development, meaningful relationships with coworkers and involvement in assignments that give a sense of purpose, a sense of belonging, and a sense of identity. Thus, when a person believes that he or she is engaged in difference making, the individual feels inspired to do more of it. As an outcome, fulfilled people are more likely to produce breakthrough thinking. In one study, for example, employees working in two companies underscored the positive and noteworthy relationship among organizational identification and feelings of vitality, sense of positive regard, reciprocity, and self-esteem as elements that led to creativity in the workplace. These employees took more risks in suggesting new ideas, producing more ways to do things, and experimenting with alternative approaches.[8] Typically, people who strive for self-actualization are not threatened by ambiguity, volatility, complexity, or uncertainty. They embrace such challenges. They are also inclined to be more spontaneous and natural, so they leave their egos at the door.[9] Motivated to overcome self-imposed constraints, they can ignore the background noise that often gets in the way of creativity. When their personal fulfillment aligns with organizational goals, they become idea-generating machines without even being aware of it.

Dream New Possibilities With Personal Exploration Approaches

Many individual-oriented approaches to creativity draw on Eastern ways of thinking. These approaches emphasize the opening of consciousness as a means of tapping into a hidden pool of brain resources and experiences. For example, studies have shown that meditation practices, such as transcendental meditation (TM), can lead to significantly better scores on the Torrance Test of Creative Thinking (TTCT) when compared to control group participants who did not practice such mind-expanding methods.[10] Results suggest that the TM-trained groups also showed significant improvement in the generation of mental models useful in solving a problem. Whereas formal training in TM would appear to have a positive effect on creativity, it is also likely that you can capture new and intriguing connections when engaging in "soft" awareness during those nonwork activities that often lead to an aha moment, such as exercising, driving, or bathing. Take, for example, a study by a researcher who was able to boost creative flexibility (as measured by the TTCT) by intentionally inducing hypnagogia, which is a restful state between wakefulness and sleep.[11] This finding points to the value of incubation (i.e., a complete disconnection from the problem-solving effort) and breaks for play, daydreaming, and napping as a means of producing a breakthrough idea.

Thought Starter
Hypnagogia

The first author of the book you're reading now designed the complete outline for his TEDx talk by engaging in such an incubational activity. Feeling frustrated while actively working on his speech, he decided to take a nap. But before napping, he posed a challenge to himself to allow his mind to continue to work on his speech. While in the drowsy state before falling asleep, the author's mind began to review some of the recent reading he had done on evolution, which was soon followed by some new connections to creativity. Remaining relaxed, he gently explored this connection and how it might become the main thesis to his TEDx speech.[12] The speech unfolded in his mind, and after about 10 minutes of this hypnagogic state, he got up and outlined the entire talk. A review of many great creators' biographies shows that they often build breaks into their creative routines—taking walks, going swimming, completing crossword puzzles, and such. By making these active, nonwork-related breaks part of their daily routines, it is likely that they take advantage of incubation by preparing their minds to develop a soft awareness.[13]

Recent research into the inner workings of the brain supports what great creators have known for centuries—an incubation break promotes increased mind wandering, leading to the formulation of new neurological connections and greater creativity. A word of advice: Not just any old break promotes mind wandering.[14] Research shows that routine tasks, those that have low cognitive demands such as doing the dishes, going for a jog, or making a peanut butter and jelly sandwich, as opposed to defusing a nuclear bomb or engaging in brain surgery, work best. The latter tasks require in-depth concentration and cognitive engagement, thereby discouraging mind wandering. Although mind wandering boosts creative thinking, it can be dangerous when diffusing bombs or operating on a patient.

Embody Ideation Through Personality

One of the oldest areas of exploration into creativity has been the assessment of the personality qualities associated with individuals who generate breakthrough ideas consistently. Such research has produced a consistent list of characteristics possessed by highly creative individuals. Here are some of the most often cited personal characteristics. Being honest with yourself, reflect on the degree to which you possess each of these traits. Creative people are open to new experiences (how often do you intentionally seek something new simply because it is unfamiliar to you?); tolerate ambiguity (how comfortable are you when limited information or guidance is available?); and take risks (to what degree do you pursue activities and ideas that make you slightly uncomfortable?). Some might argue that these are trait-based qualities and therefore innate—meaning you either have them or you don't. We would counter this view by adopting the growth mindset discussed in the previous chapter and noting that researchers have shown that creative attitudes and behaviors can be developed through training and practice.

Whereas the previous personality characteristics are consistently associated with creative and entrepreneurially-minded people, we would be painting a simplistic picture if we stopped with this description. Creators, entrepreneurs, and innovators are complex people. As described in Chapter 3, they often possess qualities that seem to be opposites. MacKinnon's study of famous architects showed that they were both unconventional and planful, original yet precise, and spontaneous while also efficient.[15] Embodying what appear to be contradictory personality characteristics would seem to have several advantages. It promotes quick adaptability to new and different situations. It also encourages the kind of thinking that sees shades of gray, rather than simply forcing situations into black and white. By embodying opposites you can better develop what Roger Martin, dean of the Rotman School of Management at the University of Toronto, calls integrative thinking.[16] With this kind of thinking you are able to seriously consider two opposing ideas, seeing the merits in both and thus enabling you to create a synthesis, a blend, or springboard into a newly formed alternative. This is a very different way of thinking from how many managers are trained to make decisions, using critical thinking to carefully analyze the pros and cons leading to the "obvious" best solution. Often the most innovative breakthrough results from a combination of elements and ideas. Embracing seemingly contradictory personality characteristics can go a long way in facilitating your own integrative thinking.

Imagine a Positive End State With Cognitive, Rational, and Semantic Approaches

Cognitive, rational, and semantic approaches generally take the view that creativity is a logical and understandable thought process; to make it explainable and productive requires the use of words, semantics, and verbal representations.[17] Within the cognitive set of theories is a specific approach called associative thinking that maintains the key to creative thinking is an ability to link or combine two or more thoughts, ideas, or elements. Indeed, it might be argued that all creative ideas, solutions, and innovations are the result of new combinations and twists on old ideas. David Kord Murray, a highly successful entrepreneur and former head of innovation for the software company Intuit, argued that you can significantly improve your creative thinking by learning to borrow ideas from a range of sources.[18] As he suggests, "You can't make something out of nothing; you have to make it out of something else." He goes on to provide a useful metaphor: "Every chef knows the ingredients in your kitchen will determine the recipe and dinner you serve your guests. Where you get these ingredients from, the places you shop, determine the opinions you and others have of your new idea."[19] He encourages innovators and entrepreneurs to actively borrow ideas from competitors, your observations, other people, and remote fields. The further afield you go to borrow ideas, the more innovative the breakthrough is likely to be.

Generate: Knowing How to Produce Many Alternative Ideas

Key to effective creative problem solving is to generate many alternative ideas, so that when making a decision, you are not left to choose among too few options. Whereas this is a natural skill for all humans, as we have argued in previous chapters, this innate ability atrophies over time for many, and for various reasons, few individuals maximize this ability to the fullest. Over time, various approaches have been developed with the goal of helping people regain and extend their idea-generating prowess. Humans are born with the innate potential to swim; certain strokes have been invented that capitalize on and improve our ability to swim. Just like you can learn these strokes to maximize your swimming ability, so too can you learn approaches to maximize your brain's natural ability to generate ideas. We share four approaches that have been successful in uplifting people's natural idea-generating skills.

The Extended-Effort Principle

When it comes to ideation, or the act of producing ideas, research into the extended-effort principle shows that a simple law of thirds can be applied to the ideas produced in the typical idea-generating session in organizations today.[20] That is, whether generating ideas alone or in a group, the most creative ideas usually come after the initial set of ideas has been produced. In fact, the most original ideas are typically found in the last third of the ideas produced. It is simply the case that when we are faced with a challenge, the first third of the ideas that come to mind are ideas that are already familiar to us or are safe. Unfortunately, because people are too busy, are not well trained, or are under pressure to make a quick decision, they often stop their thinking while in the first third of the ideas that might be produced. In other words, they cut short their idea generation—never extending their imaginations in a way that generates the more original, riskier, and breakthrough ideas. Moreover, the quantity of ideas is critical because, for most businesses today, the road from ideation to product launch is much more of a marathon than a sprint, as Jay Rao and Jim Watkinson describe in the blog *Innovation at Work*. "The reality is that out beyond the world of software and virally driven adoption, innovators must travel a long and difficult road before reaching even the beginning stage of success."[21] For example, Rovio, the maker of the well-known game *Angry Birds*, took 8 years—and 51 different game releases—to create a hit, which is now a multibillion-dollar media franchise. If you want to heighten the creativity of the ideas you produce, and if you want to improve the probability of developing an innovative breakthrough, one surefire way is to remember the rule of thirds and go beyond the initial set of ideas you produce.

Hitting the first third will vary from individual to individual. A good rule to follow is to count the initial set of ideas you produce in response to a challenge, that is, the initial blast of thoughts you can generate until your thinking runs dry. That's your first third. Now generate twice that number. If your initial brain blast resulted in 12 ideas, challenge yourself to generate 24 more ideas. Yes, it's possible—that's why it is called the extended-effort principle.

Divergent Thinking

If you are ever in a brainstorming session with a well-trained divergent thinker, you'll observe that this person's idea-generation process is a disciplined and strategic approach. It's guided by four interdependent goals: (1) to refrain from early critique; (2) to strive for a large quantity of ideas; (3) to allow "freewheeling," or to nurture unusual, outside-the-box ideas; and (4) to search for combinations or synergies as one idea builds on another. This approach is known in the literature as divergent thinking, and these four principles are described in detail in Chapter 5. We return here to divergent thinking, for it is an essential skill when it comes to idea generation. The research is clear. Those who learn and apply these principles can profoundly improve their capacity to engage in divergent thinking—the ability to generate many, varied, and original options.

Lateral Thinking

A more philosophical approach to idea generation, lateral thinking, is a mindset employed to deliberately stretch individuals' perceptions of the problem. Lateral thinking is about shifting one's thoughts in a new direction, pursuing completely new avenues toward the solution, whereas vertical thinking is about going deeper into existing approaches to the problem. Conceptualized by Edward de Bono in the late 1960s, lateral thinking is as much about learning to see the problem anew as it is about generating a large quantity of ideas.[22] This type of thinking is especially critical when a problem is recurring or intractable. The lateral thinker comes to the problem intent on changing his or her own concepts, thoughts, and biases by viewing it in an unconventional light.[23] He or she does this with a two-step process: (1) provocation to dislodge thinking from old patterns and (2) movement to lead thinking down a new path of discovery. Metaphorically, the thinker tries to jump his or her train of thought off a logical, sequential track and move in a new direction, down an unexplored track, just to see where it will go. He or she is more prepared to change directions in search of new possibilities, hidden positive aspects, and valuable circumstances. Some well-known lateral thinking methods include looking up random words (i.e., provocation) in a dictionary or book to see what new insights and ideas each word might suggest in terms of your challenge (i.e., movement). Another approach is to look at randomly selected images (i.e., provocation) and ask yourself what new ideas each picture suggests relative to the problem at hand (i.e., movement).

Learning Activity
Recognizing Moments of Incubation

Incubation is a natural part of the creative process. What are all the ways in which you provide yourself with incubation breaks? Make a list. Another way to think of this is to identify where you are and what you are doing when you get your best ideas. How does this relate to incubation? Great creators make incubation a habit. How might you make this a habitual part of your daily routine?

Doing—Using Associative Thinking to Visualize Anew

If you think you are a visual person, take a minute to read the work of Alexandra Horowitz, and think again. Horowitz is the author of the 2010 bestseller *Inside of a Dog: What Dogs See, Smell, and Know* and 2014's *On Looking: A Walker's Guide to the Art of Observation*.[24] She teaches psychology, animal behavior, and canine cognition at Barnard College, Columbia University. In this most recent book, she takes readers through 11 urban walks in the company of various experts, including doctors, architects, and even a toddler. "Poised half off the bottom step and half onto the sidewalk, my son squatted—a young weight lifter's pose, or the spring-loading of an infant rocket," she writes after a walk with her young son in an essay that will open the eyes of any parent who has ever wondered what tiny tykes actually see.[25] Horowitz not only shows us anew how to see, she helps us understand the link between science and human perception. Horowitz helps us to see that mindfulness and curiosity are intricately related. Paying attention is one thing. To do something with your observations is another. To that end, we recommend paying attention through all the senses.

A strategy shown to improve individuals' ability to visualize new possibilities is to take advantage of our minds' natural tendency to make connections and associations between concepts, even when those concepts seem unrelated. Associative theory proposes that highly creative people access stored information and working memories from a variety of sources.[26] Idea production, therefore, draws on varied and rich life experiences, which create a stored reserve of knowledge for constructing future interconnections. For example, one study found that multicultural experiences were positively linked to problem-solving performance, in particular, insight learning, remote association, and idea fluency.[27] A neuroscience study found that new and unexpected experiences in different realms could boost creativity. Researchers subverted the laws of physics and then embedded these physics in a 3-D virtual space familiar to the subjects. For example, as the subject approached a virtual table with a suitcase on top, the suitcase got smaller as the subject got closer. Subjects exposed to this new experience scored higher on tests of creativity than subjects assigned to the control groups, who had not had the virtual reality experience.[28] This research tells us that building up a catalog of rich experiences serves as a springboard for future ideas. Want to be more creative? Attend conferences outside your field, join interdisciplinary networks, shadow a manager from a different department, or subscribe to magazines outside your professional niche.

Making connections comes naturally to us. You hear the word *salt*, and you might immediately think *pepper*. You hear a song, and it brings back an old memory. You see a billboard, and you suddenly remember something you need to do. Because our minds naturally free associate, you can leverage this ability by making deliberate and facilitated associations. Free association is unguided, natural, without purpose, and therefore unpredictable. Facilitated association, in contrast, is formulating connections that are regulated by some desire, design, or intention. Great creators do this all the time. Picasso borrowed ideas from African art as he formulated a new movement called cubism. The black uniforms and shape of the helmet worn by Nazi Germany SS soldiers were the inspiration for how George Lucas visualized Darth Vader. And his love of the cowboy heroes in Western movies helped him to formulate the Han Solo character.

Many tools and creativity models are based on the concept of facilitated association; we focus on one particularly useful approach that borrows ideas from nature. Nature has successfully solved problems for millions of years and therefore provides humans with a ready supply of solutions that can help solve our problems. For instance, in 1825 engineer Marc Brunel was tasked with digging a tunnel under the River Thames. Tunneling work then was haphazard, slow, and dangerous. Brunel reasoned that there had to be a better way and came up with a solution still being adopted by engineers today. It was a small worm that inspired Brunel's big idea. Brunel observed that when a worm bores through timber, it ingests the wood on the front end and then excretes a shell that lines the tunnel wall on the other end. This observation led Brunel to develop a tunneling machine that worked in an analogous manner.[29]

Thought Starter

Inspiration From Nature

Countless other inventors, innovators, and great creators have used nature for inspiration. Why not learn to deliberately facilitate associations by borrowing from nature to improve your own ideational skills? Facilitating associations with nature to solve human problems is exactly the premise behind an innovative new science called biomimicry. Janine Benyus helped to popularize this creative methodology in her book *Biomimicry: Innovation Inspired by Nature*.[30] Whether it's the cooling system of termites, the traffic flow of ants, or the water distribution network of a leaf, nature's processes offer today's problem solvers insight into designs and systems that have evolved successfully over millennia. For example, Speedo, the company that developed sharkskin swimsuits, is now making sports news with its new Nemesis Fins. The fins are inspired by those of the humpback whale; like the whale's, Nemesis Fins create more surface area for water to pass over for enhanced propulsion. There is even a special website designed to make facilitated associations with nature easier. Simply go to www.asknature.org, enter the problem you need to address, see nature's solutions, and then make your own new connections.

Learning Activity
Applying Biomimicry

Imagine you are a restaurateur who wants to attract more customers during off-season periods. To facilitate deliberate associations with nature, go to www.asknature.org and look up ways in which animals attract mates. Use the list of solutions found in nature to inspire ways in which you might attract more customers to your restaurant. Apply divergent thinking and adopt a playful attitude to create the right mindset for finding possible solutions. Once you have diverged on alternatives, select those you believe are most likely to solve the problem of attracting more customers. In what ways did using the process of making associations help your ability to ideate (as opposed to simply trying to generate ideas without borrowing ideas from nature)?

Being—Living Like an Idea Generator

People who live the life of idea generators constantly visualize new possibilities and generate novel ideas. But how do they do it? To be sure, they employ the techniques previously mentioned in this chapter, and they do so in a myriad of individual ways. Yet research shows that they also have two important qualities in common: They have rich recreational or play lives, and they possess the ability to improvise or think on their feet.

Consider, for example, the research of Stuart Brown, a medical doctor who has engaged in a lifelong pursuit of the biological necessities of play. The author of the 2010 book *Play: How It Shapes the Brain, Opens the Imagination, and Invigorates the Soul*, Brown looked at life histories of 6,000 highly creative and successful people from all walks of life and saw a clear pattern of an active recreational life.[31] By contrast, when he studied the pathology of homicidal males, he found that most had been effectively deprived of play as children and adults. "Play-deprived adults are often rigid, humorless, inflexible and closed to trying out new options," Brown explains in the *New York Times*. "Playfulness enhances the capacity to innovate, adapt and master changing circumstances. It is not just an escape. It can help us integrate and reconcile difficult or contradictory circumstances. And, often, it can show us a way out of our problems. There are numerous examples of difficult, deadlocked negotiations that were broken open by a joke or humorous incident."[32] Play is beneficial not just because it offers the brain a respite from work, adds Brown, who founded the Center for Childhood Creativity and the National Institute for Play; play also "*reshapes* our rigid views of the world."

In fact, Brown's institute lists seven patterns of play on its website:

- *Attunement play:* laughing together, making faces at each other, staring contests

- *Body play:* leaping, wiggling, dancing, climbing, and other movements

- *Object play:* tinkering with an appliance, building a model, skipping rocks

- *Social play:* board and card games, team sports, tag

- *Imaginative and pretend play:* charades, role-playing just for fun, day-dreaming

- *Storytelling-narrative play:* telling campfire tales, writing poems, keeping a journal

- *Creative play:* painting, sculpting, making up music, inventing for the fun of it[33]

The comedian Brian Regan is a master at transforming his observations into comical hyperbole, which works as a kind of attunement play. In one of his comedy routines, for instance, Regan mentions his experience calling United Parcel Service: "Ya, I have ten boxes; can you come pick them up?" "We need the weight and the girth," the representative replied. "Okay, I don't know what the weight is, and um, I don't know what girth means. . . . So now what's the procedure?" "So this guy talks to me like I'm four years old." "Well, do you have a bathroom scale?" "Uh, ya, but if I put the box on the scale, it's gonna cover up the NUMBERS!"[34] Creating humor from observations has several effects. One, it creates a positive mood, which has been shown to support creativity. Two, comic hyperbole based on attunement with the environment can help identify opportunities for product and customer service improvement.

In addition to play, the ability to improvise is a core creative competency for our times. With wave after wave of disruptive products or technology, organizations must respond to competition in the time it takes to answer a customer's e-mail. Nimbleness is the new norm. But not all members of the organization are ready to make a switch in their approach to doing business, including leaders. In what is termed the marathon effect, leaders at the head of the pack see the finish line but do not realize that the others who are running behind cannot see the horizon because the traffic blocks the view.[35] The more adept runners are the ones who learn faster how to respond to what appears on the horizon, who can improvise on the spot and outwit their competitors. From trailblazing comedians like Tina Fey to veteran actors like Alan Alda, who now teaches improv to scientists at Stony Brook University, improv is hailed as good practice for real-life problem solving.[36] Things rarely go according to plan. So, in essence, improv superimposes ambiguity, complexity, and psychological vulnerability on any situation. Tom Yorton, the CEO of Second City Communications, explains that the idea of working without a script, building on others' ideas, creating something from nothing, and the crucial challenge of balancing the needs of individuals and those of the group is a skill today's leaders must attain to react in the moment. As Yorton observed,

> I come out of corporate ranks—not from the world of improv or theater. In fact, I often say that I'm the most unfunny guy at Second City. But my experience—and in fact, my scars—are from bumping up against the same organizational hurdles that improv is so effective at helping companies get over—challenges that include connecting with customers, engaging employees around change, moving into new markets, innovating new products and services and working without a script.[37]

Looking for a fun way to work improv into your life? Try the Yes-And thinking described in Chapter 2 with a friend, colleague, partner, spouse, or one of your children. Take turns, for example, weaving a story together by having one person start with an improbable situation, with the next person building on this by responding with "Yes, and" . . . followed up with a statement that extends the story. Go back and forth practicing improvisational storytelling. Playing charades or popular board games on the market, such as the Improv Comedy Game, is another great way to practice the skill of improvisation in a deliberate manner.

Learning Activity
Your Play Inventory

The capacity to play is crucial to creativity and makes life richer. As Stuart Brown says in his book *Play,* "When we stop playing, we start dying."[38] Brown gives himself at least 3 to 4 hours of play each day. Take some time to reflect on the ways you engage in play and try to incorporate play into your life. Further inspiration can be gained by looking to others as models. Ask your friends or family about their play lives, or research the play lives of those you admire. Name three ways in which you have seen, or experienced, play encouraged in the workplace. If you have experienced play at work, what have you found to be the benefits (if you haven't had this experience, what would you imagine the benefits to be)?

Introduction

Great ideas are often an innovator's retaliation to an intractable problem, and the story of Intezyne—a clinical-stage biotechnology company—is one such example. The intractable problem that launched Intezyne into existence involves the terrible side effects that accompany the ubiquitous cancer-fighting tactic: chemotherapy.

Millions of people around the world are diagnosed with cancer each year, and every individual receiving chemotherapy treatment—the most commonly applied treatment for most tumor types—is vulnerable to a multitude of vicious side effects brought on by the cancer-fighting drugs themselves. The problem is that the cancer-combating drugs cannot effectively distinguish between cancerous cells and the healthy cells surrounding them. Side effects of chemotherapy are varied but include immunosuppression (a drop in white blood cells, red blood cells, and platelets), gastrointestinal distress (nausea, vomiting, anorexia, diarrhea, abdominal cramps, and constipation), fatigue, hair loss, infertility, organ damage, and neurological effects such as intense pain and hypersensitivity to cold. At minimum, it's pretty rotten stuff, and at worst, these side effects can be deadly.[39]

Enter Intezyne's patented IVECT approach to cancer therapeutics—a drug-delivery methodology poised to revolutionize the way oncologists treat many types of cancer. Intezyne's portfolio of oncology assets comprises individual compounds that have either cellular or molecular targeting capability or have tumor-specific release mechanisms.[40] In a nutshell, this means that the medicine that goes in affects only the areas that need it. This is no easy task, because the delivery vehicle must be nontoxic, biocompatible, nonimmunogenic, and biodegradable and must remain undetected by the built-in defense mechanisms of the human immune system.

At the root of Intezyne's innovative approach to cancer treatment are polymer micelles, which provide a means of encapsulating and preserving the cancer-fighting drugs until they reach the tumor. Intezyne cofounder and chief scientific officer Dr. Kevin Sill compares the polymer micelles to a koosh ball: "There's a core with stringy arms coming out," he says. "The drug goes inside that core. The koosh ball strands are the polymer chains."

The problem facing Intezyne was that synthetic polymer delivery systems—which have been around since the 1970s—faced some primary challenges: (1) achieving stability of the micelle after being introduced into the body (previous attempts by researchers became diluted in water and/or blood) and (2) the micelles' general inability to target specific tissue (in this case, tumors). Prior to Sill's discovery, upon interacting with blood proteins and phospholipids, micelles would dissolve and fall apart—and once the micelle had broken down, the delivery vehicle and the toxic drugs would seep throughout the body. "We had to figure out how to keep that from happening," Sill says.[41]

(Continued)

(Continued)

Backstory: Designing a Nano-Scale Trojan Horse

Friends in graduate school, Kevin Sill and Habib Skaff (Intezyne cofounder and chief executive officer) were studying polymer chemistry at the University of Massachusetts. On a return trip by train from the American Chemical Society fall meeting in New York City, Habib leaned over to Kevin and said, "Forget this academic stuff, I'm going to start a company; you should come with me." Moments later, Sill had agreed to join him. The decision to create a biosciences start-up company wasn't something whimsically undertaken by the pair, however. As a graduate student, Skaff had been working on projects at Kodak and witnessed mass layoffs of 25,000 employees in a single day. This experience pushed him away from comparable opportunities at other popular landing spots for chemistry grads such as Royal Dutch Shell, DuPont, and the Dow Chemical Company. In addition, Skaff and Sill had discussed at length the challenges of working inside academia—the relentless pursuit of laboratory funding through grants, perpetual pressure to publish in peer-reviewed journals, and the sometimes complicated balance between doing great science and the politics of promotion and career advancement. Their decision was a calculated one, one that would change their lives forever.

With a verbal agreement in place to launch a new venture, Sill and Skaff began discussing how they could use their skills in polymer chemistry to make an impact and to better others' lives. They began by listing 15 technology areas they could venture into, such as quantum dot informatics for asset identification and security tracking applications, wastewater treatment,

the design and development of artificial blood, synthetic cell design, and drug delivery vehicles. From there, they applied criteria to their list to help narrow their options. Their evaluation criteria included feasibility (*Do we think it can be done?*), time to market (*How long do we think it will take?*), skill-set relevance (*Is this something we feel skilled enough to tackle?*), financial upside (*Is there a significant market opportunity for a solution to this problem?*), and altruistic motivation (*Are we going to feel good about dedicating our time and energy to this?*).

After scoring and discussing their options, a top choice emerged: Skaff and Sill would set out to solve the micelle instability problem of oncology drug delivery. "We honed in on oncology as a good use for that, given the reduced toxicity and delivering more of the drug to the site where it's needed," Skaff says. "That's really the Holy Grail," says Sill, "to be able to treat cancer without the vicious side effects."

Success did not find them overnight, however. They had been attending academic and industry conferences and learning everything they could from experts working in the field of polymer assembly, and by listening between the lines, they discovered that a reversible stabilizer for drug delivery applications had been eluding scientists in the field. Because of immersing themselves in the frontiers of their domain, Sill and Skaff had learned what needed to be done and identified what needed to be invented.

Next they engaged in an exhaustive review of the literature, probing history for lessons learned. Armed with their laptops and supported by the Google search engine, for 6 months, they hunted; nights and weekends, they sifted through thousands of pages of chemistry research. Sill estimates their consumption at hundreds of, or perhaps even thousands of, research articles. When they weren't working independently, they'd get together to discuss what they'd found, and they developed a habit of collaboratively sketching out molecule designs inspired by their reading. The work was grinding, and it finally paid off when, one night, they were rewarded with that often elusive flash of genius, the instance of insight often referred to as an aha, eureka, or lightbulb moment.

The breakthrough emerged from an unlikely source: Sill had stumbled upon an article published in 1938 in the *Journal of the American Chemical Society* that described a chemical reaction used for, of all things, zinc throat lozenges. Cough drops!

That article and the chemical reaction contained within were just what he was looking for. Sill was able to match the chemical reaction describing the dissolving cough drop in the article to his understanding of the dissolving polymer micelle problem that had been plaguing drug-delivery researchers.

This insight set the stage for the development of Intezyne's IVECT method, which stabilizes the polymer micelle as it travels through the body until it is exposed to acid, the trigger that breaks it apart, releasing the drug. A pH of 5.5 to 6.5 is the "sweet spot" for triggering the release, which also happens to be the pH range of a tumor. Eureka! For the breakthrough, Sill was awarded the Young Innovator of the Year award by *R&D* magazine in 2009.[42]

As a result of Dr. Sill's aha moment, Intezyne has raised millions of dollars of investment capital, hired and inspired the minds of many aspiring researchers, and with a bit of luck, they will continue to evolve the development of targeted cancer therapeutics for people around the world.

Closing

The story of Intezyne is a classic example of two highly driven, persistent scientist-entrepreneur hybrids and their journey through the creative problem-solving process. They took six critical actions:

1. Invested years of their time and energy in learning their craft (polymer chemistry)

2. Analyzed their career options and decided that entrepreneurship was the right path forward for their personal and professional aspirations

3. Generated a list of opportunity areas where they could apply their skills, then applied success criteria to their list of options to zoom in on a promising direction

4. Identified and targeted an important gap in the polymer chemistry technology landscape (the micelle instability problem) that, if addressed, could impact quality of life and health outcomes for millions of people

5. Demonstrated grit, persistence, and resilience throughout their 6-month literature search for insight into how to solve their intractable chemistry problem

6. Practiced visualizing molecule designs by sketching out their concepts and discussing the images and models

(Continued)

(Continued)

Discussion Questions: Knowing

1. From the description of Sill and Skaff's journey, can you identify the crucial factors that led to their breakthrough insight?

2. Knowledge plays an important role in producing creative breakthroughs. In what ways did knowledge promote or inhibit creative thinking in this case?

Application Questions: Doing

1. In reviewing the six critical actions undertaken by Sill and Skaff outlined in the conclusion of the case study, are you able to consider the actions through the lens of the dynamic balance between divergent and convergent thinking? Are you able to notice specific examples of each? If so, which ones?

2. Do you recall the process mash-up presented in Chapter 5? The four stages in this universal creative process are Understand (Observe & Define), Ideate (Visualize & Generate), Experiment (Develop & Validate), and Implement (Get Buy-in & Drive Change). Did you notice any examples of Sill and Skaff demonstrating or engaging in any of these stages? If so, which ones?

3. What did you learn about the aha moment from this case that you can apply in your own life?

4. Think about a tough problem you are facing in your own life. Do any of the theories, strategies, and tactics in this case help you get closer to generating a breakthrough solution? If you were to spend some time thinking about solving your challenge, where might you start, and in what direction(s) might you take your problem-solving process?

Thinking Ahead: Being

When Dr. Sill was an undergraduate student, he took 9 months off from school to work in a research lab in a co-op setting. He believes the hands-on application helped him to identify his passion, as opposed to merely chasing what he was already proficient in. What steps have you taken to help align your skills with your passion? Are you currently working on a project that helps you feel like you're "shaking hands with tomorrow"? If not, what types of projects or activities might you get involved in to move closer to this goal?

Experiment

Strategies to Develop and Validate the Best Solutions

Knowing—Developing and Validating Through Experimentation

It is no secret that developing good ideas is a process of continual experimentation—test, fail, learn, and retain the best. Anyone who has ever watched a dog show or simply admired how a pet Labrador chases and retrieves a Frisbee understands instinctively how far these animals have come from wolves and how nature evolves through experimentation. Charles Darwin first documented evolutionary development in 1859 after observing unique yet strangely familiar species of life on the volcanic Galápagos Islands off the western coast of South America.[1] Whereas evolution in nature balances two primary functions, generation of novel variations and testing these variations to see which is most adaptable, humans can, and do, adopt a similar process when developing novel ideas into workable solutions. In fact, humans use a similar process to speed up evolution; it's called selective breeding. Where nature helped our friendly Frisbee-catching Labrador to develop its physical and dispositional characteristics, humans have intervened to selectively breed dogs to produce more than 150 breeds. DNA testing now shows that dogs evolved from wolves about 130,000 years ago; this process of developing into the uniquely distinct breeds we have today occurred only over the last 150 years.[2] Just as humans can deliberately speed up evolution through breeding, so too can we speed up innovation by deliberately breeding our ideas through experimentation—quickly testing and learning from success and failure.

J. K. Rowling, who took 7 years to write the first Harry Potter book, can identify with purposeful tinkering in both life and work. In 2008, upon receiving an honorary degree from Harvard University, she offered words of wisdom on this topic to new graduates. In a now-famous speech, "The Fringe Benefits of Failure, and the Importance of Imagination," she recalled how years earlier, rebounding from divorce, poverty, and single motherhood, she found the courage to see what

Learning Goals

After reading this chapter, you will be able to do the following:

- Identify what creative scientists and entrepreneurs have in common when developing good ideas into great solutions
- Describe a system for vetting and validating the best ideas
- Discuss the benefits of prototyping, and other approaches, for developing robust solutions
- Appraise the value of failing fast
- Apply a set of key questions for soliciting feedback from stakeholders to improve an idea

others might call a counterfactual view of reality—herself as a novelist. "That period of my life was a dark one. . . . So why do I talk about the benefits of failure? Simply because failure meant a stripping away of the inessential . . . I was set free, because my greatest fear had been realized, and I was still alive, and I still had a daughter whom I adored, and I had an old typewriter and a big idea." Rowling concedes that others do not have to fail on the scale that she did to appreciate her point. But, she added,

> It is impossible to live without failing at something, unless you live so cautiously that you might as well not have lived at all—in which case, you fail by default. . . . Failure taught me things about myself that I could have learned no other way. I discovered that I had a strong will, and more discipline than I had suspected; I also found out that I had friends. . . . The knowledge that you have emerged wiser and stronger from setbacks means that you are, ever after, secure in your ability to survive. . . . Such knowledge is a true gift, for all that it is painfully won.[3]

From J. K. Rowling we see that a willingness to fail is essential to adopting an experimenting mindset.

Many of today's entrepreneurs demonstrate a penchant for purposeful tinkering in their attempts to discern and develop the best ideas. Consider Sara Blakely, the founder of Spanx, who revolutionized the modern undergarment business with technologically advanced, skinlike underwear that trims pounds and years off the wearer. In 2012, Blakely was named to *Time* magazine's annual list of the 100 most influential people in the world, and she also made the *Forbes* 2012 list of the world's wealthiest people, including its youngest self-made billionaire.[4]

At home in her Atlanta, Georgia, apartment, Blakely experimented with different designs for what she began to call "shapewear" but suffered the rebuff of male hosiery makers until one manufacturer discovered that his two daughters liked her ideas. With his help, Blakely developed several prototypes, and wore them, as did her friends and family members, before settling on her first product line. From the creation of the company name to writing her own product patent, she researched, tested, and tinkered. She even modeled the product—slipping into the bathroom to trim down with Spanx under her slim white pants—in a sales pitch to Neiman Marcus. After landing on the cover of *Forbes*, Blakely told the magazine's readers that her belief in the value of her own product carried her through early years of experimentation. "I did not have the most experience in the industry or the most money," she said. "But I cared the most."[5]

Key to Blakely's success is an intuitive understanding of mental models and how to shift her customers from the idea of buying underwear to desiring shapewear. The concept of models—that both *guide* and *inhibit* our thinking—dates back to the early 20th century and Jean Piaget, a well-known European psychologist and early researcher into cognitive science. As Piaget played with his own children, he studied how they and other children learned. Based on keen observation and experiments, Piaget believed that a child progressively detaches herself (steps back and reflects) to construct models that help her to master and control the environment she is exploring. He stated, "The more the child progresses in adaptation, the more play is reintegrated into general intelligence, and the conscious symbol [i.e., a shape or a letter] is replaced by constructions and creative imagination."[6] These observations served as the basis for the development of a popular learning theory known as constructivism, which conceptualizes a person's acquisition of new knowledge; he or she is basically constructing and testing a hypothesis.

Thought Starter
Testing and Failing

More recently, Seymour Papert, a brilliant mathematician, educator, and computer scientist at Massachusetts Institute of Technology (MIT), studied under Piaget and advanced his theory of constructivism. As described in Papert's seminal 1993 book *Mindstorms: Children, Computers, and Powerful Ideas*, learning must allow people to make connections and develop their own mental models.[7] Learning cannot be static and facilitated through lecture or explanation, but, rather, learning happens through personal engagement. In a classic set of studies, Papert created lovable robots, for instance, a turtle that moved in response to commands based on calculations made by children learning the principle of a geometric angle. "The goal of children's first experiences in the Turtle learning environment is not to learn formal rules but to develop insights into the way they move about in space," he writes in *Mindstorms*. "This method tries to establish a firm connection between personal activity and the creation of formal knowledge."[8] Further, he states:

> The understanding of learning must be genetic. It must refer to the genesis of knowledge. What an individual can learn, and how he learns it, depends on what models he has available. This raises, recursively, the question of how he learned these models. Thus the "laws of learning" must be about how intellectual structures grow out of one another and about how, in the process, they acquire both logical and emotional form.[9]

What creative scientists and entrepreneurs share is a willingness to acquire new mental models that give good ideas a chance to incubate or develop and to devise a system for vetting and validating the best ideas. In the sections that follow, you will learn the key strategies and tactics for employing these essential creative behaviors, how to practice them to develop your skills, and what living the creative life as an idea developer and validator might look like. As you move through life and work, you will begin to see new opportunities to incorporate these practices into your own habits as well as notice other people who use them as second nature.

Development: Refining Ideas
Through Play, Sketching, and Prototyping

For Helene Cahen, the word *prototype* is a verb. It's also an adjective. Never mind that, lexically, it's a noun. People who know her do not see this semantic conversion as strange but as forward thinking. Cahen is an innovation consultant with the firm Strategic Insights. A facilitator, trainer, and lecturer at the University of California, Berkeley, Haas School of Business, she specializes in guiding her clients toward user-centered innovation with design thinking. She is convinced that you and I, nondesigners, can also use highly effective mindsets and processes employed by designers. Three mindsets—being human centered, engaging in visual thinking, and adopting a prototype attitude—make the biggest difference. "The mindset of being human-centered with a focus on empathy has impacted the way I work on projects," she says. "I now start with an observation and/or interview phase first. When facilitating creative projects, I suggest that the participants learn more about the product or service in an experiential way in addition to the traditional secondary research, talk to customers or users and observe people." Second, she encourages people to overcome any hang-ups they might have about their artistic abilities and to engage in more visual thinking. "I had to overcome my personal belief that since I cannot draw any better than a five year old, I should not use visuals to communicate with others, or even when I was thinking for myself," she admits.[10]

> In the past few years I have been challenging myself to use visuals and drawings in my presentations, to use Mind Mapping for taking notes or organizing my thoughts, and to encourage people to draw in my training or facilitation sessions. I found out that drawing is a powerful problem-solving tool and it has helped me find solutions that I had in my mind but was not able to put in words.[11]

Third, the adoption of a "prototyping attitude" makes it natural to ask questions like, How can I create a small version of the solution to test it quickly and cheaply? "A prototyping attitude means that when I am facilitating a group and we are developing solutions, we start making fast prototypes (by fast I mean done in 10 minutes) which help tremendously with narrowing down options, getting group buy-in and equally important, selling to management."[12]

Cahen's thinking is supported by recent neuroscience research using a functional magnetic resonance imaging (fMRI) machine, which shows more brain activity when we read a sensory term, a descriptive metaphor, or an emotional exchange than when we read about simple objects or abstract concepts. Anatomically, then, we know that our mind maps are shaped by our connectedness—physical and emotional—to people and our environment.[13] But how does that knowledge translate across an entire business or organization? Perhaps more easily than we think, argues Peter Senge, author of the classic 1990 book *The Fifth Discipline: The Art and Practice of the Learning Organization*.[14] Mental models help make sense of things, but by no stretch of the imagination are they always correct. In fact, having only one mental model fixes you to see and then interpret things in narrow and dated ways. Senge, a leading systems scientist and senior lecturer at MIT Sloan School of Management, says the good news for organizations is that their mental models are socially constructed by all the members. This social reconstruction means organizations have the potential to continuously update their mental models to adapt to the times, if individuals, especially creative leaders, understand their own potential to expand models and if companies approach learning in a systems-like way. As Senge and colleagues explain,

> Through learning we reperceive the world and our relationship to it. . . . This then, is the basic meaning of a "learning organization"—an organization that is continuously expanding its capacity to create its future. "Survival learning" or what is more often called "adaptive learning" is important—indeed it is necessary. But for a learning organization, "adaptive learning" must be joined by "generative learning," learning that enhances our capacity to create.[15]

What the research and experts' experience shows, then, is that three strategies are essential to generative learning and idea development: (1) serious play, (2) sketching, and (3) prototyping.

Serious Play to Engage More of Your Brain

Recent research shows that even when you are resting, or tuning out the external environment, your brain engages its "default network." In this default state, it continues to process existing internalized knowledge, incubating, reflecting on, and experimenting with ideas.[16] In a 2013 synthesis of takeaways from brain research for the *Harvard Business Review* (*HBR*), Adam Waytz and Malia Mason highlight the importance of serious play, which many companies now recognize as a source of innovation. "Having unfocused free time is an important (and underutilized) factor in breakthrough innovations. That notion obviously calls to mind the '20% time' policy at Google, under which the company's engineers get a day a week to work on whatever they want," they write.[17]

Thought Starter
Serious Play

Few companies understand the seriousness of play like Pixar Animation Studios, the award-winning movie start-up housed in a glass atrium in Emeryville, California. Here, creativity is not just desirable, it's the actual product, says Josh Cooley, Pixar story artist.[18] Cooley describes the process of making a movie for a company that encourages its employees to take classes in yoga, sculpture, musical instruments, and other creative pursuits that engage their default networks. This type of serious play ensures that ample amounts of incubation, reflection, and experimentation go into each and every movie, reports Cooley, who has worked on movies like *The Incredibles*, *Cars*, *Ratatouille*, and *Up*. Typically, his creative day calls for hand-drawing several drafts of a storyboard, presenting it to a team of other story artists, listening and debating, then allowing for further expansion of the group's ideas in subsequent iterations. "Storyboarding is story [reboarding]," explains the artist, who went through 81,772 storyboards for *Ratatouille* alone, a typical number of revisions for a Pixar film.[19] Back at *HBR*, Waytz and Mason concede that not all companies can or will institute creative free-time programs, which they may find hard to assess. However, they recommend that people who want to be more creative embrace total detachment from their work environment on a regular basis. Often only with serious play can you engage your default network, assimilate the ideas of another person, envision a different time and place, and free-associate without interruption.

Finally, no one is more serious about play than Dale Dougherty. If the name is not familiar to you, how about the national, now international, maker movement? Mr. Dougherty is credited with starting this movement in 2006. If you are not familiar with the maker movement, it grew out of the DIY movement and has resulted in the development of makerspaces in libraries and other public venues. Makerspaces allow patrons the opportunity to play with technology and tools. People are encouraged to play, invent, and experiment with ideas; they can work alone, collaborate with others, or receive expert advice. The intent is to encourage adults to engage in hands-on play, to develop their own ideas into tangible products. And now this movement endeavors to influence educational practices by encouraging schools to participate in makerspaces. The maker movement and makerspaces bring together both play and prototyping into a powerful innovation laboratory. Mr. Dougherty's description of makers closely parallels how we have described innovators and entrepreneurs. He observed, "Makers are likely to see themselves as outsiders, like some artists and writers, who do not follow the traditional paths. They create their own paths, which is what innovative and creative people do."[20]

Sketching to Explore
Reinterpretations of Your Idea

Sketching aids in formulating new or half-baked ideas into great ones in a variety of ways. First, it serves as a prerequisite to prototyping by teasing ideas out of your head and into a more concrete form. Second, sketching overrides the distracting attention you may give to details. Thus, by drawing out ideas quickly, sketching better positions you to see what might work and explore ideas. Third, sketching helps you see something you thought you knew well in a new light. For example, one researcher from a design school in the Netherlands found that sketching has a positive influence on reinterpretation, which helps to create new insights when studying an old problem.[21] Each sketch in a series produced an understanding of a new representation. Sketches can also produce a second important product; they reveal scenarios that point to a potentially negative result. Time and money saved can make the difference between success and failure in today's business world.

Prototyping to Jump-Start Innovation

Without prototypes, you can't test for possibilities. Without the ability to test, it is difficult to experiment and begin to develop new mental models. This explains why prototyping is essential to jump-starting innovation, argues designer Todd

Zaki Warfel, who helped popularized the creative practice in 2009 with his book *Prototyping: A Practitioner's Guide*.[22] A hands-on treatment, the book offers tutorials for prototyping with paper, slides, software, and other media; discusses the pros and cons of the tools; and walks readers through the usability testing process, which the author says can boost idea approval into the 90% consensus range. With missionary zeal, Warfel extols the multiple benefits of prototyping: (1) it produces much-needed variation; (2) it expands mental models to help make sense of uncertainty and ambiguity; (3) it offers something that you—and your customers—can see, touch, and try; (4) it allows you to fail early, learn cheaply, and rework an idea quickly; and (5) it reduces the chances for misinterpretation.[23] When ideas are only described in words, readers may glean different understandings. However, when ideas are transformed to visible, tactile models, requests for clarification and rework are reduced. Whether it's an origami mock-up or a life-size 3-D print, a prototype helps you to own an idea and to quickly recognize its strengths and weaknesses.

Validation: How to Refine and Select the Best Options

So far we have introduced to you the benefits of idea development and techniques for experimenting with and testing ideas. But how do you refine and select the best? By what criteria do you evaluate ideas when in search of breakthrough concepts? The very word *breakthrough* suggests that the novelty of the idea defies prediction, hence, critique. But novelty is one thing and usefulness is another. What is needed, therefore, is a type of thinking that permits you to evaluate ideas in a way that transforms an idea into something more tangible and of value to the users.[24] To move into the validation phase, four key activities must be employed: (1) design thinking, (2) idea refinement, (3) product comparison, and (4) solution assessment.

Design Thinking to See More Critically

Few people have shaken up the field of innovation—and the perennial discussion of product quality—like Eric Ries, an entrepreneur and author of the *New York Times* bestseller *The Lean Startup: How Today's Entrepreneurs Use Continuous Innovation to Create Radically Successful Businesses*.[25] Since 2010, Ries has been entrepreneur-in-residence at Harvard Business School and an IDEO fellow. But his start in business was less than auspicious. After failing, or perhaps even flopping, at two early start-ups, including one in college, he went on to succeed spectacularly with the avatar-creation website IMVU. There he began to employ design thinking, or a brand of innovation based on the idea of creating "minimum viable product," with the aim of improving the product through continuous customer feedback. As Tim Brown, the popular CEO and president of IDEO, defines it, "[Innovation is] powered by a thorough understanding, through direct observation, of what people want and need in their lives and what they like or dislike about the way particular products are made, packaged, marketed, sold, and supported."[26] For Ries, it was not necessary to start with the perfect product, nor was it wise to fast-track a shoddy product. His goal was to put the best prototype in front of critical users as soon as possible to learn as much as he could from their feedback before creating the next iteration. Today, Ries gives conferences preparing entrepreneurs for the quick and chaotic pace of iterative product launches and testing, stressing that the payoff is worth the early failure and experimentation.

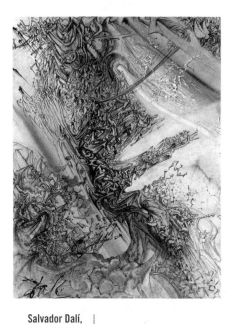

Salvador Dalí,
*Pi-mesonic
Angel,* 1957–58
ink and wash on
paper, image:
15 3/8 in ×
11 1/2 in.

© Salvador Dalí,
Fundació Gala-
Salvador Dalí, Artists
Rights Society (ARS),
New York 2017

© Salvador Dalí
Museum, Inc.

Idea Refinement to Edit and Polish

Three critical cognitive functions—forecasting, appraising, and revising—relate to the evaluation of creative ideas, based on modern creativity research.[27] Forecasting triggers the process of idea evaluation. It calls for imagining your idea in its future state. You try to envision, and then predict, the idea's consequences and reactions from those who will be impacted by your idea. From these rehearsals, you gain insights that aid in appraising your idea. Appraisal involves assessing the consequences and the reactions of others against assumed performance metrics; from this process, you then decide to advance the idea or to stop it. The third function is revising your undeveloped idea to meet new expectations. At this point, you must generate new thinking to recast and expand the original idea to improve its chances of survival.[28] Many of Dalí's sketches reflected raw and untested ideas. The accompanying sketch, by contrast, shows a highly detailed and complex image.

Comparing Products to Evaluate Creativity

In the practical world, what really excites innovators is a creative outcome that meets customer needs and has a useful social purpose.[29] To that end, scholars have created and tested a set of criteria to critically compare and assess the creativity of products, known as the Creative Product Semantic Scale (CPSS).[30] The CPSS criteria include novelty, depicted by originality (i.e., uniqueness), and surprise (i.e., acceptance and appreciation). These product qualities allow an innovator or entrepreneur to determine the degree to which the proposed idea is truly distinctive and unique. The next set of criteria is called resolution, namely logical (i.e., adherence to established standards), useful (i.e., clear and practical applications), valuable (i.e., meets intended needs), and understandable (i.e., ease of use). These criteria help the innovator or entrepreneur get into the mind of the end user and determine how easy it will be for him or her to adopt the proposed product or service. The final set is called style, which includes organic (i.e., elements form a complete whole), well-crafted (i.e., attention to detail), and elegant (i.e., elements are refined). Often those who design a new product or service sometimes underestimate the importance of style. If you are familiar with Apple products then you know the competitive advantage that style can achieve. Before launching a new idea, these criteria can be applied to refine and reshape what appears to be a good idea into a great creative breakthrough.

Assessing Solutions to Predict Creative Value

Other scholars have forwarded another set of criteria to identify functional creativity that specifically targets engineered artifacts or manufactured goods.[31] They, too, have created and scientifically tested a set of criteria to appraise the creativity in products: the Creative Solution Diagnosis Scale (CSDS). The four CSDS criteria of functional creativity are relevance and effectiveness (knowledge of existing facts and principles), novelty (problematization, existing knowledge, and new knowledge), elegance (both external and internal elegance), and genesis (forward looking). Both sets of criteria linked to the CPSS and the CSDS serve as important discussion points for team members exploring ways to test and refine breakthrough concepts. You could, of course, create your own rubric for your own industry, but the value of using a proven metric is that your evaluations have greater reliability and validity.

Learning Activity
Mind Mapping the Chapter

We reviewed a lot of information in the Knowing section of this chapter. To organize, sketch, and visualize this material, we encourage you to use a tool mentioned in this chapter—mind mapping. Mind mapping is a method for concretizing information and thoughts in a visual way. A mind map is a diagram that shows relationships between the whole and its parts. Follow these steps to use mind mapping:

1. Start in the center of a blank horizontal page.

2. Draw an image in the center of the page that represents the main concept.

3. Identify, draw, and label the main branches connected to the central idea (use different colors for different branches).

4. Drill deeper by extending main branches into second, third, or more levels.

   It is recommended that simple images, single words, and multiple colors be used throughout the mind map. For examples of mind maps, we recommend a quick Internet trip. A useful site is www.tonybuzan.com/about/mind-mapping. What themes did you spot in your mind map that give you a sense for how ideas are transformed into great solutions? Which approach to validating ideas did you like the most? Why? How might you take the approach that you liked the least and turn it into a more amenable approach? In what ways was it helpful to sketch and visualize this section of the chapter?

Doing—Acting Like an Idea Developer

Honing Your Idea Development Skills

One of the fastest ways to develop ideas constantly is to adopt the mindset of a rapid prototyper. Once you have tested your assumptions on a few partners and close friends, you are in a position to construct and test prototypes with another level of stakeholders, which will, in turn, lead to more ideas that are sorted and converted into a new prototype. Rapid prototyping is designed to communicate a proposal in the most efficient method to further explore, test, and refine it.[32] Prototypes can take the form of flowcharts, storyboards, metaphorical prototypes (e.g., a poster with images), interactive building blocks, "junk" material prototypes, overhead film sheets to layer concepts, or role-plays. For example, partners at IDEO created a prototypical mobile "minibar" for a health care client demonstrating how hospital patients and their family members could eat when desired. The minibar could be reordered and stocked daily. While they were testing this idea, they discovered that the prototype would impact ordering, fulfilling, and maintaining the minibar. These discoveries led to other issues, namely that the minibar would impact patient room design, the admissions process, and food service design. Collectively, these tests identified all the elements in a unified meal experience for the patients and their families, something that product designers would have been unable to imagine on their own.[33] As your stakeholders examine your idea, be prepared to ask questions such as, What are your thoughts? What is your preference? What is your take on it? How do you feel right now? Does this matter to you? What could help you in this instance? You may even convert naysayers to fans in this process.[34]

In addition, for the inventor, rapid prototyping can have the positive effect of quieting doubts, your own and those of others. Think of the times you have allowed the negative chatter in your head to get in the way of further exploring your ideas. All it takes is that one comment from a key stakeholder, and fear and doubt creep in. Only this time, you can decide to proactively generate counterfactuals on a variety of ways your idea can fail. Because the prototypes are presented as drafts and are positioned to include the feedback of others, you are less likely to incur premature and unfavorable decisions. Thus, rapid prototyping permits a low-risk manner of quickly exploring alternative uses of and directions for ideas, prior to committing any resources to the most attractive ones.[35] We have one word of caution, though. Although prototyping can greatly aid in the improvement of an idea, it can also contribute to a fixed view of your idea if you do not have enough ideas or move quickly enough.[36] To avoid stereotyping, work ahead to prototype versions of several ideas. By doing so, you'll receive feedback on several prototypes in parallel, which enhances learning and fosters more opportunistic exploration. In fact, one recent study indicated that participants who prototyped in parallel produced higher-quality ideas (as judged by raters) and more diverse work and had greater confidence in their ability to complete the task than participants who approached prototyping in a serial manner.[37]

Honing Your Idea Validation Skills

Embracing mistakes is not easy. Most of us have been extensively trained to rely on evidence and numbers, yet instinctively we know that sometimes we reach a point where data ends and determination begins. Designer and architect Best said it best: "True innovation requires the adoption of a belief system that sometimes must prevail in the face of other data metrics."[38] Too much reliance on data paralyzes us. This is why we must view mistakes as a creative art form. Even if an idea is tested, and not validated, much is learned from the prototyping process. As creativity expert Sir Ken Robinson has argued, "If you are not prepared to be wrong you will never come up with anything original."[39] For one, prototypes, even those with mistakes, permit you to speed up feedback and failure. Both serve as markers to find another pathway. Two, prototypes help you let go of an idea so that you can move on to the task of constructing another prototype that incorporates your learning and ultimately will likely lead to something original.[40]

In addition to mastering the art of making mistakes, it is necessary to remember the scientist inside of you. Your idea contains hypotheses that must be proven or disproven. Fortunately, according to Jeanne Liedtka and Tim Ogilvie, authors of the book *Designing for Growth: A Design Thinking Tool Kit for Managers*, a set of four tests allows us to examine hypotheses in almost all industries.[41] The value test determines whether users will embrace your idea with votes or money (at an acceptable price). If you believe your idea has appeal, then move on to the next two tests that focus on the viability of the new idea. The execution test decides if you can create and make the idea deliverable (at an acceptable cost). The scale test helps to determine whether the idea or service can be produced in a manner that meets demand. The final test, defensibility, gauges whether competitors could easily copy your ideas. Here is where knowledge about intellectual property becomes crucially important.

Above and beyond these basic tests, you will probably want to design product-specific tests to determine the strategic outcomes you seek and how they fit the organization's strategy. Remember, stakeholders are more inclined to support ideas if they perceive them to shorten their to-do lists and not add to them. To that end, we suggest you first test your idea with trusted allies and friends. With each wave of feedback, continue improving your idea. Importantly, some feedback will confirm what you already know about the assumptions of your idea. This category of information includes facts and should not be muddled with beliefs. A second category of feedback makes obvious what you do not know because its nature is uncertain; in such cases, all you can do is predict. The remaining category of feedback includes what you don't know but could find out if you made the attempts to get it.[42] To enhance your feedback, your trusted circle of friends should be introduced to criteria as measured by the CSDS, whose criteria can serve as discussion starters.[43]

In Chapter 1 you were asked to imagine that 5 years into the future you are the head of a thriving start-up (see the learning activity in the Doing section). Use prototyping to visualize and validate your start-up idea. To make your start-up idea concrete, we suggest using a prototyping method that is visual; either draw the concept or build a model of it. Once created, this tangible representation of your start-up concept can be used to evaluate its strengths and limitations. What did you learn from prototyping that will help you improve your start-up idea?

Being—Living Like an Idea Developer

Sir Ken Robinson asserts, "We're all born with immense, natural, creative abilities. Children demonstrate them all. We all feel them. But we feel they slip away from us as we get older. And I think it's vitally important for personal and every other kind of reason that we focus on them and try to develop them."[44] Based on the way children learn through exploration, Uribe and Cabra developed an elegant and playful model of creative behavior that can help us understand how tinkering plays an important role in our lives. Using a child's tricycle as a metaphor, Uribe and Cabra call their model TRYCycle.[45] As depicted in Figure 8.1, each wheel of the bike signals an attribute of creative behavior that promotes an attitude of exploration (i.e., trying things out), which is why the word *TRY* (tri→try) is modified. These behaviors are *experimentation* (a recursive and applied approach to exploration), *reflection* (which shifts weight from a focus on results to a focus on sense making), and *incubation* (which shifts weight from conscious work to unconscious work). Attitude, curiosity, and play inspire the rider to hop on, pedal, steer, and power the bike. The pedals stand for a child's attitude as demonstrated through energetic pedaling. They metaphorically represent adventure, risk taking, passion, and openness to experience. The handlebar characterizes curiosity. Children scan the horizon for things that pique their interest. As they move the handlebar toward the one that most captures their imagination, the handlebar represents a focused attention to surroundings. The seat stands for play, which shifts weight from "perilous" risk taking that comes from experimentation to a more secure risk taking. It is precisely why play involves a suspension of self-consciousness so that the child can engage in a purposeless activity that provides joy.[46]

Thought Starter
TRYCycle

Though not explicitly denoted in the metaphor, the fender represents a shield that protects the rider from emotional setbacks—those that stem from idea rejection, for example. As such, the fender symbolizes the ability to bounce back from defeat; this relates to Dweck's growth mindset, introduced in Chapter 6.[47] When we consider J. K. Rowling's act of overcoming personal failure to reinvent herself, Eric Ries's determined pitch to investors to start his third company, or Josh Cooley's

Figure 8.1 TRYCycle Model

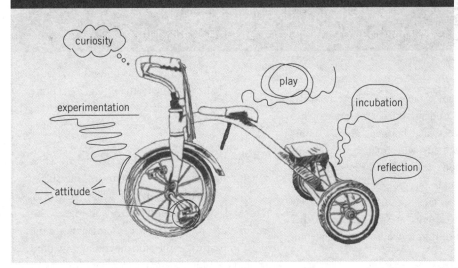

patient work, hand-drawing the 80,000th storyboard for *Ratatouille*, we see people who have not forgotten how to ride a tricycle, people who remember the endless options of childhood and people who trust the process of experimentation. Ask anyone what they do when they are creating, and many responses include, "I try experimenting with an idea, and then I think about what happened, and then I try again. I let it go. I try it again." All the permutations of that initial idea are sparked by curiosity. They describe a personal process that includes trial and error, which continues until curiosity has been quenched. After that, they go on to the next thing that sparks their inquisitiveness. As T. S. Eliot wrote, "We shall not cease from exploration. And the end of all of our exploring will be to arrive where we started and know the place for the first time."[48] Learning to develop and validate creative ideas are essential skills for creativity and the great experiment called life.

Learning Activity
Applying the TRYCycle Model

In Chapter 2 the learning activity in the Being section asked you to engage in a new activity or experience. We asked you to do this without any coaching or preparation. The TRYCycle model can be used to develop a spirit of exploration and therefore guide you to get the most out of new experiences. Identify something that you've always wanted to do but have not done. Use the TRYCycle framework to plan for embarking on this new adventure. Considering the behaviors outlined in this model, write up a plan for how you might successfully pursue this dream. Then pause to reflect: How did this model help you to get set up for success?

Introduction

Reuben Pressman wanted to be more involved on campus. An undergraduate entrepreneurship major, he decided that helping his on-campus student government with marketing support might be a good way to spend his extra time. After all, he'd get to meet lots of new people and learn about the interesting student organizations and events on campus. It was a decision that would shape his future and eventually make him a millionaire.

Helping student organizations raise awareness of their events and drive attendance is no easy task; according to Pressman, students are often busy with conflicting class schedules (ever try to organize calendars for a team project?), event space can be limited on campus, there are lots of rules to follow that few people understand, and the student leaders of each organization who technically *should* understand those rules—the elected leadership team of each organization—tend to rotate out every year as the seniors graduate and the positions are backfilled by juniors and underclassmen facing a steep learning curve.

Pressman successfully ran for student government office and transitioned from marketing director to vice president. In this newfound role his influence within student government grew as he began attending higher-level meetings with campus administrators and leaders. Now privy to conversations about challenges facing the institution, Pressman realized that student event management wasn't just a student government

problem but that the entire university faced a similar challenge when attempting to capture student engagement data. After all, handwritten sign-in sheets at events were the preferred tool of the day.

Additionally, the school struggled when attempting to figure out how to use the sparse and inconsistent data they did have access to. These data are important to consider when making decisions about which programs are the most impactful on the student community (and should therefore be eligible to receive funding in the next budget cycle).

Pressman realized that this was a meaningful and recurring problem: "Feeling these problems firsthand made me passionate about improving the situation," says Pressman, "and it was during that time that I realized that the overarching problem of data capture and decision support was actually an opportunity in disguise."[49]

From an early age, Pressman had been interested in technology and how it could be used to solve problems, and now he'd realized that his university was facing what he'd determined was nothing more than a student data challenge. He decided it was time to explore the ways in which technology might be applied to solve this problem.

First, he would assess whether other schools faced similar issues. If they did, it would demonstrate support for a larger market opportunity than just his own university. It turns out there was a larger market opportunity: Student engagement data were being directly identified by other institutions as a key driver of one of their most important institutional metrics, student retention. Importantly, Pressman also learned that these schools were yet to obtain (or build) sufficient tools to achieve their retention goals.

This insight led Pressman to ask what factors impacted student retention. And how much of a pain point is this *really* for schools? In search of an answer, Pressman set out to interview other student government leaders at similar (and dissimilar) institutions whom he had networked with through student government meetings and conferences. His hunch was correct; institutions across the entire state of Florida were experiencing the same problem: How to capture and leverage data to inform student engagement programming decisions and to help retain more students?

Pressman knew he was on to something: "We had an advantage in that we had already felt the pain points they were experiencing, but we also kept an open mind because we knew we didn't experience them at the level that others did on a daily basis. Once we had validated the problems with other student leaders at other institutions, it became about problem solving for us. Entrepreneurship is all about problem solving. It's not just having an idea. Coming at it from an angle of solving a problem creates a much bigger advantage for a start-up; it's about presenting a solution for your customer—something they really need, something that creates value for them."[50]

With three letters of purchase intent in hand, Pressman recalls, each stating something to the effect of, "Dear Mr. Pressman, if you build a solution to this problem that we have, we will buy it from you," he entered his start-up concept into a university-sponsored business pitch competition and tied for first place.

From there, Pressman pooled his prize money with some local angel investment funding and began recruiting a team of people to help him build a data capture and campus engagement solution for schools. "Our minimum viable product was designed to simply collect information and analyze it," he said. "We were inspired by Square's card reader technology—which we realized they didn't actually build themselves—so we built our solution on top of similar third-party technology and focused on creating value by making sure that our solution was the easiest to use for students and administrators."

With his solution, schools would get *free* student ID card readers that let students and administrators swipe student IDs to collect information on things such as engagement and event attendance. With a philosophy of simple and accessible, Pressman and Check I'm Here went on to land contracts with 10 institutions in the state of Florida and then shifted their focus toward developing a nationwide sales model.[51]

Entering a growth stage, Check I'm Here was presented with an interesting problem: Clients were excited to sign up and begin using the platform (and, most importantly, to pay!), however, they began asking for an increasingly wide range of specialized support features to be added to the product to solve school-specific integration and optimization problems. From a technology development perspective, this presented the Check I'm Here team with a dilemma: Which features should get priority? Should they focus on serving the requests of their largest accounts? Or maybe focus on problems they felt

(Continued)

(Continued)

were more universal across a larger number of smaller schools? Perhaps they should dedicate resources to supporting third-party platform integration or maybe develop their own application program interface (API)?

"From the start, we had already ideated hundreds of features we thought might be cool and useful, but we also knew it was critical to focus on the foundations of the core problems we were trying to solve for our clients. Doing so allowed us to only build the most basic features that we needed so that we could then use that early customer feedback to iterate our product and prioritize the building of additional, follow-on elements."[52]

Often attributed to Henry Ford, the following quotation inspired Pressman to think critically about customer feedback: "If I had asked people what they wanted, they would have said faster horses." According to Pressman, "We use customer feedback to learn about the problems that they feel, but then we largely ignore their feedback when it comes to designing solutions that we could build. For us, it just makes more sense to do our own ideation and convergence to build what we think needs to be built to tackle the customer challenges they've described to us. We'll listen to their problems all day, but when it comes to solutions building, we want to do that ourselves."

"For us, it comes down to trying things and testing and investing meaningful time and energy into validating our ideas; an idea alone isn't worth anything. As a start-up, we need to *know* that what we are building is going to be a solution for our clients. Does it provide value to our customers? That's the difference between good ideas and great ideas; it's often a case-by-case basis, but it's definitely something that you and your customers are agreeing upon when you are exchanging money."

In reflecting on the process of starting his company, building and growing a team, and what it takes to create new ideas and bring them to life in the world, Pressman believes, "I think it ultimately comes down to determination and ambition: Simply, how much do you want it? It's the ability to singularly focus, to put everything you can into whatever you're doing. The people who will be the most focused because they want to do it intrinsically, they are the ones who succeed."[53]

Company Trajectory

Stage	Date
Problem framing and opportunity recognition (imagining student ID card reader solution)	Fall 2010
Pressman wins start-up pitch competition	December 2011
Early product development (customer interviews and solution prototyping)	July 2012
Launch of public beta product	May 2014
Capital raise from local angel investors; small team of sales and marketing onboard	May 2014
Current snapshot	68 institutions, 22 states, 13 employees
Stretch goal	200 institutions by January 2017

Discussion Questions: Knowing

1. A minimal viable product contains just enough attributes to aid in gathering information about the product and its further development. Create an ultimate guide to building a minimal viable product. What tips would you include?

2. How do you interpret and explain how Reuben Pressman was able to validate his business idea?

Application Questions: Doing

1. Think of a time you successfully tested a solution. Identify the steps you completed to make this happen. What content from this chapter might enhance the process steps you identified? How is your system similar to the system Pressman applied?

2. Criteria are standards that are used to evaluate ideas. What criteria did you use to determine which school would be the best for your formal education? What did the school say or do that influenced you?

Thinking Ahead: Being

1. Reuben Pressman's success was attributed to his mindset. As you reflect on this case study, what mindset contributed to Pressman's success? How is that similar and dissimilar to yours? How is that similar to the mindsets described in the chapter? How might you find ways to further develop the mindset in the areas that do not come naturally to you?

2. Consider your next brainstorming meeting. Be deliberate about taking ideas that are vocalized or documented and then take it a step further by creating a sketch and a prototype of the sketch. Once completed, solicit feedback from others using the prototype as a discussion starter. Where are the opportunities you can do this?

Implement

Gaining Buy-In and Driving Change

Learning Goals

After reading this chapter, you will be able to do the following:

- Recognize the value of presenting ideas in different ways to open minds
- Explain how finding common ground contributes to gaining buy-in
- Name eight steps to lead change
- Examine methods for managing influence
- Appraise the degree to which you actively permit learning anxiety to resist change

Knowing—Everyone Is in the Business of Sales

There is a common saying today—everyone sells. Yet most of us do not see ourselves as "selling," being skilled in sales or remotely able to close a big deal. How, then, does one singer convince eight governments from among the world's 11 largest national economies to cancel the debt of the 52 poorest countries ($350 billion) *and* increase aid to them by $50 billion? Especially when the stakeholders initially think he is acting in self-interest or, worse, conning them? That was the challenge faced by Bono, the front man for rock band U2, when he persuaded U.S. president George W. Bush, U.S. Treasury secretaries Paul O'Neill and Lawrence Summers, and Prime Minister of Canada Jean Chrétien to do just that. Bono's foray into public policy and philanthropy showed that he was not only a brilliant musician but also a laser-like spotter of opportunities, an empathetic workaholic, a diffuser of tension, and an implementer of big ideas, as Michka Assayas writes in an astute analysis of the musician's creative leadership.[1]

Conservative politicians have a traditional distrust of rock stars and entertainers, but Bono recruited them to the cause by doing two things extremely well: getting buy-in and driving change. As you will see in this chapter, these two processes are essential steps in implementing any creative idea. If you fail to attend to them, good ideas, especially big ones, never have a chance. When it came to getting buy-in, Bono excelled at managing influence by understanding that the rock star's point of view would not carry the day. Instead, he had to learn to see things from a different perspective, that of the politician and economist, spending large chunks of time with them and getting to know their concerns and perspectives.[2] Economists, poverty specialists, World Bank leaders, politicians, and a chairperson of the Federal Reserve, to name a few, became Bono's tutors. When it came to driving change, Bono's understanding of both the urgent famine problem and the long-term economics of poverty transformed a one-time aid effort into aid plus debt relief for future generations. Intuitively, he followed many of the essential steps outlined by Harvard Business School professor John P. Kotter in his groundbreaking 1996 book *Leading Change.*[3] For example, in the face of naysayers, Bono began with a sense of urgency and formed a powerful coalition to guide the Live Aid effort, with the goal of continuing it in some form.

To top it off, Bono captured the feeling of global giving in a dramatic act that music lovers the world over—and one young woman in particular—will never forget.[4] While U2 was singing in front of 72,000 London Live Aid fans and 2 billion television viewers, Bono purposefully dropped his microphone. Heading to a lower tier of the stage to dance with someone there, Bono saw a young woman, among other people, getting squashed by the crowd. He signaled to the ushers to lift her onto the platform, and fans erupted in cheers as he slow-danced with her—their physical embrace a symbol of the bond he wanted to make with the whole audience. Bono, who garnered *Time*'s Person of the Year award in 2005 along with Bill and Melinda Gates, was not done influencing and driving change after that one concert.[5] Today, he is cofounder of DATA (Debt, AIDS, Trade, Africa), an organization that fights global poverty and HIV, including the ONE Make Poverty History campaign. "Music," he has famously said, "can change the world because it can change people."

Perspective Taking Replaces Sales Bluster

In the new world of influence, perspective-changing skills trump old-fashioned bluster, writes Daniel Pink in his provocative 2012 book *To Sell Is Human: The Surprising Truth About Moving Others.*[6] Outdated, Pink recently told *Forbes*, is

> the idea that selling is about some slippery character in a plaid sportcoat trying to stick you with a crappy used car. But if we recognize that all forms of work—whether you're pitching ideas in a meeting or asking your boss for a raise—are a form of sales in a broader sense, we can get past this outdated stereotype. What's more, success in this realm now depends much, much less on tricks and hoodwinkery than on some fundamentally human capabilities.[7]

Pink, who holds a law degree and worked as a political speechwriter, is now a best-selling author and leading business thinker. He brings the latest social science research to the book *To Sell Is Human*, and his argument for perspective taking holds important lessons for everyone in the business of persuasion. Whether you are a salesperson on a monthly quota or a parent with a rebellious teenager, Pink recommends first reducing your position of power to increase your perspective. He suggests this because research shows an inverse relationship between power and accurate perspective taking, which is why Bono gained insight when he sought out politicians and economists, as well as Ethiopian villagers, to tutor him. Importantly, says Pink, perspective taking is a cognitive, not emotional, skill. That is, one should focus on understanding the other person's interests, not the person's emotions. In addition, the more your posture and vocabulary mimic theirs, the more accurately you will take their perspective.

Although Pink offers many strategies of persuasion, depending on particular situations, here are a few of his favorites, as told to *Forbes*.[8] First, spend more time on finding hidden problems than solving existing ones, because these new discoveries can create powerful change in today's complex and fast-moving world. Second, maintain your personal "buoyancy" to ensure that you can quickly learn and recover from failures (explained as temporary setbacks caused by external, unique, or one-time conditions). In contrast, if you habitually see mistakes as something personal, pervasive, or permanent, you become less buoyant, eroding your influence potential. Third, when the facts are on your side, questions are more persuasive than statements. Questions prompt active responses, whereas statements prime passive responses. In short, the simple words, "Why not give it a try?" might be more powerful than "It's a no-brainer."

Thought Starter

Creative Buoyancy

Influence Management: The Fine Art of Getting Buy-In

Anyone who has ever tried to change someone's thinking about an idea realizes what the common expression "a closed mind" means. We form mental models in childhood, and they become more difficult to change as we mature. However, one way to open minds to change, according to the well-respected developmental psychologist Howard Gardner, is to present an idea in different forms, such as new linguistic, numerical, metaphorical, and graphic ways that an audience finds familiar.[9] For example, Bono used this persuasive rhetorical strategy with a common biblical reference to get buy-in from leading conservative Christian senator Jesse Helms. Initially Bono began his pitch with an impressive array of facts and figures. But as Bono noticed Helms drifting, he intuitively switched his pitch to stress Jesus's commitment to the sick and the poor, suggesting that AIDS could be the 21st-century equivalent of the leprosy referenced in the New Testament.[10] It was a cathartic moment for the senator; afterward, Bono had no trouble recruiting the senator's support in the global fight against AIDS.

By understanding other people's values and recasting their own ideas in mutually compatible ways, creative leaders can find common ground and gain influence. This strategy, however, calls for gathering evidence from important players, which means knowing and systematically employing proven methods of research and analysis. These methods do not have to be complicated or expensive; rather, they include widely accepted standards, such as force field analysis, stakeholder analysis, the new ABCs of sales pitching, and social proof theory, wisely applied. Taken together, these approaches will help you create a formidable tool kit for managing influence.

1. Start With Force Field Analysis

When facing a decision about change, one common, seemingly analytical, approach is to weigh the pros and cons. But as most of us know, this approach can lead to erroneous conclusions if items are not accurately weighted in terms of value and consequence. With force field analysis, a tool described in Chapter 4, it is easy to conduct this analysis with rigor and make good decisions while persuading others to do the same. In the 1940s, respected social psychologist Kurt Lewin, founder of the Research Center for Group Dynamics at MIT, developed this classic analytical tool, which offers a quantitative way of identifying and assessing factors both helping change and hindering change. "Force Field Analysis . . . helps you make a decision by analyzing the forces for and against a change, and it helps you communicate the reasoning behind your decision," wrote James Manktelow and Amy Carlson of the popular website Mind Tools, which offers an easy tutorial in the technique.[11] "You can use it for two purposes: to decide whether to go ahead with the change; and to increase your chances of success, by strengthening the forces supporting change and weakening those against it," writes leadership coach Jim Dezieck. Additionally, this type of analysis helps you identify and lower barriers between a person's status and the goal or desired change. "This lowers the total energy needed to achieve change and thereby makes change easier," notes Dezieck.[12]

2. Add Stakeholder Analysis

The higher you climb in your career, the more people you affect and the more interaction you have with higher-ups or clients with influence over your projects. These people can be fans or enemies of your next big idea. But they are not a monolithic group; rather, each holds different positions and interests as they relate to you and your success. "Stakeholder management is critical to the success of every project in every organization I have ever worked with. By engaging the right people in the right way in your project, you can make a big difference to its success . . . and to your career," advises career coach Rachel Thompson.[13]

The sketch of the lion is a tribute Dalí made to a private collector and design consultant, Stephan Lion, who provided instrumental support to the artist during the 1940s and 1950s. It is said that Dalí conveyed his regard for this patron through this sketch, perhaps expressing his appreciation to this important stakeholder. How might you express your appreciation to those stakeholders in your life?

University of Southern California business professors Mason and Mitroff introduced a tool useful in systematically identifying, analyzing, and planning actions relative to key stakeholders.[14] Essentially, this tool has you begin by generating a list of key stakeholders followed by an assessment of each stakeholder's position on the change you wish to propose (scale of evaluation is strongly opposed, moderately opposed, neutral, moderately supportive, strongly supportive). Using the same scale, you determine what level of support would be useful to increase the probability of implementing your new idea. Action steps are then generated to move the stakeholder from the current position to the desired position. This activity not only allows you to plan to use stakeholder opinions to shape the project (both in concept and positioning), it also helps ensure more resources, support, and eventual buy-in. It allows you to spot and prepare for opposition in advance. For example, the analysis concludes with a stakeholder map that gives you a solid understanding of the most important players; you can then anticipate their responses using a second tool for stakeholder planning. Useful descriptions of the stakeholder analysis can be found in Puccio and colleagues' book on creative leadership and in the Mind Tools site identified earlier.[15] Figure 9.1 displays a typical stakeholder analysis worksheet.

3. Learn the New ABCs of Sales Pitching

Social science research into "pitch archetypes" shows it is time to rethink the ABCs of how we propose or market a new idea with a revised focus on being "**A**ttuned, **B**uoyant, and **C**lear," writes Daniel Pink.[16] In an interview with the *Harvard Business Review* about his book *To Sell is Human*, Pink reminds us that "every email is a pitch. . . . And what [the research] shows, very much, is that, when you pitch, effective pitches don't convert [the other person] in the pitch. What I do, essentially, is, I invite you to participate and co-create it."[17] For example,

Figure 9.1 Stakeholder Analysis Worksheet						
Stakeholder	**Strongly Oppose**	**Moderately Oppose**	**Neutral**	**Moderately Support**	**Strongly Support**	**Required Action**

Key: x = Where are they now?   O = Where do they need to be?

in describing the social science behind this, Pink turns to Carnegie Mellon researchers' investigation into a kind of everyday pitch, an e-mail subject line, to find out what makes it effective.

> They sat with people looking over their shoulder as people opened their email. And these people narrated why they were making decisions about opening email and so forth. . . . And what they found—actually, pretty clear results. There are two categories of subject lines that tend to get opened the most, namely subject lines that appeal to utility and subject lines that appeal to curiosity. When people have a lighter email load, curiosity is effective. When they have a heavy email load, you've got to go with utility.[18]

In his book (and in videos on his website at www.danpink.com/resources), Pink offers six simple pitches and examples, based on the best argument, or ammunition, and the situation at hand.[19] His first is the "one-word pitch," as immortalized in the movie *The Graduate*, when the aimless college student played by Dustin Hoffman is advised to consider a future in plastics. A more current example, says Pink, is MasterCard's one-liner: *Priceless*. Second, he suggests "the question pitch," such as Ronald Reagan's famous line, "Are you better off than you were four years ago?" The third is a "rhyming pitch," which may not sound cerebral but can stick nonetheless. Pink's example, "If the glove doesn't fit, you must acquit," was famously said by Johnnie Cochran in the O. J. Simpson murder trial. His fourth favorite is what Pink calls "the subject line pitch," which calls for improving e-mail messages to appeal to usefulness or curiosity. For example, he recommends the template "4 tips to improve (e.g., golf, test scores, client sales) today." Fifth, he suggests tightening up "the Twitter pitch" to 120 characters (20 characters short of the maximum) so others can easily retweet it. Sixth, he recommends "the Pixar pitch" and rules from story artist Emma Coats, especially Rule #4, which is to create a compelling narrative of your story.[20]

4. Employ Social Proof Theory

Finally, the newest research on "social proof"—or the opinions of other customers—shows that it speaks much louder than the voice of the producer or the company. This is especially true with online content, which gives most consumers today instant access to reader reviews, surveys, comments, and blogs. For example, 70% of consumers report reading product reviews before buying, and these product reviews are "12x more trusted than product descriptions from manufacturers," according to Ed Hallen in a recent article in the online magazine *Fast Company*.[21] Other examples of social proof include (1) expert social proof, (2) celebrity social proof, (3) user social proof, (4) wisdom of the crowds social proof, and (5) wisdom of your friends social proof. Hence, whereas social proof may not be new, the Internet and social media have made it ubiquitous in marketing. Hallen suggests that a couple of quick ways to put this psychology to work right away are to add customer testimonials to websites and stress follower/subscriber numbers in blogs. He adds that it is helpful to "find experts who are interested in what you're doing, build relationships and work together to find ways that they can help promote you."[22]

Drive Change: Bridging and Managing Four Critical Aspects

Tradition is comfortable, stable, and predictable, especially when it's tied to your identity. If what you're doing is not broken, then why mess with it? Well, the next time you hear someone say, "We've always done it this way," remind them of the attendant truism: If you always do what you've always done, you will always get what you've always got. In today's fast-moving, technologically driven, and competitive business world, "what you've always got" may no longer be a viable service or product. To innovators, then, new ideas suggest the change needed to keep pace with the larger environment, hence, to survive. But to others, these same ideas suggest a destruction of familiar ways of doing things. To a large degree, the concerns that preoccupy the latter group stem from learning anxiety, and they underscore why some people resist change. To successfully drive change, you will need to understand this type of anxiety and to bridge and manage aspects of transformation in at least four important ways: (1) help individuals replace learning anxiety with survivor's anxiety, (2) take a step-by-step approach to creative destruction and reinvention, (3) cultivate a learning/helping organization that transcends culture, and (4) understand how collective creativity permeates the innovation process.

1. Replace Learning Anxiety With Survivor's Anxiety

Learning anxiety, studies show, comprises a combination of fears, such as fear of temporary incompetence, fear of punishment for incompetence, fear of loss of personal identity, and fear of loss of group membership,[23] or what some experts call the "Death Valley" of change.[24] When people go through transitions, it is not uncommon for them to experience a sense of risk and, as a result, relapse to what is familiar and comfortable. If these fears are not addressed, then defensive responses typically follow. Such responses may include confusion, immediate criticism of the proposed changes, denial, malicious compliance, subtle sabotage, easy agreement, silence, and deflection.[25] This topic receives little attention in organizations. It is messy and time consuming to address the psychological bases of learning anxiety. It is much easier to "shake it off" and get on with the matters of business at hand that you are paid to do. But until survival anxiety (i.e., the acceptance of an imminent threat brought on by a sense of urgency) supersedes learning anxiety, your ideas will likely be dead on arrival.

2. Take a Step-by-Step Approach
to Creative Destruction and Reinvention

Few people understand organizational change and its structure and processes better than retired Harvard Business School professor John P. Kotter, author of the definitive 1996 book *Leading Change*.[26] When he launched his book, Kotter wrote in the *Harvard Business Review* that it grew out of watching more than 100 companies, large and small, try to reinvent themselves to compete on the world stage. "These [change] efforts have gone under many banners: total quality management, reengineering, rightsizing, restructuring, cultural change, and turnaround." Whereas a few had succeeded and others had failed, most fell "somewhere in between, with a distinct tilt toward the lower end of the scale," he wrote. Kotter drew two general lessons from his observation and analysis. First, in successful cases, "the change process goes through a series of phases that, in total, usually require a considerable length of time. Skipping steps creates only the illusion of speed and never produces a satisfying result."[27] Second, Kotter observed that because few people have experience in renewing organizations through change, even the most capable people will make missteps that can undermine successful momentum.

Managing change is a delicate process. To assist change leaders, Kotter outlined eight critical success factors that remain staples in the leader's tool kit today. These factors are to (1) establish urgency for change (from examination of crises, potential crises, or major opportunities); (2) form a leading coalition (with enough power to implement the change plan and the ability to work as a team); (3) create a vision of the new ideal (that serves as a motivational goal and keeps everyone headed in the right direction); (4) communicate that vision (using every means possible to convey the new future and the strategies and behaviors necessary for getting there); (5) free others to act (by getting rid of obstacles that undercut the vision), encouraging risk taking and nontraditional ideas, activities, and action; (6) create short-term wins (by establishing visible performance improvements and recognizing and rewarding those involved in meeting them); (7) consolidate improvements/produce more change (by using victories to continue to transform organizational elements that don't support the vision, hiring change agents, and announcing new projects); and (8) institutionalize new approaches (by telling the story of the new behaviors and corporate success and developing leadership teams and succession plans to support the vision).

3. Cultivate a Learning/Helping
Organization That Transcends Culture

The topic of corporate culture has preoccupied leadership for nearly two decades, since Edgar H. Schein, known as the father of organizational psychology, began writing about who we are in organizations, why we resist change, and how we learn in a series of provocative books, such as the essential *Organizational Culture and Leadership*,[28] *The Corporate Culture Survival Guide*,[29] and his latest,

Humble Inquiry: The Gentle Art of Asking Instead of Telling.[30] Recently, in an interview with *Forbes*, Schein advised that corporate culture is not as important in today's fluid organizations and international workforce as "macro cultures" and "micro cultures."[31] Macro cultures are evidenced by nations and nationalities, including the many international employees and clients with whom we interact with daily. Micro cultures surface between occupations and disciplines in organizations, causing problems in the operating room, for example, or in the design studio.

Schein says he is often called in as a consultant to help companies change cultures, when that is not really possible or practical. The more pressing questions are, What problem are we trying to solve? How are our multicultural teams learning from and helping each other as they try to solve it? Says Schein, "To help leaders deal with multi-cultural teams two things need to happen—leaders have to become much more humble and learn how to seek help, because the subordinates under them will be much more knowledgeable than they." Second, he adds, leaders will have to become "culturally literate" by understanding the frames of different occupations and nationalities and creating "cultural islands" where people can drop their nativist guards and speak directly about what is hampering them without fear of repercussion. He concludes, "If leaders can't create those kinds of cultural islands, they won't be able to create teams that can actually work."[32]

4. Understand How Collective Creativity Permeates the Innovation Process

If you are getting the feeling that creativity is everyone's job, you are right. But this may be news to some people in your organization. In the old days, innovation was viewed as two distinct stages, discovery and implementation, and "responsibility for creativity [was] partitioned into separate departments," explains leading creativity scholar Tudor Rickards.[33] The award-winning Rickards, who has written extensively on innovation and creativity, is based at the University of Manchester (England), Alliance Manchester Business School, where he is professor of creativity and organizational change. Today, he argues, innovation involves new social procedures that thrive on creativity through all phases of discovery and learning. Hence, we are all innovators. This recasting of the role of creativity, he writes, has two important implications. First, organizations do not have to stop and retool to begin innovating. They can inventory and reflect on their proven behaviors in creativity and innovation, deepen understanding, sharpen focus, and build on these collective skills. Second, they can dismiss the old social-engineering model and replace it with a creativity-constructs-meaning model, wherein everyday brainstorming, experimentation, and risk taking lead to learning and, importantly, innovation. In his blog, *Leaders We Deserve*, Rickards asserts that the primary challenge of creative leadership today is facing ambiguities—in the marketplace, the workplace, and the research and design process.[34]

Revisit the story of Bono's success in selling the idea of canceling debt of the 52 poorest countries and at the same time increasing aid to them by $50 billion. Using the knowledge you were introduced to in this section, explain how Bono was able to overcome the resistance to this idea. What lessons can you extract from your assessment of Bono's approach that might be useful to you in the future?

Doing—Acting Like an Influencer and Change Agent

Honing Your Pitch Skills

If you have ever tried to explain a new idea to a client, a coworker, or even a new acquaintance, and taken your listener through a litany of technology code and business platitudes, you realize at least one thing about pitching. Even if you know a great deal about the market and have spent months nurturing and shaping your ideas, you may be all over the place when talking about what you do or hope to do. That's where Jason Shen comes in. Shen is a marketing manager at Percolate and previously cofounded Ridejoy. He's like a pitching coach for professional baseball players, only he trains entrepreneurs to transform weak and dry pitches into something unexpected that seals the deal. Shen says most people still rely on the standard pitch, or the problem-solution story, which is a serviceable standby when you're out of other ideas. But in his popular blog, he encourages readers to think much more creatively about telling the story of their companies and has identified 11 start-up "pitch archetypes." Because every business is unique, the pitches don't sound scripted. They sound like good stories, and they can help you effectively lead the discussion and frame your points. However, Shen does offer an important qualification: "These pitches are not magic. Nothing works unless you do."[35]

Following are Shen's 11 pitches, which can apply to any kind of start-up, whether you are launching a business or just trying to sell an idea for a new product or service inside your existing company.[36] Practice different ones until you find the one or two that work best for you, your style, your situation, and the audience receiving the pitch. If you lack confidence in pitching now, you will be surprised at how good you will get with a little storytelling practice.

Archetype 1: "Traction," or the rapid-growth "everyone has started to use this new product" pitch, which works perfectly as long as you have the data to back up the story.

Archetype 2: "X for Y," or the comparison with a proven model/service/product for a growing new customer segment/market/platform, as evidenced by the saying "brown is the new black."

Archetype 3: "Personal Story," or the anecdote about how the company's creators were trying to solve a personal or business problem (that many others also wrestle with) and invented this product/service with mass appeal.

Archetype 4: "Pivot/Offshoot," or the discovery of a new idea that comes out of work on another, related or unrelated, project and shows your investor how you can see customer needs and new ideas from the ground up.

Archetype 5: "Evolution Next," or showing the evolution of a successful idea in the marketplace and predicting the next trend and phase in development so investors want to position themselves for future upsides.

Archetype 6: "Painting the Future," or the ability to imagine a new future, such as the paperless office, like a time traveler, complete with pictures of how your service/product will be used.

Archetype 7: "Service at Scale," or a service, such as accounting or recruiting, that is often outsourced to small shops but can be transformed into one scalable product with software or some other technology.

Archetype 8: "Wouldn't It Be Cool If?," or a novel idea (like Twitter in 2006) that did not exist because the technology or know-how was not there but now can be developed due to some recent innovation that you have access to.

Archetype 9: "Insane Tech," or a new set of breakthrough technologies that topples the traditional way, transforms the operational landscape (making something 30 times faster/bigger/smaller), and opens up entirely new possibilities.

Archetype 10: "The Dream Team," or the opportunity to work with a rare group, like Dr. D'Agostino created in his lab (see Chapter 5 case), assembled for this market to build this product/service because no other outfit has the right mix of people, connections, and resources to make it work.

Thought Starter
Creative Pitching

Archetype 11: "Consumerfication of Enterprise," or a product or service that used to be expensive/slow/complicated that you make affordable/fast/easy, opening up a whole new market, like Weebly, the easy-to-use website builder.

Honing Your Change Skills

As we saw previously in this chapter, especially with Tudor Rickards's research, making one area of a company, such as the R&D division, responsible for generating innovation is simply a huge mistake.[37] This view is narrow-minded and risky because competitors who instill a true culture of innovation are advancing with better ways to do things in every unit of the organization. As the Chicago-based consulting group Doblin asserts, "Creating new products is only one way to innovate,

Table 9.1	Doblin's Ten Types of Innovation®
1. PROFIT MODEL: How you make money	6. PRODUCT SYSTEM: How you create complementary products and services
2. NETWORK: How you connect with others to create value	7. SERVICE: How you support and amplify the value of your offerings
3. STRUCTURE: How you organize and align your talent and assets	8. CHANNEL: How you deliver your offerings to customers and users
4. PROCESS: How you use signature or superior methods to do your work	9. BRAND: How you represent your offerings and business
5. PRODUCT PERFORMANCE: How you develop distinguishing features and functionality	10. CUSTOMER ENGAGEMENT: How you foster compelling interactions

Source: Larry Keeley, Ryan Pikkel, Brian Quinn, and Helen Walters, *Ten Types of Innovation: The Discipline of Building Breakthroughs* (Hoboken, New Jersey: John Wiley & Sons, 2013). www.doblin.com/tentypes

and on its own, it provides the lowest return on investment and the least competitive advantage . . . companies that integrate multiple types of innovation will develop offerings that are more difficult to copy and that generate higher returns." To that end, Doblin has identified ten types of organizational innovation (see Table 9.1) that, once made a set of best practices, allow creative thinkers anywhere in the company to identify new opportunities and develop "defensible innovations."[38]

In addition to understanding the breadth of your innovation potential, it's important to practice scanning, in both a keen and constant fashion. Pay attention to organizational paradoxes and dilemmas (e.g., efficiency versus effectiveness). Challenge yourself to find an alternative response that does not compromise. Go for a "yes-and" idea, not an "either/or." Keep a journal that captures challenges as mentioned in trade journals, newspapers, social media, and conferences. Take time to log ideas in response to these challenges. Remember that this will not be easy. In many cases, what blocks success is an environment defined by volatility, uncertainty, complexity, and ambiguity (VUCA).[39] As Edgar Schein recommends, training multicultural teams to deal with VUCA problems will bring to the table the creative potential of everyone involved.

In the process of implementation, your ideas will face hurdles. So, first and foremost, let go of your need to have it come out perfect. Handle any rejections with calm, reflection, and a sense of humor. In short, be buoyant, as author Dan Pink calls it. To get started, try one of Pink's exercises for building buoyancy, the Rejection Generator Project, as he describes in his newsletter. "Just choose your favored style of repudiation, type in your email, and in minutes you'll receive a dream-destroyer in your inbox," Pink writes, only half-jokingly.[40] Additionally, become a staunch listener, and make adjustments according to feedback. Embody tolerance for ambiguity, or risk getting stuck in the quicksand of inertia.

In Chapter 2 you identified a start-up idea, and in Chapter 8 you were asked to test the viability of this idea by creating a prototype. We now wish you to think about how you will sell this start-up idea. Use force field analysis, described both in this chapter and Chapter 4, to examine the factors that will either support or resist your start-up concept. Replicate the Force Field Analysis worksheet presented in Table 4.1 in Chapter 4. Looking at the forces for and against this idea, how might you pitch this start-up idea in a way that will improve the likelihood of success? Take the perspective of one of your key stakeholders and complete the force field analysis again, but from that stakeholder's perspective. What new insights did this provide or reinforce?

Being—Influencing and Leading Change

Two decades ago, *The Executive* published an article on how to become an influential manager with these sage words, "Managers who choose rational ideas based on the needs of the target, wrap them with a blanket of humor or anecdotes, and cast them in the language of the person to be influenced, are much more likely to see their influence objective achieved."[41] Fast-forward to today, and you will see that today's writers and scholars offer similar advice when it comes to persuading others. In her popular TED Talk, Nancy Duarte presents an approach to making a convincing connection with your audience so that they are moved to a purposeful action—*resonance*.[42] Howard Gardner, in his book *Changing Minds*, asserts the significance of taking a rational approach to change minds—*reason*.[43] Dan Pink, in *To Sell Is Human*, persuades us of the importance of understanding stakeholder perspective and being able to detach germane pieces of information from noise or distraction—*attunement*.[44] In *The Art of Woo*, the authors identify the honoring and managing of relationships as paramount—*credibility*.[45] Great influencers aren't born; instead, what enables them to maximize their influence is reflective and adaptive persistence.

Consider one of the most celebrated groups of creative people today—MacArthur Fellows, 21 people who are chosen each year for their track record in innovation and their potential for future contributions. MacArthur Fellows receive a $625,000 stipend paid over 5 years as a type of incubator capital for continuing to explore their best ideas. "Those who think creativity is dying should examine the life's work of these extraordinary innovators who work in diverse fields and in different ways to improve our lives and better our world," said Cecilia Conrad, vice president of the MacArthur Fellows Program, when she announced the 2014 genius awards. "Together, they expand our view of what is possible, and they inspire us to apply our own talents and imagination."[46]

Whether MacArthur fellows are tackling social issues like secure and affordable housing or redefining paradigms in art, the labor movement, or documentary filmmaking, they all have one thing in common: They understand how to model the creative way by championing solutions for themselves and others. Key to living this kind of life is "contextual thinking," as described in Puccio, Mance, and Murdock's *Creative Leadership: Skills That Drive Change*.[47] Contextual thinking results from taking an intentional environmental scan and factoring it into your thinking and decision making to create responsive products and services. According to Puccio and colleagues, "Contextual thinking enables you to notice what is happening around you. . . . It is not to have a good solution; being able to implement it depends on whether the timing is right, the resources are available, and if those around you are supportive."[48] Without contextual thinking, you can make serious miscalculations, as we have seen in the history of business failures, from the introduction of the ill-fated Ford Edsel to the more recent dot-com boom and bust. In the end, the ultimate result of learning how to be the influencer and change agent in your own life is your own satisfaction. As MacArthur fellow Pamela O. Long, an independent historian, said recently in an interview for the History News Network about how she found her own creative path, "Think outside the box. Everyone is different and in a different situation, so everyone's solution will be different. The important thing is, if you have found something you love to do, be flexible in figuring out the best way for you to do it."[49]

Thought Starter

Contextual Thinking

Learning Activity
Honing Your Selling Skills

As Pink suggests in *To Sell Is Human*, selling takes many forms, from negotiating a salary to bargaining with our loved ones. We constantly use our persuasive powers and thus have ample opportunity to refine them. When the need for buy-in arises (in any context, personal or professional) practice honing your skills, perhaps structuring a pitch around one of the many archetypes provided in this chapter. Use one or more of Pink's strategies, such as perspective taking. With this in mind, how would you approach this situation? Try it out, then write about it in your journal.

Case Study
ChappellRoberts: Creative Ideas

Introduction

When it comes to implementing new ideas successfully, gaining buy-in from others to drive change may be one of the most challenging tasks facing an innovator. The ability to be persuasive, to wield influence over those whose opinions or involvement can help make your creative idea happen (or, alternatively, die on the vine), and to see situations from perspectives other than your own are all tools an innovator can use to increase the likelihood of driving productive change in an organization.

Getting buy-in involves influencing a buyer. Driving change involves speaking from a place of power. In the case of a start-up company or a new creative idea being pushed by an intrapreneur, these might mean leveraging expert opinions and evaluations or developing deeper authority on the subject at hand. For Tampa, Florida–based advertising agency ChappellRoberts, it's a little bit of both.

In 1978, two friends, Colleen Chappell and Deanne Roberts, founded the full-service creative agency, ChappellRoberts, with the aim of standing out within the industry. Today, the award-winning agency thrives in the city's eclectic Ybor City neighborhood and works with clients including Fortune 100 brands; telecommunications firms; health care leaders; and professional baseball, football, and hockey teams. Graphic designers, copywriters, managers, marketers, and account executives all support this endeavor and embody their company tag line: "We create change."

None more so than ChappellRoberts founder and CEO Colleen Chappell, whose more than 25 years of industry experience has helped to establish the executive as a standout in the field of advertising. An award-winning expert in brand development, and marketing and advertising strategy, Chappell knows what works and what doesn't. She also knows how to get buy-in and how to drive change in partnership with her clients.

Before bringing on a new client, ChappellRoberts employs a custom-built "brand discovery" process. This allows the team to fully evaluate the client relationship potential and gain insight into the perspective of the company and its customers.

As part of this process, Chappell explains, the agency lets clients in crowded industries like health care "get the expected out of their system" when it comes to campaigns or branding, "and then we say, let's throw that all away now!"

Encouraging clients to share (and then dismiss!) their prior conceptualizations of their advertising and marketing strategies may sound risky, but at the same time, it allows space for ChappellRoberts to then introduce a novel, dynamic solution or strategy that can help the client drive future change. How?

Process

Earlier in this chapter, we discussed the notion that we are all salespeople—to sell is human. Sales comes down to persuasion, as author Daniel Pink noted in *Forbes*.[50] Persuasion, Pink suggests, comes down to a combination of finding hidden problems (which can be catalysts for quick-moving change), developing a thick skin to recover from setbacks, and choosing questions instead of statements when the facts are in your favor.

At ChappellRoberts, the persuasion process unfolds in a similar fashion: First, the "brand discovery" process, which allows the agency's team to tackle the deeper, hidden problems that Pink suggests can drive change; second, a brief that contains several ideas or strategies, minimizing potential setbacks; and finally, an open approach to the question of "What is the right answer?"

To truly understand the perspective of the client or the client's customers, there can be no right answer, Chappell says. "The agency shies away from pinpointing: 'This is the one concept, the one idea, the one answer.' We do a spectrum. There's always more than one answer."

In fact, Chappell is quick to quote award-winning *National Geographic* photographer turned motivational speaker DeWitt Jones: "His philosophy is that there's more than one 'right' answer. He shows you visually, through moving camera angles so that the sun or shadows shift and a new perspective is revealed, creating multiple right answers."[51]

Subjectivity is a filter that all of us share, Chappell says, but the agency works to keep clients focused on the strategy contained within collaborative briefs. With that extra layer of transparency, too, ChappellRoberts distinguishes itself among creative agencies: After creating and refining the brief in-house, they share it with the client, who can add another layer of perspective.

Perspective taking, or truly seeing client needs and perspectives, can go a long way toward helping a client feel comfortable making the shift from tried-and-true traditions to a new, reimagined creative idea or product.

What does perspective taking mean for ChappellRoberts? Going beyond the client to the client's customer: "If I can put myself in the mindset, in the shoes of who they're selling to, then I'm giving them an advantage," Chappell says.

As Kotter, author of *Leading Change*, noted in the *Harvard Business Review*, leading change is one of the most difficult tasks creative people face in the implementation of a new idea.[52] Because change requires both time and a series of steps, it cannot be moved along to meet a deadline. ChappellRoberts approaches change through, above all, a thorough and immersive approach that stacks smarts and strategy above showy pitches. Because Chappell is a chief marketing officer, big agencies pitch to her regularly. Flashy approaches and dramatics didn't appeal to her; smart approaches did. Turns out, most ChappellRoberts clients agree: "Every client likes a smart approach. If you can show them that this approach is smart, it goes far more than big dramatic pitches."

Building a smart creative brief, Chappell says, is the heart of the creative process for the agency and the foundation of the strategy upon which new ideas are built. Through the process of building a creative brief, ideas are refined, readjusted, and developed in a formal process. Like creating a great soup, Chappell explains, adding ingredients in stages and letting herbs—or ideas—simmer for a while will help draw more flavors out of the dish.

This collaborative process results in more strategic ideas through multiple iterations of

(Continued)

(Continued)

editing and brainstorming, Chappell says. "You've got to embrace the process—don't fight it. Ultimately what you come up with is far more strategic and profound."

When it comes down to the client taste test, of course, things become less a matter of perspective and more a matter of subjective taste. But knowing what tools to use to discern which strategy or platform is right for the time, and the tone, can go a long way toward implementing creative change.

Chappell cautions agencies against potentially overreaching. Know what you're good at, and know what a good client match is, she says. The key to success for Chappell: "Being very clear about what our model is. We're about full-service integration. We need to strategically work with you for this to be a success."

Acting like an influencer will achieve the dual role of getting buy-in and successfully leading change to implement your ideas. But another way to influence change is to recognize when a relationship with a client is draining resources or is in some other way working against the values of your company.

Parting ways with an ill-matched client can be embraced as an opportunity to hone your change-driving skills. At one point, Chappell fired the firm's largest client with no backup, because a continued relationship "was more of a compromise to what we stood for as an organization and as people than it was worth the money."

The ChappellRoberts team bounced back through a focus on securing new business, developing a deeper understanding of their existing clients, and honing an understanding of modern technology and industry trends. Even so, they're not immune to hearing no. Walking away from clients who aren't the right fit for your company or ending unsatisfactory business relationships can help shape your perspective of hearing no from another client into a question of how you can meet that client's needs.

Chappell recounts a piece of early advice she received when in business sales: "If you're not hearing no, you're not working." But rather than giving in to rejection, she says, "I immediately change my mindset to 'Now I'm closer to the next yes.'"

Conclusion

Getting buy-in and leading change are persistent challenges that fly in the face of innovators and entrepreneurs. For Colleen Chappell and the ChappellRoberts team, there are proven ways to help influence creative change: Earning and wielding influence, using creative persuasion methods, and deliberately taking on the perspective of others are all ways to gain buy-in, lead change, and drive business for the firm.

Discussion Questions: Knowing

1. Kotter outlined eight critical success factors to manage change. Which steps closely relate to those applied by the ChappellRoberts team?

2. How does the ChappellRoberts team approach to influencing others resemble that of Bono's process?

3. In what ways does Chappell overcome resistance to change?

Application Questions: Doing

1. Think of a time when you faced a criticism of your idea. Which tactics in this case would have helped you to rebound from that criticism?

2. Imagine a scenario where you can introduce a smart creative brief. What would your brief look like? Speculate on what kind of feedback you might receive to improve the smart creative brief.

3. What did you learn about the buy-in process from this case that you can apply in your professional life?

Thinking Ahead: Being

1. What daily habits can you identify to empathize with those whom you associate? Imagine you were offering advice to someone you know based on the pain points you discovered as they related to annoyances and problems to be solved at work. How might you shape your advice by connecting with these pain points?

2. It is easy to fall back to your initial responses to harsh criticism. What are the ways to prevent yourself from unraveling in the face of harsh criticism?

Being

**Ways to Sustain Yourself
as a 21st-Century Innovator**

The Emotionally Intelligent Leader

Learning Goals

After reading this chapter, you will be able to do the following:

- Recognize research that makes the case for emotional intelligence
- Explain how emotional intelligence contributes to effective leadership
- Apply methods and strategies that enhance awareness of emotions, both one's own and others'
- Describe the blocks that get in the way of self-creative leadership
- Appraise the degree to which you actively work to regulate the type of thinking that hinders creativity

Knowing—Emotional Intelligence Is *Not* a Soft Skill

A Story About Managing Emotions

Have you ever felt overwhelmed by emotions? Did you notice how you were unable to do your best thinking in these moments? Have you ever regretted one of these moments? We start this chapter with a short story, one drawn from Indian animal fables.[1] A long time ago, there lived a priest's assistant and his wife. They had a young son who, due to their busy work schedules, was alone much of the time. The assistant thought extensively about his son and the time he spent alone. He wondered how to protect and give his son company during the times both parents worked. A pet, he thought, would help with both matters. The following day, he purchased a mongoose from the market. As time passed, the mongoose grew into a wonderful pet. The priest's assistant and his wife considered the mongoose another member of the family. But despite their enjoyment of the pet, the wife at times feared they were putting their son in harm's way. After all, it was just an animal!

One day, she needed to leave her home to retrieve water from a pond nearby. With some trepidation, she left the child with the mongoose. While she was away, a king cobra entered the home. Sensing the danger to the child, the mongoose leaped into action and fought the cobra to its death. As the mongoose would typically do, it ran to the door upon the return of the child's mother. But on this day, she entered her home in horror. The mongoose's mouth was painted with blood. It had to be her son's blood, she concluded. She picked up a heavy box and slammed it on the mongoose, killing it. In a frenzied state, she began to look for her son, only to find him sleeping soundly. To her surprise, next to her son's bed were the remains of the dead cobra. The shock was immediate; she realized that the mongoose had saved a life, whereas she had taken one. The mother was filled with sadness and repentance at her hasty action. Many lessons can be extracted from this old fable; we believe this story serves as a good example of how runaway emotions can undermine good decision making. The story's lesson is important, because if we do not learn to manage these biologically driven processes—our emotions—they may derail our success and our ability to meet important goals.

This chapter, therefore, explores the topic of emotional intelligence[2] (EI)—which is defined as the ability to manage oneself and one's relationships with others[3]—and its relationship to professional success. For example, what do leaders do to regulate the emotions that stand in the way of their creativity, and what do they do to nurture the creativity of those whom they lead? To be precise, in this chapter we examine how EI is important for organizational success. We further show why this topic matters today. Emotional *unintelligence*, as we dub it here, *can* generate a lifetime of blocks to creativity. As you discovered in the opening story, the priest's assistant's wife allowed herself to become emotionally hijacked. Had she instead paused for a moment to check on her son, she would have avoided years of remorse. Too often leaders make damaging decisions based on unchecked emotions. They hold too tightly to an emotion, which in turn blocks their ability to formulate productive thinking. Learning to manage your emotions opens the mind to more possibilities.

Some readers may think this fable is too exaggerated to fit an organizational context. We would counter this view by suggesting that "emotional hijacking," that is, when one's thinking is overwhelmed by emotions in a manner that serves to undermine effective decisions and progress toward meaningful goals, is a regular occurrence in organizations. Take, for instance, the well-publicized firing of Steve Jobs from Apple Computer. John Sculley, former president of Pepsi-Cola, was brought in as a senior executive at Apple, where his management approach clashed with the undisciplined leadership style displayed by Jobs. Apple's board sided with Sculley and voted for Jobs's removal. Then CEO John Sculley, whom the board had hired to oversee Jobs and grow the company, was tasked with stripping Jobs of his responsibilities.[4] It was not just Sculley who allowed his emotions to get the best of him. The board also struggled with Jobs's appearance and unusual lifestyle. As one of the board members commented many years later, he had found Jobs and his Apple cofounder Steve Wozniak to be very unappealing people. "Jobs came into the office, as he does now, dressed in Levi's, but at that time that wasn't quite the thing to do. And I believe he had a goatee and a mustache and long hair—and he had just come back from six months in India with a guru, learning about life. I'm not sure, but it may have been a while since he had a bath," he said.[5] Sculley later recounted his unsuccessful attempt to turn Apple around. Regretfully, he wished he had reached out to Jobs for help. But because Jobs had stopped talking to him, Sculley had felt awkward. Like the mongoose in the story, Jobs was initially seen as a threat. Rather than check the veracity of the threat (perhaps examining the downsides of removing Jobs), the board decided quickly and erroneously to fire him. Like the mother in the mongoose story, Sculley and the board could have checked their assumptions and then found another alternative to calm their worries. Both the fable and the business example show how strong emotions can overwhelm people's ability to see alternative possibilities. In the next section, we review some of the research that makes the case for emotional intelligence.

Research Support of Emotional Intelligence

Here's an interesting fact. A 2005 study that examined why new hires failed revealed that four out of five factors were not related to technical competence. The results of this study showed the following:

- 26% of new hires failed at their job because of issues related to coachability (the ability to accept and implement feedback from bosses).

- 23% lacked the emotional intelligence to understand and manage their own emotions.

- 17% were devoid of the motivation needed to achieve their potential and excel on the job.

- 15% lacked the temperament and attitude for the job.[6]

Another study specifically related to job performance showed a relationship between EI and greater increases in merit pay, whereas lower company rankings were associated with organizations whose workers had received lower scores on an EI measure.[7] Additionally, emotionally intelligent employees, those who possessed higher levels of interpersonal facilitation (i.e., relating to others in a way that improves or sustains productive collaboration) and stress tolerance also received better peer and supervisor evaluations. In another study involving sales agents for a national insurance company, results suggested that those who had less self-confidence, resourcefulness, and empathy sold insurance policies with an average premium of $54,000. On the other hand, agents with higher measures of these attributes sold policies worth $114,000.[8] A study conducted by the top-ranked global provider of executive education offers yet more support for the value of EI. Specifically, the Center for Creative Leadership discovered that executives who lacked emotional competencies had higher rates of professional derailment (e.g., in areas such as difficulty in managing change, trouble working well in a team, and poor interpersonal skills).[9] Leaders who easily detect and comprehend the emotions of others are in a better position to gain their acceptance because individuals who feel understood are more likely to support their leader.

Elsewhere, leading organizational researchers Zhou and George have argued that leaders high in emotional intelligence are more likely to draw creative ideas out of their followers.[10] Specifically, they believe that emotionally intelligent leaders are much more likely to support the thinking strategies, like those described in Chapters 5 through 9, necessary for employees to produce innovative outcomes. For example, Zhou and George argue that emotionally intelligent leaders are more sensitive to employees' dissatisfaction and can channel such frustration toward the identification of problems that need to be resolved and new opportunities that might be seized.

There is no shortage of studies that highlight the positive impact of emotional intelligence on work-related performance. The challenge, then, is to change the belief among many leaders that soft skills (such as EI) undermine their ability to engage in effective leadership. For example, some leaders mistakenly believe that showing compassion diminishes their ability to analyze data or hold people accountable for poor performance. Ironically, it is the avoidance of EI behaviors that compound and, in some cases, grow problems. Remember that EI does not suggest *replacing* thinking skills with affective skills but balancing the two. So, we provided a definition of EI. We made the argument for EI through case studies supported by empirical evidence. But what exactly are the abilities that drive emotional intelligence?

Emotional Intelligence Abilities

Adele Lynn, author of *The EQ Difference: A Powerful Plan for Putting Emotional Intelligence to Work*, breaks down EI into five sequential components (i.e., skills that must be mastered in turn). They are self-awareness and control, empathy, social expertness, personal influence, and mastery of purpose/vision.[11] The five components are described next.

Self-Awareness and Control

Individuals with high EI have a good sense of self. They are keenly aware of and understand their strengths and areas of development. They are aware of their preferences, feelings, values, interests, and triggers that lead to emotional hijacks. But self-awareness is not enough. The emotionally intelligent person also acts on the information drawn from self-awareness by controlling himself or herself in a manner that supports relating to others so that mutual goals are maximized.

In an extensive research study involving interviews with dozens of business school deans and executives, the results were unambiguous that leadership development programs often do very little to develop introspection and self-awareness. Instead, much more focus is given to logic and general knowledge (e.g., IQ) and analytical decision making.[12] One of the interviewees asserted that leaders cannot effectively understand others if they do not take the time to understand themselves. To belabor the point inferred by these deans and executives, introspection is crucial to leadership development.

Self-doubt can get in the way of healthy introspection—truly embracing one's talents, skills, and character. Low self-confidence and poor self-esteem feed a negative and incomplete awareness of the self and can lead to misinterpretation of others and an inability to form healthy relationships. Therefore, the foundation to high EI starts with a healthy sense of self. David Walton, a leading behavioral science consultant, provides four simple and practical tips to improve self-esteem: (1) stop comparing yourself to other people; (2) don't put yourself down;

(3) get in the habit of saying and thinking positive things about yourself; and (4) don't deflect, accept compliments.[13]

Empathy

Individuals with high EI are able to understand the perspectives of other people. They have a way of making others feel that they have been understood and validated. We need to be clear here. By empathy, we suggest that the listener understand without necessarily agreeing with what has been shared. Like self-awareness, empathy is an internal skill that first must occur inside an individual seeking to make social interactions more effective. In the book *Rethinking the MBA: Business Education at a Crossroads*, empathy is identified as a skill that is neglected but crucially important for managing and leading.[14]

Social Expertness

This aspect of EI is the ability to construct a strong and healthy social bond with others. The relationship is genuine and communicates caring, concern, and disagreement in healthy ways. This ability is an external skill because it involves interaction with others. Let's take a look at an example to stress the importance of social expertness. Robert Nardelli and James McNerney, both executives, had each worked for General Electric (GE). Talented and with very successful track records, both worked within the Jack Welch system. Both left GE to take on CEO positions, Nardelli at Home Depot and McNerney at Boeing. Contemplate how these two executives made their debuts as CEOs. Based on insider reports, Nardelli came across as pompous; in one meeting he stood up and scolded his staff, "You guys don't know how to run a *f*****g* business." On the opposite end of the spectrum, McNerney dedicated his first few months on the job chatting with employees so that he could learn as much as possible about the Boeing units. There was no yelling or public humiliation. In fact, McNerney pushed for teamwork and shared the credit with the former Boeing CEO.[15] As one executive shared, McNerney was adored at Boeing. Meanwhile, Nardelli ultimately was forced out of Home Depot. His data-driven, confrontational management approach got on the nerves of many experienced executives. Although he had impressive numbers, Nardelli's temper, ego, and controlling leadership approach led to his downfall.[16] We would suggest that Nardelli's inability to create healthy social bonds led to his undoing.

Personal Influence

Highly emotionally intelligent people are able to lead and inspire themselves and other people, too. And once you are able to build healthy bonds with others, then you are in a much better position to accomplish goals. In *Rethinking the MBA: Business Education at a Crossroads*, Datar and colleagues report that executives identify the ability to influence others as a key professional performance challenge.[17] They assert that MBA students need to learn ways to persuade others when faced with resistance. It is not uncommon for students, when faced with dissenting points of view, to struggle.

However, at the moment of truth, effective leaders must be able to communicate their ideas in a powerful way, across the organization or up the chain of command.

Mastery of Purpose/Vision

This aspect of EI is the ability to sustain an authentic life that is true to the values you espouse. Maintaining effectiveness in this area requires you to have a clear understanding of your life's purpose. Furthermore, you have to be willing to go after your life's purpose and to take action within an organizational context so that your life's purpose is aligned with that of the organization.

A poignant example of this skill is found in the Powell doctrine. The doctrine was named after General Colin Powell in the lead-up to the 2003 American invasion of Iraq; it outlines a list of questions, and five tenets, that should be answered satisfactorily before engaging in war.[18] For example, two questions ask, "Do we have a clear attainable objective?" and "Is there a plausible exit strategy, to avoid endless entanglement?" Virtually *every* Powell doctrine tenet was violated. There was no clear vision of an exit strategy, and the objective was not clear either. The pressure to conform politically led influential stakeholders to support the decision to go to war, despite intense reservations and, in some cases, against their will. Mastery of purpose creates a clear picture of the hope and desire for a future state. The end in mind is so strong that you can taste and feel it, as if every attribute of the dream had already come to life. Yet for some, imagining a future state is difficult. There are those who do not create a strong sense of purpose or vision for themselves, for they wish to avoid the feeling of being let down should the vision not manifest. In short, too much management of expectations limits the vision. Under these psychological conditions, consider that the head (cognition) leads the heart (feelings), instead of the other way around. Dreams, hence, must lead the formation and articulation of a vision. Not convinced? Let us present a leadership example.

Thought Starter
Emotional Intelligence

Transformational Leadership

Herb Kelleher is the quintessential transformational leader. Let's examine more closely the profound influence he had on his employees, whom he thought of as his family. Kelleher is retired, but his legendary status as Southwest Airlines' founder and CEO lives on through folklore and its corporate culture. Southwest Airlines was one of the few airlines, if not the only one, to make a profit during difficult economic times. Kelleher humbly credits his people. But Southwest employees are quick to reply that it was Kelleher's tenets on how to run a business that contributed to Southwest's extraordinary success.

- He focused on building a lasting relationship with his customers. He pressed for a positive customer experience. To that end, Southwest would screen—and still does—for flight attendants who could make customers laugh during flights. From rap-singing preflight safety instructions to cracking jokes, nothing was too absurd.

- He stressed simplicity. For example, Southwest Airlines flew one type of aircraft, namely the 737. With one aircraft type, they reduced the costs related to training and maintenance.

- This next tenet is directly related to transformational leadership through the lens of EI. Kelleher was truly committed to his people. At the time of his tenure, Kelleher could be seen loading bags onto airplanes on hot summer days. Kelleher did not use words such as *caring, trusting,* or *liking* to describe how he felt about Southwest employees. No! He used the word *love.* In fact, Southwest's New York Stock Exchange ticker symbol is LUV. They paint hearts on all their airplanes. They brand themselves as a company that loves its people and its customers.

It is no wonder that Kelleher was voted at the time as the most admired CEO and that Southwest has shown one of the most formidable financial and service results in the entire airline industry.[19] We would suggest that Southwest, due to Kelleher's high EI, exhibits a positive culture and as a consequence is a profitable company.

Blocks and Barriers to Creative Thinking

In an earlier chapter we noted that creativity can be thought of as one's ability to overcome self-imposed constraints.[20] This conception of creativity aligns well with our discussion of EI, especially in that self-awareness serves as a foundation to EI. With this in mind, we build on our EI discussion by reviewing ways in which people block their own creative thinking through mental and emotional barriers. Self-creative leadership is the ability to be self-aware of intrapersonal blocks and then to do something to overcome them. For example, the notion that your organization is too bureaucratic, or too conservative in the ideas it promotes, or highly political, or that you have no influence, runs counter to your empowerment. What EI factors may be lurking in your self-doubt? In fact, when you ignore these voices, you set yourself up for a potential emotional hijacking. If you think these forces are true, then you enable them. Instead, we suggest that you attempt to disable them by confronting your self-imposed constraints and engaging them with new habitual thoughts and thought patterns that approach problem solving in open and appreciative ways. Put in simple terms: Create new habits by shifting your frames of mind into more productive ones—ones that sideline your fears and open new possibilities.

Consider Salvador Dalí's famous portrait titled *Gala Contemplating the Mediterranean Sea Which at Twenty Meters Becomes the Portrait of Abraham Lincoln–Homage to Rothko.* When you can on your own, pull up this multilayered and complex painting (see the link in the footnote).* What do you see? Do you see the artist's wife, model, and muse Gala standing with her back to you? Perhaps the sun glows

---

* Martinez-Conde (2014, June 17). Dalí masterpieces inspired by *Scientific American.* Retrieved December 20, 2016, from https://blogs.scientificamerican.com/illusion-chasers/dali-masterpieces-inspired-by-scientific-american/

for you in a way that presents an ascending, Christ-like image from above? Or, perhaps if you squint a bit, the bust of President Abraham Lincoln becomes clear—the sun now representing the exit wound of a bullet? This surrealist masterwork was inspired by an article in *Scientific American* magazine that described the minimum number of pixels a brain would require to "see" (or frame) a human face. The artist, Salvador Dalí, took the answer (believed at the time to be 121) as a challenge and produced this masterpiece in response. It's a compelling example of duality in nature, of our ability to represent parallel realities in our minds and of the immense power of framing. Digging deeper into the concept, one might argue that *what* you see has a great deal to do with *how* you are looking; in the world of creative problem solving, choosing to see through productive frames is a particularly compelling strategy.

The previous example illustrates the important role played by perception when it comes to solving challenges creatively, but an important question still remains: Are all matters of creativity driven primarily by perception alone, or do we need to be aware of other roadblocks and barriers that sometimes get in the way? The short answer is, it depends. If we are talking about your own personal, individual-level creativity, then the answer mostly has to do with you and the way your mind perceives problems and opportunities. If we are considering team-level creativity, then communication, collaboration, management practices, and technology also have important roles to play. And if we zoom out even farther and consider the creativity of entire organizations, then policies (and politics), procedures, diversity, culture, leadership, and macro technological and economic systems are relevant, too.

But let's not get ahead of ourselves; after all, this book is about you, and the development of your personal creative-thinking abilities and your ability to drive creative change. As we've expressed in previous chapters, it is our belief that creativity is a human trait (everyone has it, including you!), and at the same time, this chapter intends to demonstrate that there is perhaps no greater enemy to your own creativity than the constraints put on your imagination by your own mind. In the words of French philosopher Paul Valéry, "Everything that is masks for us something that might be." In other words, you are both the wellspring of your creative genius and also its biggest impediment, and you will need self-awareness to overcome the self-imposed barriers to your own creativity. In the same way that the Surrealist painting by Salvador Dalí highlights examples of self-imposed perceptual blocks to creativity, the rest of this chapter showcases further examples of blocks and barriers to your creativity. Additional issues of perception (beyond framing) that affect your personal creativity are also explored, as well as approaches to overcoming blocks and barriers to creativity that occur when you are collaborating with others inside organizations.

Fear: The Silent Killer

Palliative care is a form of medical therapy that focuses on symptom management as opposed to curing illness. It's often intended to help patients maintain an acceptable degree of quality of life as they approach the end of their lives. As a palliative care nurse, Bronnie Ware spent a great deal of time in close quarters with individuals preparing for the end. In her popular blog *Inspiration and Chai*, a post titled "Top 5 Regrets of the Dying" resonated with a global audience of readers, so she developed it into a book, recently published. The top regret of the dying, she reports, is "I wish I'd had the courage to live a life true to myself, not the life others expected of me."[21] These powerful words are striking in similarity to the charge of creativity research pioneer Dr. Ellis Paul Torrance's popular 1983 *Manifesto for Children*: "Learn to free yourself from the expectations of others and walk away from the games they impose on you. Free yourself to play your own game."[22]

One must wonder, however, if researchers know it, and the dying are openly communicating it, then why aren't we, the living, listening and acting upon the advice? Why do we continue subjecting ourselves to the games of others? Why aren't we manifesting lives more truly aligned with our creative selves? What's stopping us from overcoming these self-imposed constraints? The answer may have to do with an ancient yet useful and hard-wired ingredient of the human experience—fear.

Fear is essential for life—without it we'd be walking into oncoming traffic, consuming rotten foods, and befriending poisonous critters. Throughout time, the story has been the same; fear the "right" things, and you just might live long enough to pass on your genes. Rinse. Repeat.

The problem is, most of the threats humans have evolved to fear are no longer relevant to our daily lives. Consider the following question: Should your brain really be flooding your body with fear-response chemicals because of a passive-aggressive e-mail from a colleague? In fact, we rarely find ourselves having to evade or fight off predators, yet the same fear programming that has helped us persist and evolve into modern-day humans has not yet had an opportunity to evolve into something more suited for the complexities of a 21st-century life. Evolution is an extremely incremental process, and it takes time—a *long* time. As a result, fear and its conceptual cousin, anxiety, linger on as constant and significant contributors to our human experience.

It's important to distinguish between these two closely related concepts, fear and anxiety, for they are often misused interchangeably. One way researchers attempt to separate them is by focusing on the timeline of each.[23] For example, fear takes on a more immediate quality in the sense that your body is almost instantaneously reacting on a biological level to an immediate threat (think saber-toothed tiger bearing down on you!). It is a chain reaction in the brain that starts with a stressful stimulus and ends with the release of chemical compounds—the net effect being that the body speeds up, heart rate and blood pressure increase, pupils dilate to take in as much light as possible, and veins constrict and send blood to major muscle groups as you prepare to either do battle in the moment or flee to live on and fight another day. This is commonly referred to as the fight-or-flight response. It just happens. In everyday terms, it's automatic; in medical terms, it's *autonomic*.[24]

Anxiety, on the other hand, is more predictive and unfolds over time. Consider, for example, your mind and body reacting to the idea of a saber-toothed tiger coming for you some time in the future; this is the persistent psychological and emotional result of worrying about whether you will one day be a big cat's fleshy delight.

So what? Why should you care that some leftover biological and psychological processes remain active inside your brain and body? Well, it's important to consider the role these processes play because they may be doing nothing less than actively shaping your entire day-to-day reality! If that weren't reason enough, fear and anxiety can also have the devastating effect of paralyzing your capability to think and be creative. Fear and anxiety about future "failure" and "being wrong" stop us from attempting things that might end up becoming game-changing, never-done-before successes! Indeed, new ideas have a high bounce rate, meaning they often pan out in unexpected ways. This may be especially true or likely if the idea is *really* out there, but the important factor to consider is that fear and anxiety are effectively stealing your opportunity to find out for yourself.

Regina Dugan understands this well. In her popular TED Talk, she claims, "We cannot both fear failure and make amazing new things."[25] Her words come from a place of great experience on the matter. Prior to transitioning into her current role at Google, Dugan served as the first female director of the Defense Advanced Research Projects Agency (DARPA). During her tenure she oversaw many high-risk projects, including the development of an experimental hypersonic test vehicle considered the fastest maneuvering aircraft ever created—a vehicle capable of making a cross-continental flight from New York to California in the almost incomprehensible time of 11 minutes and 30 seconds. The experimental craft has flown twice, yet "we must fly again," says Dugan, "because amazing, never-been-done-before things require that you fly. You can't learn to fly at Mach 20 unless you fly."[26] Dugan's comments are a powerful endorsement for a learning-by-doing approach to innovation, suggesting that there may be no substitute for fear-less experimentation when seeking breakthrough ideas. Accordingly, it should come as no surprise that her latest endeavors at Google embrace a similar appetite for risk and reward: electronic tattoos and ingestible passwords powered by stomach acid! Her managerial-flavored remarks on her new mission are quite telling: The team will be a "small, lean, and agile group that is unafraid of failure," and it will "celebrate impatience."[27] Celebrate impatience, indeed; team members will only work for Dugan for a maximum of 2 years so that they must feel a sense of urgency in their work—an idea borrowed from DARPA, where employees wear their future resignation dates on their name badges. Dugan is not alone in suggesting that we must be willing to overcome our inner fears to create breakthroughs.

Academic researchers have found similar results, determining that fear of failure keeps us from engaging in risk taking[28] and that creativity and risk are indeed conceptual bedfellows.[29] That is, creative ideas, as they are unproven, are always accompanied by some degree of risk.

It may be tempting to point the finger at *other* people and *other* organizations and suggest that creativity and innovation aren't happening for them because *they* are too scared to experiment with new ideas; *they* are stuck in habits and patterns and old ways of doing things; *they* are afraid to fail. In response, we challenge you to consider the seminal question posed by Dugan in her TED presentation: "What would you attempt to do if you knew you could not fail?"

This question is important because it challenges us to consider the intoxicating parameters of our comfort zone—the safe spaces within which the vast majority of our life experiences unfold. To answer it faithfully is to venture inward, to stand toe-to-toe and do battle with our excuses for not tackling bigger and more important challenges with our lives. Again, consider: What would you attempt to do if you knew you could not fail? Another useful risk-mitigating question might be: What would you do if you believed no one cared if you failed?

In reflecting upon your answer(s) to the admittedly provocative question just posed, you might begin to wonder, *What exactly is risk, and how does it affect me?* It turns out that risk comes in several varieties. Consider the following categories:

1. *Financial risk:* of losing economic value

2. *Social risk:* of losing one's position in the social hierarchy

3. *Emotional risk:* of exposing oneself to uncomfortable and/or extreme emotional states

4. *Physical risk:* of enduring bodily harm

5. *Intellectual risk:* of coming up on the losing end of a debate

As you were reading through the bulleted list, you may have begun to consider your own appetite for each of the various forms of risk. Are you a daredevil when it comes to adventure sports? Did you borrow the maximum amount of interest-free student loan money to invest in the stock market while you were still in college? Do you often find yourself engaged in heated or contentious dialogue within online forums or in-person debates? Do you comfortably extend yourself emotionally in relationships with friends and others close to you?

Everyone has a different level of comfort with each of the various types of risk; think of it as a unique-to-you "risk profile." Regarding creativity, this is important because each type of risk plays a meaningful role in moderating (either stifling or supporting) your creative thinking, behavior, and expression.

Indeed, your unique risk profile and your hard-wired biological mechanisms of anxiety and fear play a critical role in shaping your ability to be creative and to do creative work. If you are too anxious and/or afraid to bring the products of your imagination to life because you are unwilling to risk experiencing the feelings associated with not being successful (especially in the beginning), or you are uncomfortable investing time and resources into your creative work (and creative play!), then you are likely setting yourself up for a creativity-limited life, while simultaneously handicapping your potential for future learning and development within your field or industry. The question remains: What would you do if you knew you could not fail? And, perhaps even more importantly, What's stopping you from doing something about it?

The emotionally *unintelligent* blocks and barriers to creativity come in all shapes and sizes, and they vary greatly depending on the level of analysis being considered (e.g., individual, team, organization). This Knowing section was designed to help you get to know thy enemy, and reading it is a good start toward being able to overcome these blocks on demand. Moving forward, the next section of this chapter describes some approaches to *Doing* just that.

Learning Activity
Linking Emotional Intelligence to Transformational Leadership

List five ways in which Herb Kelleher demonstrated emotional intelligence as a transformational leader at Southwest Airlines. To add to your knowledge, we strongly recommend conducting further research on Herb Kelleher.

Doing—Tools and Strategies for Overcoming Creative Blocks

There is a popular image, that some would call a meme, of a horse tied to a blue plastic chair that has been widely circulated through cyberspace. If you haven't seen this photograph, then use your mind's eye to imagine a powerful horse tied to a flimsy plastic chair. What's the point? Why would such a powerful beast remain connected to, indeed anchored by, such a small object? Surely a creature of such strength and power could outmuscle the relatively lightweight and insignificant chair. Yet, oddly enough, it doesn't. The horse remains in place, accepting its immobilizing circumstances and telling itself (somehow) that it cannot break free. This isn't just an equestrian issue, however; as we've discussed throughout this book, human beings are highly susceptible to self-imposed constraints on their imagination as well. Given our dependence on language-based communication, we may be especially vulnerable to the creativity-killing concept known as negative self-talk. Negative self-talk is the inward, private-to-you conversation that unfolds in your mind. Put simply, it's the voice of doubt, and when it comes to creativity, it's especially important to consider the role of negative self-talk because of how truly crippling it can be. Interestingly, understanding the power of *negative* self-talk may also provide an opportunity for going on creative offense, for it leads us to the following question: If negative self-talk can kill creativity, can affirmative (positive) self-talk help to enable possibilities and bring creativity to life?

We think so. For example, let's unpack the oft-paraphrased statement attributed to celebrated inventor Thomas Edison describing the lengthy trial-and-error process leading up to the invention of the lightbulb: "I have not failed; I've just found 10,000 ways that did not work." Did you notice the affirmative (positive-first) spin? This technique sets a creative tone, invites further participation toward the task at hand, and, contrary to devaluing all the other attempts that didn't work out (by calling them failures), Edison's statement instead celebrates the discovery of *all* the outcomes—independent of whether they produced a working lightbulb. This is a fundamentally different way of recasting the old phrase "trial and error" into something more positive—*trial and learn*. Another clever example of reframing is captured by the newly coined word *nearling*.

The illuminating notion that the words we choose to use might be impacting our ability to be on creative offense isn't just the relic of a late-19th-century inventor. Creativity educator Edward de Bono has explicitly suggested that the English language itself might be a barrier to creativity, for he believes it is missing a very important word. Specifically, de Bono argues that the English language does not contain a word to describe a "fully justified venture which did not succeed for reasons we could not predict and over which we had no control."[30] Instead, argues de Bono, our default approach is to describe *all* attempts that don't result in "success"—including all the early experimental versions that helped Edison inch ever closer to the final breakthrough design of a working lightbulb—as "failures." To overcome the limitation of language, a new word has been invented and is being used in Europe—*nearling*. Nearling refers to a new attempt or idea that was undertaken with the best of intentions but as of yet has not produced the right result. The word connotes being nearly there and learning something from the experience. Rather than calling it a mistake or failure, consider using the word *nearling*.[31] Ignoring this advice and continuing to blanket your self-talk with the "failure" label may not hurt you directly, but it also won't help you should you ever find yourself tied to a plastic chair (metaphorically, we hope).

Upon interviewing founders of 200 successful ventures, Stanford Graduate School of Business lecturer Amy Wilkinson discovered an insight she calls "the Creator's Code," described in her recent book by the same name. She observes that founders of successful companies tend to "fail wisely," that is, they choose to wear their earlier misfires as badges of honor while they commit to learning throughout the process and strengthening their future chances of success. Wilkinson suggests that the goal should be to reflect on your individual risk profile to determine what you are and are not comfortable with—and to just know that if creativity and innovation are the goal, then the answer can't be zero![32] Successful entrepreneurs in Wilkinson's research understand the intimate connection between failure and learning.

Thought Starter
Failing Wisely

Embracing and Internalizing the Terror of the New

What do Thomas Edison and Elon Musk have in common? For starters, they share an omnipresent belief that they will be able to bring their ideas to life regardless of roadblocks and setbacks. David Kelley, cofounder of the globally celebrated product development and industrial design firm IDEO and cofounder of the world-famous d.school at Stanford (officially known as the Hasso Plattner Institute of Design)—a unique academic structure that supports students from business, engineering, medicine, law, and other diverse disciplines to develop the requisite "thick skin" for bringing new ideas and prototypes to life—has recently developed a term to describe this belief: *creative confidence*. Inspired by a recent, life-altering cancer diagnosis, Kelley organized the lessons learned during his lifetime of experience in industry and academia to coauthor a book by the same name. The goal of the book and accompanying movement is to help as many people as possible reach a place of creative confidence in their lives—to overcome the negative self-talk that crushes creativity before it has a chance to emerge.[33]

If there is one thing Kelley knows, it's "no's." Having spent his entire career designing countless prototypes for client-sponsored creative products and services, he understands the immense importance of skillfully and productively interpreting negative feedback on a new idea. It's worth mentioning that it's an important skill for everyone to develop, not just designers. For example, if you are unable or unwilling to keep going in the face of "no," then you will have a very difficult time bringing any creative ideas into the world around you. One technique for overcoming a "no" is to actually dig into it further—to learn more about the objections and concerns being expressed by the naysayers and to get comfortable reframing the "no" into a "not yet," "not under the current circumstances," or "not without feature x, y, or z." In effect, the doubters and critics are transformed into your teachers and product advisors who can help you redesign for improvement and product-market fit. Finally, consider the no-riddled path of some extraordinarily successful companies that are wildly popular with consumers and are currently reshaping their industries (e.g., Zappos, Airbnb).

In this section, we've reiterated the importance of practicing your creativity fundamentals to strengthen your emotional intelligence, while also introducing some new approaches that describe what it means to be *Doing* creative offense. If your goal is to untie yourself from the mental plastic chairs in your life, then overcoming the negative self-talk of doubt, reframing the word *failure*, regaining your creative confidence in the face of judgment (and particularly the word *no*), failing wisely, getting started before you're ready, embracing the terror of doing something new, and teaming up with other like-minded innovators in safe spaces for entrepreneurial experimentation are now all tools you have in your tool kit. Perhaps Amazon founder Jeff Bezos said it best during a media interview following a very public and high-profile technical failure that occurred within one of his portfolio companies, Blue Origin. Instead of explaining the technical details of the fiery explosion in the sky, or speaking about the setback in financial terms or business jargon, Bezos calmly looked at the interviewer and replied, "Step by step, ferociously."[34]

Recruit a partner for this activity. Sit back to back and ask your partner to speak for 3 minutes about any topic he or she wishes. Listen to your partner without interrupting and write down the emotions you hear. What deeper emotional insights can you glean from your partner's words and tone of voice? How did not being able to respond affect your ability to listen? Afterward, share your insights with your partner. Were they correct?

Being—Actively Learning From Failure

If it hasn't happened already, somewhere along the line someone is going to tell you that if you want to get a job, you're going to need to create a résumé. The problem is that a résumé doesn't actually "get" you anything—except for maybe a foot in the door of a potential employer. At least this was something that one of your authors discovered when he worked as an administrator in the College of Business before becoming a professor.

Specifically, his role was to connect students seeking employment opportunities with local companies who wanted to hire them. The primary communication tool exchanged between them was—you guessed it!—a résumé. What he learned during this experience was that (a) undergraduate students often lack sufficient professional experience to effectively showcase all their hard-earned skills, abilities, and wisdom and (b) that résumés tend to artificially emphasize the purely positive things that have happened during what is often a very limited professional scope of activity (to mention nothing of the very serious issue of embellishment). Because of these factors, a résumé represents a very limited opportunity for candidates to differentiate themselves from others seeking the same position. To make matters worse, it's also of limited utility for employers because it doesn't actually help them identify the best candidates for the positions available.

For the author, this led to a realization that a student could do better with a little creativity. In addition to the cover letter and traditional résumé, students could also present a complementary, job-specific *failure résumé* (alternatively, you could call it a *nearling résumé*). Instead of a traditional résumé—one that touts all the accomplishments and credentials a person has achieved—a *failure résumé* showcases experiences that didn't go to plan. Even more importantly, it showcases what someone has learned from the process, while also going on to demonstrate how the person applied that unique, valuable, and perhaps painful learning as he or she has moved on to larger and more challenging projects.

A failure résumé is especially powerful if you can demonstrate specific examples of how you've leveraged the key learning from your failures by successfully applying them to future challenges—specifically ones like the challenges you'll encounter within the defined duties and responsibilities of the position you are applying for. To recap, consider the benefits of presenting a failure résumé.

1. *Differentiation.* You stand out from all other candidates who didn't invest the time, effort, and creativity to submit a unique product to assist the employer in making an informed decision.

2. *Humility.* You demonstrate that you are a thoughtful and reflective learner with confidence in your ability to take on challenges and learn from your mistakes.

3. *Experience.* You prove that you already have experience learning and growing in the specific skill and knowledge areas that the position you're competing for requires.

4. *Hustle.* In a world where you are competing for opportunities against global talent, there's no reason you shouldn't be doing everything possible to get your application to the top of the stack; this also helps an employer get excited about the prospect of you bringing the same level of energy and ingenuity to their organizational challenges and opportunities.

How do you create a failure résumé? Well, that's really up to you; this is a creative exercise, after all! Images, text, charts, and graphs all seem like fair game. Perhaps it is worth considering the experience from the recruiter's or hiring manager's perspective, in which case you might want to create something that he or she will be familiar and/or comfortable reviewing. Regarding themes, you might include coverage of professional, academic, and perhaps personal/relational experience; again, the goal is to match your experiences to the specific skills, responsibilities, and maybe even keywords advertised in the position description. To structure your failure résumé message, consider the following approach.

Step 1. Recount the critical incident of what happened.

Step 2. Describe your key learning and/or takeaways from the process.

Step 3. Demonstrate how you applied your newfound learning in another situation.

Richard Branson got started selling Christmas trees and publishing a student newsletter. Mark Cuban sold garbage bags and taught disco dancing lessons. Billionaire casino mogul Sheldon Adelson sold newspapers and operated vending machines. In addition to their humble business beginnings, each of these astronomically successful individuals has also started and/or invested in a variety of projects and companies that have failed. But this book isn't about industry giants like Branson, Cuban, and Adelson; no, this book has always been about you, and we hope this chapter in particular has really turned your attention inward. After all, what could possibly be more personal (and you-focused) than exploring strategies for embracing the principles of emotional intelligence and understanding the implications of facing your inner fear(s) and anxiety when trying something new? As much as we'd like to make it easier for you, we know better. In the words of abolitionist Frederick Douglass, "If there is no struggle, there is no progress." We just hope that your creative struggles, from here on out, occur firmly within your learning zone. In the timeless and ever-potent observation of American author Anaïs Nin, "Life shrinks or expands in proportion to one's courage," and we therefore encourage you onward to make glorious, learning-filled mistakes and to do so with great creative courage—understanding that it won't be easy. You might recall earlier references to Regina Dugan and her work with DARPA and Google. Her words ring true on the creative battle within:

> Now I want to say, this is not easy. It's hard to hold onto this feeling, really hard. I guess in some way, I sort of believe it's supposed to be hard. Doubt and fear always creep in. We think someone else, someone smarter than us, someone more capable, someone with more resources will solve that problem. But there isn't anyone else; there's just you. And if we're lucky, in that moment, someone steps into that doubt and fear, takes a hand and says, "Let me help you believe."[35]

If you aren't ready to create something new in this exact moment, then maybe it's a great time to grab someone else's hand and help them believe.

Learning Activity
Create a Failure or Nearling Résumé

Following the description provided in the Being section, prepare your own failure résumé. When it's completed, ask yourself, What was the best and worst thing that happened? What am I now aware of? What do I understand better about myself? What did I learn? What can I take from this and apply in the future?

Case Study
Airbnb

Introduction

Barriers to creativity and innovation present themselves in many ways, from the intrapersonal fear (and anxiety) of failure experienced by individuals to the managerial and organizational frameworks that impede or hinder creative thinking and behavior in organizations. For Airbnb, the blocks to creativity in the pivotal early years as a start-up company just kept on coming. In fact, the very idea of paying to sleep in a stranger's home once caused potential Airbnb investors to literally laugh out loud during a pitch meeting.[36] So, perhaps understandably, the team behind the (now extraordinarily successful and rapidly growing) international social lodging company was on the verge of packing up and walking away. But when the going got tough, the team behind Airbnb got creative.

It may have been tempting to move on, to go and get "real jobs," but the team didn't; instead, they applied for entry into an exclusive start-up program, Y Combinator (YC). YC is an intensive 12-week start-up accelerator that offers access to resources and asks the tough questions to help founders think through the inherent challenges and opportunities within their business models.

The opportunity to participate in YC didn't just fall into the team's lap, however, and neither did the first round of funding from Sequoia Capital that eventually placed Airbnb permanently in the field of "disruptive technology" that has hotels and city officials alike feeling uneasy about taxes, regulations, and the future of lodging.[37] In fact, Airbnb only exists today because the team refused to succumb to blocks and barriers early on.

Backstory

In 2008, two former college friends who were sharing an apartment in San Francisco launched Airbnb. The inspiration? There was a design conference in town, and cofounders Joe Gebbia and Brian Chesky had heard that some visitors might have trouble booking rooms.

The new idea was so simple that it was first referred to as AirBedandBreakfast because the friends didn't even have a spare bed to offer, just a few air mattresses. Within 24 hours, they'd coded a bare-bones website, sent the link around to a few blogger friends, and then waited. That first week, they made $900.

Months after launching the website and bringing on Gebbia's former roommate Nathan Blecharczyk, though, Airbnb was stagnant. They tanked at South by Southwest in 2008, only booking five rooms from an available 60 listed near Austin's annual festival. Undeterred by the "failure" at SXSW, the team tried again: This time, they scoured craigslist and booked listings in Denver during the Democratic National Convention. There they achieved some media success, with mentions on CNN, and in the *Washington Post* and the *New York Times*, but the momentum didn't last. Again, postevent bookings slowed down. Roadblocks were forming. The team wasn't making much money, and they couldn't get big entrepreneurs to invest in their yet-to-be-proven model. Furthermore, they were taking on debt and being laughed out of conference rooms.

Creative confidence is the kind of attitude that kept Thomas Edison, Elon Musk, and Jeff Bezos looking forward, despite setbacks, roadblocks, and hearing the word *no* repeatedly. It's also the driver behind small ideas that can lead to life-altering change. In the case of Airbnb, one such revolution unfolded in the form of breakfast cereal.

Cereal Entrepreneurship

Post-DNC, prospects were grim. The team wasn't getting press anymore, revenues were low, and debt was growing. Rather than fold, however, the team reevaluated the core idea behind Airbnb—bed and breakfast—and

(Continued)

(Continued)

discovered an opportunity to strike up new media interest during the heated election year of 2008. Overnight, they "became cereal entrepreneurs," Gebbia says. The creative solution to getting back in the public eye: custom Obama-O's and Cap'n McCain cereal boxes, which they sent to reporters in a bid for publicity. In addition, they sold 800 boxes at $40 a pop, raising approximately $30,000 dollars to help them stay afloat. But by November, postelection, the allure had worn off. The team was almost ready to quit when an old friend encouraged them to apply for the YC program. It was the creativity Airbnb showed in the face of limited resources that helped them pass from struggling start-up to profitable business. YC cofounder Paul Graham stated, "We didn't love the idea of renting spare rooms to strangers, it seemed odd, but as soon as we saw the cereal boxes, we knew that we were going to work with them."[38]

YC has helped launch companies like Dropbox, Disqus, Reddit, and many more, but simply getting into the program does not guarantee success.[39] And in the 12 weeks of the YC program, Graham advised the Airbnb team to gain fresh perspective by talking to customers in New York City, a place where the company had more traction than most (a form of positive deviance).

What did they discover? For the most part bad photography. Through this deliberate analysis of their listings and booking data, Gebbia realized the biggest barrier Airbnb was facing was low-quality camera phone photos of the spaces for rent.[40] A stint in the city, meeting with renters, and personally photographing available spaces with rented, high-end photo equipment was the creative

answer to a logical solution for Airbnb. Ultimately, the team would discover that people *did* want to use the site—they just wanted to clearly see what they would be renting!

Of course, achieving popularity like Airbnb's didn't mean that the barriers stopped presenting themselves. If anything, they became more complex. The team had successfully figured out a business model that worked for most customers, but other, newer roadblocks were forming. In 2014, San Francisco and New York City passed laws prohibiting short-term rentals in certain buildings or homes.[41] The company faced a large fine in Barcelona in July 2014.

However, in other cities around the globe, such as Amsterdam, Airbnb is being welcomed. On their end, the company has remained active but has taken hotel and city complaints seriously, even going so far as to collect hotel tax in cities like San Francisco and Portland, Oregon.[42] By working with local and state governments to find solutions that allow the company to operate freely, Airbnb is both shifting the narrative of the known model and seeking to address future constraints.

Closing

Airbnb floundered, flourished, floundered again, and is now flourishing at a mind-boggling scale. Each time they gained traction with their disruptive idea, a barrier requiring creative thinking and execution attempted to get in the way. And even as an international empire today, they continue to face obstacles.

But beyond all the roadblocks and barriers, the core idea of Airbnb is a brilliant, successful solution to a pain point many individuals have experienced. It offers a simple answer to the near-universal problem of finding affordable rooms in expensive cities, with the additional benefits of meeting new people and maximizing unused space. Gebbia and Chesky's idea leveraged technology (web and mobile applications) to challenge an existing model (the hotel and vacation industries), and they pursued their vision with creative abandon.

From the early days of Airbnb's initial struggles, to YC in 2009, to the current day, the company has steadily grown to boast over 800,000 listings in 33,000 cities and 192 countries and is currently valued at approximately $10 billion.

Discussion Questions: Knowing

1. Compare and contrast the qualities and characteristics of the existing hotel-based model for lodging to the new, distributed, social model used by Airbnb. What are the advantages and disadvantages of each?

2. How does the Airbnb start-up story demonstrate the principles of problem finding, idea generation, solution experimentation, and strategy execution?

3. Describe the role of grit, persistence, and determination in the case.

Application Questions: Doing

1. Design challenge: Review one of the creative blocks (and tactics used to overcome) experienced by the Airbnb team and then visually map it through the four-stage model presented in Chapter 5.

2. Put yourself in the shoes of a city council member. Instead of blocking Airbnb, what creative ideas might you come up with to overcome *your* blocks as a council member to leverage the capability that Airbnb might bring to your community? Embrace the principles of divergent thinking to generate as many ideas as possible.

Thinking Ahead: Being

1. If you were the CEO of Airbnb, where would you take the company next? What new strategies for products and services might you recommend? What new markets might you venture into? Be sure to explain your answer(s).

2. What are the outstanding questions facing the company, site users (renters and hosts), and the countries and communities in which Airbnb operates?

3. Recall a time when you were challenged by a creative block or barrier. What helped you to overcome the situation? How did you use your creative-thinking capabilities? Did grit and perseverance play a role? Describe the process by which you overcame your challenge.

Sustaining Your Creativity

Learning to Defy
and Transform the Crowd

Learning Goals

After reading this chapter, you will be able to do the following:

- Explain the investment theory of creativity
- Appraise ways in which creative power is given away
- Predict the key stakeholders and assess their level of support for a proposed idea or creative change
- Envision a desired future and construct a descriptive story that outlines a path toward this future state

Knowing—Investment Theory of Creativity

A Story About a Sandwich That Revolutionized an Industry

Herb Peterson happened to like eggs Benedict—a buttered half of an English muffin topped with ham (or bacon) and a poached egg, all smothered in Hollandaise sauce. Mr. Peterson was a food scientist who co-owned a number of McDonald's franchises in California.[1] This was the late 1960s, and fortunately for McDonald's, a happy collision among these variables led to a massive business opportunity. Backtracking just a bit, two brothers, Richard and Maurice McDonald, founded McDonald's in 1940. In 1955 Ray Kroc facilitated the opening of the first franchised McDonald's restaurant. Soon thereafter, Kroc, an aggressive business-man, purchased the equity rights from the McDonald brothers and led the development of a global corporation that today employs over 1 million people worldwide.

Most readers are too young to recall that from the founding of this fast-food restaurant until the early 1970s, McDonald's served only lunches and dinners. That all changed, however, thanks to Herb Peterson's creativity and willingness to defy his own corporation, where there was strong resistance on the part of many franchise owners to open their doors before the standard 11:00 a.m. start. Unbeknownst to the McDonald's corporation, Mr. Peterson began to experiment with breakfast dishes. Mr. Peterson, in keeping with McDonald's focus on food you eat with your hands, tested a number of versions of an eggs Benedict–type breakfast sandwich. The original Egg McMuffin featured an egg cooked in a Teflon ring, yolk broken, with grilled ham and a slice of cheese. And it was served as an open-faced sandwich.

Of course the McDonald's corporation saw the positive reaction Herb Peterson's chain of restaurants was creating with the new breakfast item, and of course, they immediately saw a business opportunity. Right? Wrong! Instead, the corporate office reprimanded Mr. Peterson for violating the terms of the franchise agreement. He was even threatened with a number of penalties. Mr. Peterson persisted, however, and managed to introduce the Egg McMuffin to Ray Kroc during a visit to his Santa Barbara franchise. Mr. Peterson and his assistant Donald Greadel famously invited Ray Kroc to their restaurant without giving away the details of the idea they wished to share with him. That was probably wise, because Ray Kroc admitted in his autobiography that he was initially skeptical of the breakfast sandwich idea; however, when he tasted Peterson's creation, he immediately saw the potential.[2] It took some years to scale up production, and in 1972 the first corporate-approved Egg McMuffin was served.

This little sandwich, inspired by eggs Benedict, launched a new business opportunity that was reported in 2014 to account for 25% of McDonald's sales and generates billions of dollars annually.[3] One might conclude that this is history and the end of the story, but when McDonald's faced overall slumping sales in the middle of 2015, the corporation looked to breakfast to turn things around. With national surveys showing that most Americans eat and drink 1.4 times each morning, the McDonald's corporation targeted breakfast as a strategic business opportunity[4]—as have many other fast-food chains, even the likes of Taco Bell. McDonald's focused on boosting sales with their McCafé, earlier hours, the introduction of new breakfast items such as pastries, and all-day breakfast. And the plan worked; in the last quarter of 2015, the breakfast strategy proved to significantly increase sales. Just think: This all started with a simple idea, the Egg McMuffin, and the creativity of one man, Herb Peterson.

Sternberg and Lubart's Investment Theory of Creativity

We shared the story of Herb Peterson and his invention of the Egg McMuffin to illustrate a particular theory of creativity. This theory holds that creating is like investing. Sternberg and Lubart argue that like the fundamentals of investing, buy low and sell high, creativity operates in much the same manner.[5] When investing, the potential for the greatest gains generally comes when you find a stock that is undervalued and has great potential for growth. However, investing in such financial instruments is risky. The same can be said of creative ideas. As Sternberg and Lubart put it, "Buying low means actively pursuing ideas that are unknown or out of favor but that have growth potential. Selling high involves moving on to new projects when an idea or product becomes valued and yields a significant return."[6] And as with investing, buying into novel ideas with unproven usefulness or value is a risky venture. Yet this is exactly what creative people—both innovators and entrepreneurs—do. They defy conformity pressures and invest their efforts, energy, and sometimes their financial resources into developing original concepts with perceived promise but unproven widespread value or acceptance. Whereas Dalí learned to master traditional modes of artistic expression, he decided to break away, to defy the crowd and adopt a different and not fully embraced form of artistic expression—surrealism (reflected in one of Dalí's most iconic images, the melting face of a clock, and in the image of the exploding melting face of a watch found on the next page). As Sternberg and Lubart argue,

Metaphorically the creative person "buys low" by rejecting currently popular, conventional ideas that others are readily buying into, instead coming up with and championing fresh ideas. He or she then "sells high" when the idea "purchased" for a "low price" achieves societal value, as others finally recognize its worth and jump on the bandwagon.[7]

Less creative individuals, because they do not want to stand apart from the crowd, are likely to stick with the tried and true—ideas with proven value. Of course, such ideas have their advantages. They are safe. They are efficient. When mastered, they demonstrate competence. And, of course, there is a downside. When individuals make a habit of buying into accepted practices and ideas, they do not stand out. They melt into the crowd and therefore do not distinguish themselves. If you want to be average when it comes to creativity and achievement, the surest way forward is to adopt the same thinking and practices as everyone else. If you want to be a successful entrepreneur or organizational innovator, then it becomes imperative for you to break away from established practices adopted by the majority.

Recall our earlier conversation about the conformity pressures so prevalent in our society. Over time, it is likely that you have been so conditioned by your surroundings that you may not even be aware of the tendency to simply follow the crowd. Again, this is not to say that conformity is completely bad or unproductive. The reality is that people and organizations require both creativity and conformity, and the fact is there is a symbiotic relationship between the two. Creativity generates new and unproven ideas, whereas conformity then assures that those ideas perceived to be most valuable are adopted by the crowd. Creative people and organizations generate, develop, and sell breakthrough concepts. People who are effectively creative take advantage of society's conformity to disseminate their breakthrough ideas. The question most pertinent to you is the degree to which you are prepared to defy the crowd to distinguish yourself as a creative person, to serve as an organizational innovator or an entrepreneur who is a catalyst for change.

Thought Starter

Defy the Crowd

Many organizations now recognize that to survive and thrive they need members who are able to bring their creative imagination to bear within the organizational setting. Moreover, many members of society believe creativity is necessary for a healthy economy. This does not mean being creative is easy. Whereas organizations, and society in general, say they value creativity, there remain conformity pressures that can make it difficult for creative ideas, and creative people, to be accepted. To help you improve the probability that you can successfully defy the crowd and sell your creative ideas, we turn to Sternberg and Lubart, who provide a list of components of successful creative individuals. The framework outlined by these scholars highlights some of the critical points raised in this book. Therefore, we use their model to highlight some of the most important factors for you to internalize so that you might take your creativity to another level. We encourage you to use this summary to analyze the extent to which you are in the best possible position to tap into and sustain your creativity.

Intelligence

According to Sternberg and Lubart, intelligence and its role in supporting creativity can be thought of in three ways. The first is synthetic intelligence. This component of intelligence has to do with effectiveness in information processing. Synthetic intelligence can be related to the observational and problem-defining skills we discussed in Chapter 6, as well as the ideational skills described in Chapter 7. Someone high in synthetic intelligence looks at information in new ways, recombines old ideas in new formats, discovers interesting problems and opportunities, produces unique ideas, and can easily change directions. Next is analytic intelligence. This form of intelligence enables you to be skillful at the all-important solution development and validation stage of the creative process (see the skills described in Chapter 8). Where synthetic intelligence spots interesting problems and generates original responses to these problems, analytical intelligence allows you to select which possibilities will yield the greatest results. Highly creative people use their analytic intelligence to know which ideas are worth investing their time, talent, energy, and resources. Analytic intelligence distinguishes the crackpot inventors from the innovative inventors who recognize which ideas can be transformed into value propositions. The third kind of intelligence is practical intelligence. This is the ability to sell your novel ideas, exactly the kinds of skills presented in Chapter 9, to get others to recognize their value and, as a consequence, to buy into such original concepts. Also, practical intelligence enables a person to know what feedback to heed for further developing his or her novel and unproven concept. Highly creative people know what feedback to ignore and what feedback holds the key to improving the original concept.

Knowledge

Most theories and models of creativity hold that to produce creative work in some field or domain, one must understand the body of knowledge in that area. Knowledge is necessary for creativity; it is the foundation that guides the production of ideas. No matter the field, whether it is music, art, business, technology, science, or psychology, you need an awareness of the basic content to produce new work. And some research shows that the more technical the field is, the longer it takes for someone to produce creative work.[8] For example, the peak creative period for scientists comes later than it does for writers. Some have argued that this occurs because more technical fields require a longer period to amass a sufficient understanding to then make original contributions. However, knowledge is not sufficient. To create new knowledge, you must not fall victim to what you know, to assume that your knowledge is truth. Certainty kills creativity. Knowledge must be thought of as permeable and temporary, not as an absolute.

Thinking Styles

Intelligence refers to ability; in contrast, thinking styles can be characterized as a mindset for creativity. You might possess the ability to imagine and generate novel ideas, but do you also have the right attitude to leverage this ability? You might possess the speed and power to be successful at ultimate fighting, but do you hold the fearless mindset necessary to enter the cage? You may be flexible and athletic enough to do a front flip, but do you have the courage to do this on a narrow balance beam? Thinking styles are about how you think, not how well you think. When it comes to creativity, do you possess the kind of mindset that will allow you to defy the crowd?

Personality

Some of the earliest work in the field of creativity has clearly and consistently highlighted personality traits that improve an individual's chance of demonstrating creative behavior. Some of the most important traits are a willingness to take risks, the courage to stand up for one's beliefs, and a good sense of humor. In the world of financial investing, one of the crucial questions financial planners assess with respect to their clients is their tolerance for risk. As noted earlier in this chapter, the safer investments, those that are less risky, generally have modest returns. Opportunities for larger gains are more likely to occur with those investments that present higher levels of risk. It is the same with creative ideas. Buying into ideas that are already well established and proven entails no risk and generates modest return—you now own what everyone else owns. To generate and embrace something new, which provides great opportunity for differentiation and growth, requires a personality comfortable with taking risks. Beyond risk taking it is also helpful to be comfortable in taking a stand, demonstrating absolute commitment to the new idea. This trait leads to persistence and a dogged determination to overcome obstacles that stand in the way of success. Finally, study after study of the creative personality highlights the importance of humor. A good sense of humor allows for a playful attitude, which can go a long way in reducing the stress and self-doubt that might come along with the pressures associated with selling a creative idea. Individuals who pursue creative ideas are likely to experience failure. When you are skillful at generating and experimenting with original concepts, you will quickly realize that an important part of the process is failure—the idea looked good on paper, but in reality, it fell short of the desired impact and value. A good sense of humor helps one to rebound faster from such setbacks.

Motivation

Highly creative people are driven, possessing a high degree of energy. There is a stereotype about creative people being fanciful dreamers. The reality is that people who bring creative ideas to fruition are driven to achieve their goals. Motivation can come from extrinsic and intrinsic sources. Extrinsic sources include a desire to achieve some level of notoriety, acknowledgment, and reward. Intrinsic sources relate to internal rewards such as self-expression, satisfaction, and personal challenge. Both are important, but as Sternberg and Lubart say so well, "Creative people are almost always doing something they love. Likewise, distinctive work will rarely come from someone who hates the task at hand."[9]

Environmental Context

The final quality necessary for creativity to occur does not relate to an individual resource but to the environment in which the individual finds himself or herself. It is possible for an individual to possess the five qualities described earlier and yet not produce creative work. In such cases, this is almost always due to the situation. The classroom environment, for example, can squash student creativity, and an employee's ability to contribute creative ideas at work often depends on the atmosphere found in the workplace. If your creativity is important to you, be sure to find the kind of environment that will nurture, not undermine, your creative potential. And if you cannot find the right environment, then take control (as best you can) of the situation to create your own environment.

Learning Activity
Investment Theory Exercise

Summarize in your own words Sternberg and Lubart's investment theory of creativity. Next, find an example of a successful creative project, either through research or perhaps something personally familiar to you, and describe how the investment theory applies to that example. In what ways does this example validate this theory? Identify an idea that you "bought low" in your organization or in life. How did this work out? In what ways were you successful, or not, in getting others to see the value of this novel idea?

Doing—Addressing Resistance to Change

When you create, you introduce change. Your new ideas either replace old ideas or push others to go in a new direction (and often both). Creative ideas can be disruptive and therefore are not always welcomed with open arms. Given the built-in conformity bias in human nature, it is important to recognize that responses to your creativity may range from mildly unsettling to outright hostility in the face of a perceived threat. In hindsight, it is easy to spot a creative idea, that is, once its value is fully understood and accepted. Some 40 years later, the Egg McMuffin looks like a no-brainer idea; however, that's from the vantage point of seeing a thriving breakfast business at McDonald's. In retrospect, it is easy to look back with surprise, and perhaps even a bit of arrogance, at McDonald's resistance to this winning business proposition—recall that the corporation rebuked the inventor of the Egg McMuffin. At the time, the McDonald's business model was based on serving handheld meals at lunch and dinner; thus the notion of a breakfast sandwich was novel and disruptive. To be a successful innovator or entrepreneur begins with the ability to identify and develop unique ideas, but ultimate success depends on your ability to get others to buy into and embrace the value of your new proposition.

So how did Herb Peterson overcome resistance to the idea of a breakfast sandwich? Mr. Peterson's success came about as a result of selling his idea to a critical stakeholder, Ray Kroc, the man who launched the corporation. With respect to change, we define a stakeholder as anyone who is impacted by a proposed action or can influence the successful adoption of a creative idea. When proposing a creative idea in a social context, it can be extremely helpful to be aware of the stakeholders in that situation and to consider specific strategies for how you will win such individuals over. If you are going to get a crowd to adopt your thinking, you will want to target specific individuals within the crowd who, once convinced of the merits of your idea, will assist in getting others to adopt the new idea. You were briefly introduced to stakeholder analysis in Chapter 9; because buy-in is central to the success of innovators and entrepreneurs, we revisit this tool with greater detail.

To identify stakeholders, consider the following questions:

- Who has an interest in the proposed action?

- Who is most likely to be affected by the idea?

- Whose resistance would undermine success?

- Which individuals and groups have a clear role in this situation?

- Whose buy-in is necessary for success?

- Who is in a strong position to sway others' opinions of this idea?

Once you have identified the stakeholders in the situation, next you need to consider the nature of the various stakeholders' views regarding your proposed change. Some may be supportive of your idea, whereas others may stand in opposition to your proposed action. It is helpful to specifically identify the perceived level of support for any stakeholder you consider to be crucial to your success. Do not take for granted those you believe are in your corner. Instead, be deliberate about confirming their support and actively enlist them as advocates for the proposed action. This will help build positive momentum. For those stakeholders who are likely to oppose your idea, generate strategies aimed at moving their opinion from negative to positive (or at least neutral). Also, a useful strategy is to consider how supportive stakeholders might be leveraged to convert those opposed to your idea. Supportive stakeholders who have credibility and influence can help sway the naysayers.

Falling in love with your own creative ideas is natural. It is important to be committed to ideas you believe have great potential. However, it is foolhardy to naively believe that everyone else will hold the same enthusiasm for your thinking. Learning to enlist key stakeholders often means the difference between the successful adoption of your ideas or their early demise. And sometimes the most important creative thinking applied to a successful innovation isn't the creativity required to create the original idea but instead the imagination employed to sell the innovation to others. It is one thing to defy the crowd yet quite another to get the crowd to come over to your way of thinking.

Learning Activity
Conducting Stakeholder Analysis

Identify an idea, plan, or activity you need to successfully carry out in the next 60 to 90 days. Using the questions in the previous bullet points, make a list of all the stakeholders and then select the most important ones. Create a table with four columns (or simply replicate the Stakeholder Analysis Worksheet found in Figure 9.1). In the first column, list the most important stakeholders. In the next column, identify the current level of support associated with each stakeholder. In the third column, identify the level of support you will need in the future from each stakeholder to be successful. Assess the gap between where each stakeholder's support is currently and where you need it to be. In the final column, list the action steps you can take to move the stakeholder to where you need him or her. Think creatively about these action steps. If the stakeholder is strongly supportive already, then think about action steps you can take to get this stakeholder to influence others. Once the table is completed, review all action steps listed in the fourth column and create an action plan (i.e., organize action steps you wish to take in chronological order). In what ways is this tool valuable before launching an idea?

Being—Becoming a 21st-Century Innovator

Creativity, though influenced by many factors, emanates from the individual. Organizations are not creative; it is the individuals inside those organizations who create. New innovations and entrepreneurial enterprises do not launch themselves; the breakthroughs to such endeavors are born in the creative minds of a few who decide to defy the crowd. With this in mind, we wish to close this personal journey by focusing on you, for it is the individual who is the catalyst to all creative acts. Our goal here is to help you sustain your momentum on this journey. To assist you, we close this book by presenting a set of ways in which individuals give up their creative power.[10] To go on a journey, especially one that is long and arduous, one must be in the best possible shape at the outset. Furthermore, you must take care of yourself all along the way. Fortify yourself against these common personal limitations, and you will do much to retain and strengthen your creativity.

Limiting Your Options

One of the most debilitating ways to undermine your creative power is to confine yourself to a limited number of options. As you increase your options, you simultaneously increase your probability of success. If there are no options, there is no hope. One option pins all hope on only one way forward; it is either succeed or fail. Two options provide at least a fallback position but force decisions into either-or scenarios. When you create multiple options, whether they are solutions to a problem or alternative paths toward achieving a goal, you are in the strongest position possible. To drive this point home, consider an example. Imagine you are sitting across a table from someone with whom you are negotiating, perhaps trying to land a job or buying a car. Imagine the person across from you represents your only option. How much power do you possess in this situation? Now imagine that you have an alternative option, another job offer or another car dealer with whom you are working. By having alternatives, you increase the probability of achieving your goal. This is exactly what great creators, innovators, and entrepreneurs do to achieve success. Over his lifetime, Picasso produced more than 20,000 works. James Dyson tested more than a thousand prototypes before finding the solution for the bagless vacuum cleaner. Steve Jobs achieved success in multiple industries—computer technology, film animation, mobile phones, and music. Thomas Edison held over 1,000 patents. Not all your ideas will be creative breakthroughs, but the more ideas, alternatives, and options you create, the more likely you will be to achieve what you desire.

Resting on Success

Building on the previous point, one way in which we limit our options is through success. The risk in having a successful innovative idea is the fact that it is easy to become wedded to that idea or a particular way of thinking—unwilling to continuously grow and experiment with new possibilities. As Sternberg and Lubart noted, "As an individual acquires a more and more valuable portfolio of creative accomplishments, he or she faces the same danger as does a mature company— that he or she may not be able to muster the resources to deal with a rapidly changing world."[11] Nokia is a fine example of an organization that was innovative but suffered from its own success. Although primarily known as a pioneer in the mobile phone industry, at one time Nokia was (and still is) a rubber boot manufacturer (well before it entered the mobile phone market). Nokia was the first to introduce the smartphone but was unable to keep up with the competition— who introduced phones with more elegant interfaces (most notably the iPhone). Nokia saw its market share drop from 51% to 27% and its profits decrease by 40% in 2010 alone.[12] Just as Nokia went from a paragon of innovation to an after thought in the mobile phone marketplace, so too can individuals suffer from the seduction of success. Like a smart investor knows when to sell and move on to the next idea, a smart innovator or entrepreneur recognizes that innovation and creative thinking must be continuous. In the rapidly moving 21st century it does not take long for others, competitors especially, to catch on and to catch up. Curiously, Nokia is now trying to resurrect itself by leading the way in wearable smart technology. You guessed it . . . they have introduced smart boots (e.g., calorie tracking, GPS navigation, gamified orienteering). So Nokia has gone from boots, to mobile phones, and back to boots.[13] Time will tell whether this innovation will be a success. Regardless, Nokia is resurrecting its innovate mindset, which in the long term bodes well for the company. To continuously evolve, and avoid extinction, you too need to continuously generate novel variations as an innovator and entrepreneur.

Expecting Guarantees

It is one thing to have the skill to generate many alternatives and quite another to have the mindset to pursue those ideas. Another way people give up their creative power is expecting guarantees before pursuing a goal, direction, activity, or idea. In such cases, individuals decide to move forward only when they feel a sense of assurance that their efforts will yield a particular outcome. Innovative and entrepreneurial ideas, because they are new, rarely come with guaranteed returns. If you want a guaranteed return, simply follow the ideas and pursuits that are well established. However, be prepared to accept meager to modest returns, because everyone has already bought into these ideas (and prepare yourself to be surpassed by others who are generating and proving the value of new ideas, which will dramatically and drastically reduce the value of established and soon to be out-of-date practices). Expecting guarantees stops innovation before it can get started. If the pioneers of aviation, the Wright brothers and Glenn Curtis, for example, had expected guarantees, airplanes and commercial flight would have never gotten off the ground. One of the benefits of not limiting your options is the fact that you spread risk across options. Only a small number of Thomas Edison's inventions resulted in viable businesses, but, fortunately, his creative mind led to the formulation of many options that yielded a few highly successful ventures.

Letting Other People's Approval
Be More Important Than Your Own

Teresa Amabile of the Harvard Business School has led a fascinating program of research exploring the conditions that undermine intrinsic motivation and, consequently, creativity. She discovered that when people believe they are being observed or evaluated, their ability to produce creative results drops significantly. They become preoccupied with the observers and therefore invest less creative effort into their work. By seeking or becoming preoccupied with others' approval, you give away your creative power. The risk here is that another person's approval may become more important than producing an idea that is pleasing and rewarding to you. An innovation study among architectural firms lends support to this argument. It was found that when architects did not strictly constrain themselves to the brief provided by the client, they were significantly more likely to receive industry awards for their creative designs.[14] Naturally, evaluation and feedback are valuable components of the creative process. The lesson here, especially at the beginning of a creative initiative, is not to limit your dreams and aspirations by becoming overly concerned about the expectations and perceptions of others.

Not Being Clear About What You Want

Karp, upon whose work we base our ideas about these self-imposed constraints, says that any change initiative must start with a clear view of what you want. Innovators and entrepreneurs are change leaders; when successful, their ideas enable organizations and industries to change and grow. As Karp so effectively argues, "Until you give yourself full permission to want what you want, and to want all of it, there is little likelihood that you'll give yourself permission to get it."[15] It is not enough to want, you must be clear about what you want. By *clear* we mean that you possess a vivid image of that which you wish to create or the desired future you want to bring into reality. Vague and idle dreams do not compel action. Robert Fritz, a filmmaker, author, and entrepreneur, provides an elegant description of the power of a clear vision.[16] When you have a clear vision of a desired future, it creates tension—that is, tension between your current reality and the desired future you have in mind. The productive way to relieve this tension is to make choices and pursue strategies that move you toward your vision. Without a clear vision, there is no compelling force that facilitates enlightened decision making and action. And it is important that the vision be clear. Vague aspirations do little to promote action. Wanting to successfully run a marathon is more forceful than a general desire to get into shape. As Steve Jobs said, "If you are working on something exciting that you really care about, you don't have to be pushed. The vision pulls you."[17]

We present these self-limiting behaviors to help you sustain your creative power. By describing each, we hope you have become more aware of how you might be undermining your creativity at its source—you. To get you started on the next step in your journey, we build on the last point, possessing a clear vision, and guide you through a creativity tool that will enable you to envision and tell your own future story.

To close the book, we will have you create an image of a desired future and then a plan to get there. To do so, we will have you use a tool called storyboarding. On a piece of paper, create two rows of three large boxes each, like a cartoon strip. In the last box, lower right, draw an image of your desired future (label this box "My Vision"). What do you want to be doing 3 to 5 years from now? What's your dream? Don't worry about artistic ability; stick figures and symbols are fine. Attempt to be very clear, adding as much detail as possible. What are you doing? Who is with you? What's your impact? Now go to the first box, upper left, and label this "Current Reality." In this box create an image of your current reality relative to your vision. Where are you now? Once completed, you will have four empty boxes in between your current reality and your vision. In these boxes draw, in chronological order, four milestones you will need to achieve to realize your vision. This is your story—now go make it happen!

Case Study
Repeatable Magic: Sergio Fajardo and the Transformation of Medellín, Colombia

Introduction

At a time when many citizens in Medellín, Colombia, were living under an umbrella of fear, crime, and narco trafficking–inspired violence, a creative, courageous, and discontented mathematics professor decided that writing opinion pieces for a newspaper asserting how things "should be" was not the most effective approach to bringing about transformational change. Rather, he took a leave of absence from his position at the University of the Andes to organize and facilitate a series of conversations between a growing group of socially committed, politically disenfranchised, action-oriented citizens who recognized that it was politicians who made the most crucial decisions in society. Indeed, the group had had vastly different backgrounds and perspectives, but in common, they knew that the only way to have their collective voice heard was to get themselves into elected office somehow.

A connector of people, Sergio Fajardo positioned himself to lead these conversations with engaged citizens from a wide range of backgrounds including business, education, and nongovernmental organizations. They would come to serve as a brain trust that would inform

(Continued)

(Continued)

and energize a soon-to-unfold campaign for elected office.[18] From 15 to 30 to 50 to almost 200 members before the election, participants met to diagnose, analyze, and explore problems and opportunities facing the city.

Next, the group decided that Sergio Fajardo should be the name on the top of the ticket, and, soon thereafter, Fajardo began walking the city of Medellín from end to end, engaging his fellow citizens in discussion and debate about the importance of education and to ask for their vote to become their mayor. With zero political experience to his name, Fajardo rallied his closest friends and colleagues to create an entirely new, independent political party, a party that would go on to win the mayorship of Medellín (January 2004–December 2007) and propel Fajardo to become the governor of Antioquia (January 2012–December 2015)—and he just might become the next president of Colombia.

You may recall from the chapter Sternberg and Lubart's investment theory of creativity whereby a creative person metaphorically "buys low," by rejecting ideas and behaviors currently popular and accepted in society, and instead chooses to come up with and champion his or her own, fresh ideas that run counter to the status quo, even in the face of great obstacles. The investment cycle is then completed when he or she "sells high" once the creative ideas have been "purchased" or embraced by others over time, at a creative premium. For Sergio Fajardo, buying low and selling high has been a way of life.

Home to 6.6 million people, the Antioquia region of Colombia and its capital city Medellín represent a bustling economy and a thriving incubator of people and ideas. But it wasn't always this way. In fact, Medellín was once known as the most violent city in the world, struggling with tragically high per capita homicide rates,[19] a struggling economy, and an international reputation as the cocaine capital of the world.[20]

The son of a prominent architect, Sergio Fajardo could have followed in his father's footsteps and inherited the family business. Instead, he fell in love with mathematics and decided to invest in his own education, a future that would diverge greatly from his familial roots.

With great discipline and work ethic, Fajardo earned the opportunity to attend graduate school at the Universidad de los Andes–Bogotá, but he did not stop there. During his studies, he decided to travel to the United States in 1978 to attend English-intensive summer courses at the University of Buffalo, no small task for a native Spanish speaker.

Fajardo's work ethic remained on display as he continued onward to complete his PhD at the University of Wisconsin–Madison. His fearlessness to learn new things was not limited to the academic arena, however. For example, after decades of conflict between the Colombian government and armed militia groups and narco-trafficking guerrillas, Fajardo was invited to attend a series of conflict resolution workshops in Medellín. These dialogues were facilitated by Roger Fisher and were known as the Commission for Facilitating Peace. Fisher was invited to facilitate these dialogues due to an international reputation he had established as an expert in conflict resolution through the Harvard Negotiation Project and also because of the strong reputation of his coauthored book (with William Ury) on the topic of negotiation, Getting to Yes.[21]

Fajardo was initially suspicious of the idea of a foreign facilitator—an American—who he thought might be at a disadvantage when trying to understand the dynamics, history, and culture of the conflict, someone who would come in and propose a very American, *10-easy-steps-to-peace* approach to navigating the deadly and materially destructive forces in play.

What happened next though perhaps defines Fajardo as a creative person and leader. Instead of allowing his presumptions about Fisher and the inherent challenges facing a foreign facilitator who dared enter a complex and contentious situation, Fajardo instead possessed the openness and courage to invite new thinking into his own thought process, and by acquiring new information, he would eventually change his own mind. Instead of allowing doubt to shape his workshop experience, he acquired a copy of Fisher's book and dedicated the time and energy to studying it before the workshop began! This way he would be prepared to not only understand the principled negotiation method Fisher would use to facilitate the workshop, but in so doing, he could also create even more value for the group as a note taker and translator for others. It paid off. Fajardo became a de facto leader in those important peace dialogues. Looking back, Fajardo indicated, "Roger Fisher helped me learn a lot; he helped me learn how to listen."[22]

Urban Design, Park Libraries, and a Power Company

Sitting across the table from leaders of Colombia's powerful public utilities company, Empresas Públicas de Medellín (EPM), the newly elected mayor listened intently as company planners, designers, and engineers presented a compelling vision to celebrate their 50th anniversary: the redevelopment of a highway and waterfront park that would run through an upper-middle-class neighborhood in the city. The team presented a detailed description of the aesthetic beauty that would be created with the project and lobbied for their months of hard work to proceed forward, as planned. Fajardo listened and took notes. He waited until the presentation ended, and, at that moment, he paused. He knew he would have one chance—that very moment—to ask a critical question and to then follow up on that question in a way that only a creative and courageous leader could. To the leaders and design team, Fajardo asked, "How much do you think this will cost?" About 60 million dollars, they replied, at which point Fajardo followed up and said, "60 million dollars? Are you sure?" They said, yes, they were sure. Fajardo replied, "Okay, with that money we are going to build schools in Medellín." The result: EPM changed its mind and instead of spending the $60 million on the park design, worked with Fajardo to redirect those resources to organize a competition for local architectural firms to imagine and construct *parques bibliotecas* (park libraries) and schools. Since then, a network of stunning parques bibliotecas has been constructed around Medellín, and citizens of the "most humble" circumstances now have architecturally stunning centers of learning to identify with. They can say, "I live near X library," and that orientation to a place has become a point of pride and a physical representation and recognition of the value of learning and education.[23]

The Power of Understanding Stakeholder Perspectives

Sergio Fajardo has always been a reader. He speaks fondly of the bookshelves in his childhood home, recalls doodling in the margins

(Continued)

(Continued)

of his book collection, keeps a wooden school chair from his youth in his gubernatorial office, and, in addition to the local and regional media, he reads the *New York Times* daily. Reading widely and being able to tap into broad perspectives on a wide range of issues has not only helped him to gain insights into stakeholder positions during key negotiations, but it has also forced him to develop tools to organize and make sense of this vast body of information. For example, inspired by his architect father, Fajardo began sketching out meetings and visualizing conversations. Not only has this habit allowed Fajardo to organize and manage the information that comes across his desk (and mind) on any given day, but it also led to an interesting revelation when he began using Twitter to help him communicate the sometimes complex affairs of governance to the people of Colombia (and the world).

Tweets, as you may be aware, are short messages deliberately constrained to 140 characters. Feeling limited, Fajardo developed a habit of sketching notes and images he wants to share, taking pictures of them, and then tweeting images of those handwritten notes (thereby overcoming the 140-character limit and also adding a personalized touch to his communications, which has resonated with his followers and helped him authentically connect with his constituents). As a result, followers on Twitter have gotten to know the voice of his Twitter account, and this approach has helped him to simplify (without trivializing) the important information he must share.

Organizing information to better understand diverse stakeholder perspectives has not only been helpful for Sergio Fajardo to communicate from one to many (via Twitter), but it has also been influential in critical negotiations and policies that have directly impacted the lives of Colombians. For example, in 2003, 868 paramilitary narco traffickers signed an agreement with the Colombian government to demobilize and to reintegrate back into society. Soon thereafter, Fajardo won the mayoral election of Medellín and would be expected to manage their reintegration process. A hotly contested issue, debate raged within communities, and, with no precedent to follow, Fajardo and his team faced the prospect of having to create an entirely new plan. That is, they had to develop a program to not only support the hundreds of individuals who had committed serious crimes so that they could be transitioned into leading healthy, productive, law-abiding lives, but also to understand and consider the broader perspectives of community members and organizations who would become their new neighbors.[24]

"From day zero, we said we are going to work with you transparently. We were learning and devising new alternatives; these guys come in and everyone knows they were former criminals; then someone says, 'How come my kid doesn't have anything to do, and this guy, who was a criminal, has all these subsidies?' And we said, she's right. So we created a new program for people who had never been part of the conflict to take advantage of some of the same programs and offerings we were allowing for the former criminals."[25]

"We were solving things by understanding," says Fajardo. "We always acted transparently, and that's what gives us power. We were open. We worked with everyone. We have to design everything on the move. We have the power of ingenuity."

Sustaining Power and Influence

From student, to teacher, to mayor, to governor, to Colombian presidential hopeful, Sergio Fajardo has been able to not only sustain but also grow his considerable influence as a creative change maker. One of the tools Fajardo has used to help achieve this extraordinary trajectory has been to develop himself into an exceptional communicator (recall his handwritten, personalized, and visualized tweets). Furthermore, Fajardo employs no speech writers; he prepares everything himself in the same way he used to prepare his lectures as a professor. Just as he used to get to know his students so that he could personalize their lecture experiences, Fajardo explains that he always tries to get a feel for a local place and the key issues facing citizens before developing a unique presentation or a speech for that audience. Specifically, he does this by connecting with the people there, being present with how the place looks and feels with all his senses, and understanding what the people are feeling. This, and not speech writers, informs what he will say.

"Remember me?" says a man on the street to Fajardo. As a political figure and leader who travels his country and the world, Fajardo meets many people, and remembering them all is not a realistic possibility. However, when someone approaches him in the streets he does not tell him, "No, I do not remember you. I'm sorry, I meet so many people." Instead, he says, "Tell me about the time that we met, of what we spoke about, and why it was memorable for you." He cites an example of a man who suggests that education could be the platform upon which he runs for mayor of Medellín. Fajardo smiles, thinking about the possibility that when that man is at home with his family at night and hears messages of "*Medellín, la mas educada*" (Medellín, the most educated) on the television, radio, and Internet, he says to his family, "See Fajardo and that education plan? I told him to do that. That was my idea."

Another communication technique had potentially saved Fajardo's life. Although he downplays the risk of holding office during earlier days of violent times in Colombia, he suggests that he does not feel fear, because he "never talks about a person"; instead of *naming names*, he has trained himself to describe, for example, what it means to be corrupt and to express to a community that "we cannot allow people who do these things to rule us." Instead of naming names and calling out murderers and criminals individually, he depersonalizes the conversations, creates distance from the actors themselves, and shifts the focus of the conversation toward the bigger ideas as opposed to the individuals involved.

Another way Fajardo sustains and grows influence is to celebrate examples of success achieved by others. For example, when he travels he speaks of a young boy who attends a public school in a small town that used to be notorious for its narco traffickers. Instead of discussing drugs, however, Fajardo speaks of this town and the young boy who lives there because the boy has won the Antioquian Knowledge Olympics and has earned the highest grades in the entire province of Antioquia!

Fajardo has also helped to celebrate others through a collaboration with his wife, Dr. Lucrecia

(Continued)

(Continued)

Ramirez-Restrepo, a psychiatrist and professor at the University of Antioquia, Medellín. Together, and in response to high rates of anorexia, bulimia, and other eating disorders in young Colombian women (17.7% affliction rate vs. 5% in Spain and 10.2% in the United States in 2003), Fajardo and his wife have reimagined the traditional role of beauty pageants and have instead replaced them with Most Talented Women's conferences. In addition, they have also helped young women reimagine their role in Colombian society through the creation and support of the Anorexia-Bulimia Prevention Network, Teen Pregnancy Prevention Network, Sexual Violence Prevention Network, and Medellín's Women of Academic Excellence Network.

Fajardo tells these stories and shares these examples to help others see themselves as being on a growth trajectory, to help people *feel* their potential future and to be excited to the point of motivation to take action toward that future and to seek out opportunity for themselves.

Closing

Homicide rates in Medellín in 2015 were the lowest in 40 years, GDP is booming, and the World Economic Forum in 2015 recognized the transformation of Medellín as one of the Top Ten Urban Innovations in the world. With these achievements to stand on, Dr. Sergio Fajardo, Medellín, and the region of Antioquia echo together the sounds of hope, not fear. Together they demonstrate what's possible when people work together to buy low and sell high, and as a result, their communities move forward, emboldened with the powerful messages of "the most beautiful for the most humble" and "the most educated."

Discussion Questions: Knowing

1. Sergio Fajardo's oft-heard quote, "The most beautiful for the most humble," suggests the restoration of personal dignity in regions that were riddled with fear and crime. Applying your understanding of investment theory, what would you surmise were the popular ideas and behaviors Fajardo rejected to address the crime in Medellín? What were the great obstacles he had to face to buy low? What compelled him to buy low? What aspects of the environment helped and hindered the ideas he put forth?

Application Questions: Doing

1. Do you recall the stakeholder questions listed in this chapter? Identify the stakeholders that Sergio Fajardo had to consider to bring about change, and answer the questions below:

o Who had an interest in his proposed action?

o Whose resistance would undermine success?

o Which individuals and groups had a clear role in this situation?

o Whose buy-in was necessary for success?

o Who was in a strong position to sway others' opinions of this idea?

2. Think of an idea that did not agree with your understanding of the world. (In Fajardo's case, it was initially an American, *10-easy-steps-to-peace* approach to navigating the deadly and materially destructive forces in play.) Putting at bay any judgments about this idea, what aspects do you consider to be advantages? How might you reframe your concerns so that you are compelled to consider this idea?

3. Graphic recording involves profound listening at various sensory levels. When faced with complexity, Fajardo sketches to organize and manage the information that comes across his desk (and mind) in any given day. Moreover, sketches help him to communicate the sometimes complex affairs of governance to the people of Colombia. What would a sketch of this case study look like to you? How does this compare to a sketch completed by a classmate?

Thinking Ahead: Being

Sergio Fajardo had no experience in politics. Virtually an unknown, he ran against seasoned politicians. Driven by his belief that transformational change was needed, he decided to make a difference. Taking Fajardo as an inspirational example, consider the following questions.

1. What are your beliefs that can position you as a creative asset in your organization or future organization?

2. What might be some creative-thinking habits that will help you to preserve these beliefs?

3. To fully embrace your creative power, review and make a list of all the concepts, tools, principles, and content from this book that you found particularly intriguing or useful.

4. Considering your responses to the first three items, create a personal manifesto or guiding statement that will always be there to support you through the challenges associated with organizational complexity, uncertainty, volatility, and ambiguity.

5. Using your thoughts and reactions to the previous items, revisit the vision you created for yourself in the final learning activity in this chapter—your storyboard. In what ways might you strengthen this story and personal vision by reflecting on these insights? Feel free to further refine the storyboard you created for the Being learning activity.

Notes

Introduction

1. *Bob Dylan becomes founding patron of the University of Auckland's Creative Thinking Research Project.* Retrieved January 24, 2015, from www.creativethinkingproject .org/bob-dylan-creative-laureate.

2. Ibid.

3. Dyson, J. (2009, October). James Dyson on encouraging creativity [Video]. *Wall Street Journal.* Retrieved February 13, 2016, from www.wsj.com/video/james-dyson-on-encouraging-creativity/7E45B9C0–2689–40BF-9191–740442FF6A42.html.

4. Franken, R. (1994). *Human motivation* (3rd ed.). Monterey, CA: Brooks/Cole.

5. World Economic Forum. (2016, January). *The future of jobs: Employment, skills and workforce strategy for the fourth industrial revolution.* Retrieved February 12, 2016, from www.weforum.org/reports/ the-future-of-jobs.

6. Infosys. (2016). *Amplifying human potential: Education and skills for the fourth industrial revolution.* Retrieved February 14, 2016, from www.experienceinfosys .com/humanpotential.

7. Datar, S. M., Garvin, D. A., & Cullen, P. G. (2010). *Rethinking the MBA: Business education at a crossroads* (p. 9). Boston: Harvard Business School.

8. The Association to Advance Collegiate Schools of Business. *Standard 9: Curriculum content is appropriate to general expectations for the degree program type and learning goals.* Retrieved January 25, 2015, from www.aacsb.edu/accreditation/standards/2013-business/learning-and-teaching/standard9.aspx.

9. Fillis, I., & Rentschler, R. (2010). The role of creativity in entrepreneurship. *Journal of Enterprising Culture, 18,* 49–81.

Chapter 1

1. Puccio, G. J. (2012, December). *Creativity as a life skill* (TEDx Gramercy). Retrieved February 15, 2016, from http://tedxtalks.ted.com/video/ Creativity-as-a-Life-Skill-Gera.

2. Roth, G., & Dicke, U. (2005). Evolution of the brain and intelligence. *Trends in Cognitive Science, 9,* 250–257.

3. Dunbar, R., Barrett, L., & Lycett, J. (2007). *Evolutionary psychology: A beginner's guide.* Oxford, UK: Oneworld.

4. Palmer, D. (2010). *Origins: Human evolution revealed.* London: Mitchell Beazley.

5. Morriss-Kay, G. M. (2010). The evolution of human artistic creativity. *Journal of Anatomy, 216,* 158–176.

6. Hunter, J. E., & Schmidt, F. L. (1996). Intelligence and job performance: Economic and social implications. *Psychology, Public Policy, and Law, 2,* 447–472. See also Williams, W. M., & Yang, L. T. (1999). Organizational creativity. In R. J. Sternberg (Ed.), *Handbook of creativity* (pp. 226–250). Cambridge, UK: Cambridge University Press.

7. Gabora, L., & Kaufman, S. C. (2010). Evolutionary approaches to creativity. In J. C. Kaufman & R. J. Sternberg (Eds.), *Cambridge handbook of creativity* (pp. 279–300). Cambridge, UK: Cambridge University Press.

8. Pringle, H. (2013). The origins of creativity. *Scientific American, 303*(3), 5–11.

9. Mithen, S. J. (1996). *The prehistory of the mind: A search for the origins of art, religion, and science.* London: Thames and Hudson.

10. Mithen, S. J. (2006). *The singing Neanderthals: The origins of music, language, mind and body.* Boston: Harvard University Press.

11. Gau, J., & Segaller, S. (1996). *Triumph of the nerds: The rise of accidental empires* [Documentary]. Oregon Public Television and PBS.

12. Carruthers, P. (2002). Human creativity: Its cognitive basis, its evolution, and its connections with childhood pretence. *British Journal for the Philosophy of Science, 53,* 225–249.

13. Ibid., p. 239.

14. Miller, G. (2000). *The mating mind: How sexual choice shaped the evolution of human nature.* London: Heinemann.

15. Nettle, D., & Clegg, H. (2006). Schizotypy, creativity and mating success in humans. *Proceedings of the Royal Society B: Biological Sciences, 273,* 611–615.

16. Carruthers, *Human creativity,* p. 240.

17. Morriss-Kay, *Evolution of human artistic creativity*, p. 174.

18. Darwin, C. (2003). *The origin of species: By means of natural selection of the preservation of favoured races in the struggle for life*. New York: Signet Classics.

19. Ibid., p. 111.

20. Emmons, H., & Alter, D. (2015). *Staying sharp: 9 keys for a youthful brain through modern science and ageless wisdom*. New York: Simon & Schuster.

21. Darwin, *Origin of species*, p. 43.

22. Collins, J. C., & Porras, J. I. (1994). *Built to last: Successful habits of visionary companies*. New York: HarperBusiness.

23. Trilling, B., & Fadel, C. (2009). *21st century skills: Learning for life in our times*. San Francisco: Jossey-Bass.

24. Richards, R. (Ed.). (2007). *Everyday creativity and new views of human nature*. Washington, DC: American Psychological Association.

25. Colvin, G. (2008). *Talent is overrated: What really separates world-class performers from everybody else*. New York: Penguin Group.

26. Gardner, H. (1993). *Creating minds: An anatomy of creativity seen through the lives of Freud, Picasso, Stravinsky, Eliot, Graham, and Gandhi*. New York: BasicBooks.

27. Amabile, T. M. (1987). The motivation to be creative. In S. G. Isaksen (Ed.), *Frontiers of creativity research: Beyond the basics* (pp. 222–254). Buffalo, NY: Bearly.

28. Carruthers, *Human creativity*.

29. BBC. (2012–2013). *The creative brain: How insight works* [Episode 8 of 17]. Retrieved August 29, 2013, from www.bbc.co.uk/programmes/b01rbynt.

30. Rogelberg, S. G., Scott, C., & Kello, J. (2007). The science and fiction of meetings. *MIT Sloan Management Review, 48*, 18–21.

31. Rao, L. (2010, February 11). The StartupBus: The true story of 12 strangers building three startups, getting real. *TechCrunch*. Retrieved January 10, 2015, from http://techcrunch.com/2010/02/11/the-startupbus-the-true-story-of-12-strangers-building-three-startups-getting-real.

32. Strauss, K., Chen, L., Close, K., Inverso, E., & Solomon, B. (2015). America's most promising companies. *Forbes*. Retrieved January 10, 2015, from www.forbes.com/most-promising-companies.

33. Bizannes, E. (2010, February 11). *The Startup Bus*. Retrieved January 10, 2015, from http://eliasbizannes.com/blog/2010/02/the-startup-bus.

Chapter 2

1. Davis, G. A. (1986). *Creativity is forever* (2nd ed.). Dubuque, IA: Kendall/Hunt.

2. Adler, J., & Lawler, A. (2012, June). How the chicken conquered the world. *Smithsonian*, 40–47.

3. Darwin, C. (2003). *The origin of species: By means of natural selection of the preservation of favoured races in the struggle for life*. New York: Signet Classics. p. 252.

4. Carruthers, P. (2002). Human creativity: Its cognitive basis, its evolution, and its connections with childhood pretence. *British Journal for the Philosophy of Science, 53*, 225–249.

5. Kim, K. H. (2008). Meta-analysis of the relationship of creative achievement to both IQ and divergent thinking scores. *Journal of Creative Behavior, 42*, 106–130.

6. Bronson, P., & Merryman, A. (2010, July 7). The creativity crisis: For the first time, research shows that American creativity is declining. What went wrong—and how we can fix it. *Newsweek*, 44–50. See also Kim, *Meta-analysis*.

7. Zaccaro, S. J., Mumford, M. D., Connelly, M. S., Marks, M. A., & Gilbert, J. A. (2000). Assessment of leader problem-solving capabilities. *Leadership Quarterly, 11*, 37–64.

8. Kim, *Meta-analysis*.

9. Ames, M., & Runco, M. A. (2005). Predicting entrepreneurship from ideation and divergent thinking. *Creativity and Innovation Management, 14*, 311–315.

10. Wolf, K. M., & Mieg, H. A. (2010). Cognitive determinants of the success of inventors: Complex problem solving and deliberate use of divergent and convergent thinking. *European Journal of Cognitive Psychology, 22*, 443–462.

11. Walczyk, J. J., Runco, M. A., Tripp, S. M., & Smith, C. E. (2008). The creativity of lying: Divergent thinking and ideational correlates of the resolution of social dilemmas. *Creativity Research Journal, 20*, 328–342.

12. Pannells, T. C., & Claxton, A. F. (2008). Happiness, creative ideation, and locus of control. *Creativity Research Journal, 20*, 67–71.

13. Kim, K. H. (2011). The creativity crisis: The decrease in creative thinking scores on the Torrance Tests of Creative Thinking. *Creativity Research Journal, 23,* 285–295.

14. Asch, S. E. (1940). Studies in the principles of judgments and attitudes: II. Determination of judgments by group and by ego-standards. *Journal of Social Psychology, 12,* 433–465. See also Asch, S. E. (1956). Studies of independence and conformity: I. A minority of one against a unanimous majority. *Psychological Monographs I, 70,* 1–70.

15. Dunbar, R., Barrett, L., & Lycett, J. (2007). *Evolutionary psychology.* Oxford, UK: Oneworld. pp. 34–35.

16. Adobe. (2012, April). *Study reveals global creativity gap: Universal concern that creativity is suffering at work and school.* Retrieved September 2, 2013, from www.adobe.com/aboutadobe/pressroom/press releases/201204/042312AdobeGlobalCreativity Study.html.

17. Standfield, L. (2012, October). *School exams "stifle children's creativity."* Retrieved September 6, 2013, from www.parentdish.co.uk/2012/10/08/school-exams-stifle-childrens-creativity.

18. *Steve Jobs 1995 interview with Steve Morrow.* Retrieved August 29, 2013, from http://blog-next .learnboost.com/steve-jobs-on-education.

19. Damon, W. (2014). *A nation of entrepreneurs?* Retrieved May 27, 2016, from www.hoover.org/research/nation-entrepreneurs.

20. Runco, M. A. (2007). *Creativity: Theories and themes.* Boston: Elsevier.

21. Ravitch, D. (2010). *The death and life of the great American school system: How testing and choice are undermining education.* New York: Basic Books. p. 108.

22. Estrin, J. (2009). *Closing the innovation gap: Reigniting the spark of creativity in a global economy.* New York: McGraw-Hill. p. 221.

23. Ackoff, R. L., & Vergara, E. (1988). Creativity in problem solving and planning. In R. L. Kuhn (Ed.), *Handbook for creative and innovative managers* (pp. 77–89). New York: McGraw-Hill.

24. Colvin, G. (2008). *Talent is overrated: What really separates world-class performers from everybody else.* New York: Portfolio.

25. *Steve Jobs early TV appearance.* Retrieved September 8, 2013, from www.youtube.com/watch?v=FzDBi-UemCSY.

26. Ericsson, K. A., Prietula, M. J., & Cokely, E. T. (2007, July-August). The making of an expert. *Harvard Business Review, 85,* 114–121, 193.

27. Colvin, *Talent is overrated.*

28. Ibid., p. 70.

29. Colvin, *Talent is overrated.*

30. Trilling, B., & Fadel, C. (2009). *21st century skills: Learning for life in our times.* San Francisco: Jossey-Bass.

31. Heffernan, V. (2013, August 7). *Education needs a digital-age upgrade.* Retrieved September 10, 2013, from http://opinionator.blogs.nytimes.com/2011/08/07/education-needs-a-digital-age-upgrade/?_r=0.

32. Nisen, M. (2013, January 28). *Robot economy could cause up to 75% unemployment.* Retrieved September 10, 2013, from www.businessinsider.com/50-percent-unemployment-robot-economy-2013-1.

33. Frey, C. B., & Osborne, M. A. (2013). *The future of employment: How susceptible are jobs to computerisation?* Retrieved July 14, 2014, from www .oxfordmartin.ox.ac.uk/downloads/academic/The_Future_of_Employment.pdf.

34. National Center on Education and the Economy. (2008). *Tough choices or tough times: The report on the new commission on the skills of the American workforce.* San Francisco: Wiley. p. 23.

35. Wagner, T. (2008). *The global achievement gap: Why even our best schools don't teach the new survival skills our children need—and what we can do about it.* New York: Basic Books. p. 38.

36. Adobe. (2014, September). *Seeking creative candidates: Hiring for the future.* Retrieved December 19, 2015, from www.adobe.com/content/dam/Adobe/en/education/pdfs/creative-candidates-study-0914.pdf.

37. Otani, A. (2015, January). *These are the skills you need if you want to be headhunted.* Retrieved July 27, 2015, from www.bloomberg.com/news/articles/2015-01-05/the-job-skills-that-recruiters-wish-you-had.

38. Casner-Lotto, J., Rosenblum, E., & Wright, M. (2009). *The ill-prepared U.S. workforce: Exploring the challenges of employer-provided workforce readiness training.* New York: The Conference Board.

39. Scott, G., Leritz, L. E., & Mumford, M. D. (2004). The effectiveness of creativity training: A quantitative review. *Creativity Research Journal, 16,* 361–388.

40. Rickards, T. (1990). *Creativity and problem-solving at work.* Aldershot, UK: Gower.

41. Gregory, S. (2013, September 16). It's time to pay college athletes. *Time,* 38–42.

42. Rickards, *Creativity and problem-solving,* p. 134.

43. American Medical Association. *Becoming a physician.* Retrieved November 11, 2016, from www.ama-assn.org/ama/pub/education-careers/becoming-physician.page?.

44. Jefferson Health. *About Stephen K. Klasko, MD, MBA.* Retrieved November 11, 2016, from http://leadership.jefferson.edu/about.

45. M. Hoad, personal communication, January 29, 2016.

46. Klasko, S. J. *What healthcare will look like in 2020.* TEDxPhiladelphia. Retrieved November 11, 2016, from www.youtube.com/watch?v=esugL07XANg.

47. M. Hoad, personal communication, January 29, 2016.

48. Klasko, *What healthcare will look like.*

49. M. Hoad, personal communication, January 29, 2016.

50. JeffConnect mobile application. Retrieved November 11, 2016, from https://jeffconnect.org/landing.htm.

Chapter 3

1. Mozart, W. A. (1985). A letter. In B. Ghiselin (Ed.), *The creative process: Reflections on invention in the arts and sciences* (pp. 34–35). Berkeley, CA: University of California Press.

2. Ibid., p. 35.

3. Ward, T. B., & Kolomyts, Y. (2010). Cognition and creativity. In J. Kaufman & R. J. Sternberg (Eds.), *Cambridge handbook of creativity* (pp. 93–112). Cambridge, UK: Cambridge University Press.

4. Kaufman, A., Kornilov, S. A., Bristol, A. S., Tan, M., & Grigorenko, E. L. (2010). The neurobiological foundation of creative cognition. In J. Kaufman & R. J. Sternberg (Eds.), *Cambridge handbook of creativity* (pp. 216–232). Cambridge, UK: Cambridge University Press.

5. Ibid.

6. Talbot, R. J. (1997). Taking style on board. *Creativity and Innovation Management, 6,* 177–184.

7. Green, M., & Williams, L. M. (1999). Schizotypy and creativity as effects of reduced cognitive inhibitions. *Personality and Individual Differences, 27,* 263–276.

8. Ghadirian, A. M., Gregoire, P., & Kosmidis, H. (2001). Creativity and the evolution of psychopathologies. *Creativity Research Journal, 13,* 145–148.

9. Rothenberg, A. (2006). Essay: Creativity—The healthy muse. *Lancet, 368,* 8–9.

10. Plucker, J. A., Beghetto, R. A., & Dow, G. T. (2004). Why isn't creativity more important to educational psychologists? Potential, pitfalls, and future directions in creativity research. *Educational Psychologist, 39,* 83–97.

11. Emmons, H., & Alter, D. (2015). *Staying sharp: 9 keys for a youthful brain through modern science and ageless wisdom.* New York: Touchstone.

12. Burkus, D. (2014). *The myths of creativity: The truth about how innovative companies and people generate great ideas.* San Francisco: Jossey-Bass.

13. Talbot, R. J. (1993). Creativity in the organizational context: Implications for training. In S. G. Isaksen, M. C. Murdock, R. L. Firestien, & D. J. Treffinger (Eds.), *Nurturing and developing creativity: The emergence of a discipline* (pp. 177–214). Norwood, NJ: Ablex.

14. Gallo, C. (2013, August 16). *10 powerful quotes from the Steve Jobs movie and what they teach us about leadership.* Retrieved July 14, 2014, from www.forbes.com/sites/carminegallo/2013/08/16/10-powerful-quotes-from-the-steve-jobs-movie-and-what-they-teach-us-about-leadership.

15. Jobs, S. (2005). *Stanford commencement speech.* Retrieved July 15, 2014, from www.youtube.com/watch?v=D1R-jKKp3NA.

16. Schrager, J. (2013, August 19). *Take a cue from Steve Jobs's playbook.* Retrieved July 14, 2014, from http://blogs.wsj.com/experts/2013/08/19/james-schrager-take-a-cue-from-steve-jobss-playbook.

17. MacKinnon, D. W. (1978). *In search of human effectiveness: Identifying and developing creativity.* Buffalo, NY: Creative Education Foundation.

18. Csíkszentmihályi, M. (1996). *Creativity: Flow and the psychology of discovery and invention.* New York: HarperPerennial.

19. Bilton, N. (2011, November 18). One on one: Walter Isaacson, biographer of Steve Jobs. Bits. *New York Times*. Retrieved July 14, 2014, from http://bits.blogs.nytimes.com/2011/11/18/one-on-one-walter-isaacson-biographer-of-steve-jobs/?_php=true&_type=blogs&_r=0.

20. Ward & Kolmyts, *Cognition and creativity*.

21. Murray, D. K. (2009). *Borrowing brilliance: The six steps to business innovation by building on the ideas of others*. New York, NY: Gotham Books.

22. Grahame-Smith, S. (2010). *Abraham Lincoln: Vampire hunter*. New York: Grand Central.

23. Murray, *Borrowing brilliance*.

24. Amabile, T. M. (1983). The motivation to create. In S. G. Isaksen (Ed.), *Frontiers of creativity research: Beyond the basics* (pp. 223–254). Buffalo, NY: Bearly Limited.

25. Jobs, S. (2011, October 7). *Iconic quotes will keep him alive*. Retrieved July 16, 2014, from http://news.dice.com/2011/10/07/steve-jobs-iconic-quotes-will-keep-him-alive.

26. Csíkszentmihályi, M. (1990). *Flow: The psychology of optimal experience*. New York: HarperPerennial.

27. Wagner, T. (2012). *Creating innovators: The making of young people who will change the world*. New York: Scribner.

28. Amabile, T., & Kramer S. (2011). *The progress principle: Using small wins to ignite joy, engagement, and creativity at work*. Boston: Harvard Business Review Press.

29. Jobs, *Stanford commencement speech*.

30. Ekvall, G. (1996). Organizational climate for creativity and innovation. *European Journal of Work and Organizational Psychology, 5,* 105–123.

31. Ibid.

32. Ekvall, G. (1991). The organizational culture of idea management: A creative climate for the management of ideas. In J. Henry & D. Walker (Eds.), *Managing innovation* (pp. 73–79). Newbury Park, CA: Sage.

33. Puccio, G. J., Mance, M., & Murdock, M. C. (2011). *Creative leadership: Skills that drive change* (2nd ed.). Thousand Oaks, CA: Sage.

34. Amabile & Kramer, *Progress principle*.

35. Ibid., p. 54.

36. Dobrev, S. (2002). Entrepreneurs: Will they stay or will they go? Understanding entrepreneurship requires a look at both context and individual. *Capital Ideas, 3*(3). Retrieved October 31, 2013, from www.chicagobooth.edu/capideas/win02/entrepreneurs.html.

37. Kounios, J. (2013, May). *Neural precursors to creative insight. Conversations in the disciplines: A conference on creativity and innovation*. University at Buffalo, New York.

38. Amabile & Kramer, *Progress principle*, p. 52.

39. VanGundy, A. B. (1984). *Managing group creativity: A modular approach to problem solving*. New York: AMACOM.

40. Rotter, J. B. (1966). Generalized expectancies for internal versus external control of reinforcement. *Psychological Monographs: General and Applied, 80*(1), 1–28.

41. Roy, R., & Gupta, S. (2012). Locus of control and organizational climate as predictors of managerial creativity. *Asia-Pacific Journal of Management Research and Innovation, 8,* 525–534.

42. Estay, C., Durrieu, F., & Akhter, M. (2013). Entrepreneurship: From motivation to start-up. *Journal of International Entrepreneurship, 11,* 243–267.

43. MacKinnon, *In search of human effectiveness*.

44. Liu, D. N., & Shih, H. T. (2013, December 4). *The transformation of Taiwan's status within the production and supply chain in Asia*. Retrieved on August 29, 2016, from www.brookings.edu/opinions/the-transformation-of-taiwans-status-within-the-production-and-supply-chain-in-asia.

45. *Hackerspace*. Retrieved August 29, 2016, from https://en.wikipedia.org/wiki/Hackerspace.

46. G. Imreh, personal communication, February 10, 2016.

Chapter 4

1. Janszen, F. (2000). *The age of innovation: Making business creativity a competence, not a coincidence*. London: Prentice Hall.

2. Ibid., p. 3.

3. Barsh, J., Capozzi, M. M., & Davidson, J. (2008). Leadership and innovation. *McKinsey Quarterly, 1,* 37–47.

4. McKinsey & Company. (2010, August). *Innovation and commercialization, 2010: Global survey results*. Retrieved November 12, 2013, from www.mckinsey

.com/insights/innovation/innovation_and_
commercialization_2010_mckinsey_global_
survey_results.

5. Vardis, H., & Selden, G. L. (2008). A report card on
innovation: How companies and business schools are
dealing with it. In G. J. Puccio, C. Burnett, J. F. Cabra,
J. M. Fox, S. Keller-Mathers, M. C. Murdock, &
J. Yudess (Eds.), *An international conference on creativity
and innovation management: Conference proceedings—
Book 2* (pp. 239–258). Buffalo, New York.

6. Rosenberg, M. (2008, March 17). *Innovation and
creativity—beyond the mission statement.* Retrieved
November 17, 2016, from http://dns2.mediatecpub
.com/articles/view/innovation_and_creativity_
beyond_the_mission_statement.

7. *Remarks by the president in the State of the Union
Address.* (2013, February). Retrieved November
23, 2016, from www.whitehouse.gov/the-press-
office/2013/02/12/remarks-president-state-union-
address.

8. Barsh et al., *Leadership and innovation*, p. 37.

9. Colvin, G. (2008). *Talent is overrated: What really
separates world-class performers from everybody else.*
New York: Portfolio. pp. 146–147.

10. Sherman, E. (2010, September). *Blockbuster's
plight exposes a broader corporate creativity problem*
[Update]. CBS MoneyWatch. Retrieved November
23, 2016, from www.cbsnews.com/news/block
busters-plight-exposes-a-broader-corporate-
creativity-problem-update. See also Chong, C.
(2015). *Blockbuster's CEO once passed up a chance to buy
Netflix for only $50 million.* Retrieved November 23,
2016, from www.businessinsider.com/blockbuster-
ceo-passed-up-chance-to-buy-netflix-for-50-
million-2015-7.

11. Janszen, *Age of innovation*, p. 7.

12. Soo, C., Devinney, T., Midgley, D., & Deering, A.
(2002). Knowledge management: Philosophy,
processes, and pitfalls. *California Management
Review, 44,* 129–150.

13. Andrew, J. P., & Sirkin, H. L. (2006). *Payback:
Reaping the rewards of innovation.* Boston: Harvard
Business School Press.

14. Ibid., p. x.

15. Soo et al., *Knowledge management*, p. 145.

16. Carnevale, A. P., Gainer, L. J., & Meltzer, A. S.
(1990). *Workplace basics: The essential skills
employers want.* San Francisco: Jossey-Bass;
Trilling, B., & Fadel, C. (2009). *21st century
skills: Learning for life in our times.* San Francisco:
Jossey-Bass; Davies, A., Fidler, D., & Gorbis, M.
(2011). *Future work skills 2020.* Palo Alto, CA:
Institute for the Future for the University of
Phoenix Research Institute. Retrieved November
17, 2016, from www.iftf.org/uploads/media/
SR-1382A_UPRI_future_work_skills_sm.pdf;
IBM. (2012a). *Connected generation: Perspectives
from tomorrow's leaders in a digital world. Insights
from the 2012 IBM Global Student Study.* IBM
Institute for Business Value. Retrieved November
17, 2016, from www-935.ibm.com/services/us/
gbs/thoughtleadership/ibv-student-study.html;
IBM. (2012b). *Leading through connections: Insights
from the Global Chief Executive Officer Study.* IBM
Institute for Business Value. Retrieved November
17, 2016, from www-935.ibm.com/services/
multimedia/anz_ceo_study_2012.pdf; Otani, A.
(2015, January). *These are the skills you need if
you want to be headhunted.* Retrieved July 27,
2015, from www.bloomberg.com/news/articles/
2015-01-05/the-job-skills-that-recruiters-wish-
you-had; World Economic Forum. (2016, January).
*The future of jobs: Employment, skills and workforce
strategy for the fourth industrial revolution.* Retrieved
February 12, 2016, from www.weforum.org/
reports/the-future-of-jobs.

17. Davies, A., Fidler, D., & Gorbis, M. (2011). *Future
work skills 2020.* Palo Alto, CA: Institute for the
Future for the University of Phoenix Research
Institute. p. 9.

18. Marshall, A., & Kinser, C. (2012). *Connected generation: Perspectives from tomorrow's leaders in a digital
world: Insight from the 2012 IBM Global Student Survey.*
Somers, NY: IBM Global Business Services. p. 10.

19. Fillis, I., & Rentschler, R. (2010). The role of creativity in entrepreneurship. *Journal of Enterprising
Culture, 18,* 49–81.

20. Ibid.

21. Baron, R. A. (1998). Cognitive mechanisms in
entrepreneurship: Why and when entrepreneurs
think differently than other people. *Journal of
Business Venturing, 13,* 275–294.

22. Estay, C., Durrieu, F., & Akhter, M. (2014).
Entrepreneurship: From motivation to start-up.

Journal of International Entrepreneurship, 11, 243–267.

23. IBM. (2010). *Capitalising on complexity: Insights from the Global Chief Executive Officer (CEO) Study.* Portsmouth, UK: IBM United Kingdom Limited.

24. Elenkov, D. S., & Manev, I. M. (2009). Senior expatriate leadership's effects on innovation and the role of cultural intelligence. *Journal of World Business, 44,* 357–369.

25. Mumford, M. D., Zaccaro, S. J., Harding, F. D., Jacobs, T. O., & Fleishman, E. A. (2000). Leadership skills for a changing world: Solving complex problems. *Leadership Quarterly, 11,* 11–35.

26. Puccio, G. J., Mance, M., & Murdock, M. C. (2011). *Creative leadership: Skills that drive change* (2nd ed.). Thousand Oaks, CA: Sage.

27. Ibid.

28. Guilford, J. P. (1968). *Intelligence, creativity and their educational implications.* San Diego, CA: Knapp. p. 12.

29. Csíkszentmihályi, M. (1990). *Flow: The psychology of optimal experience.* New York: HarperPerennial.

30. Rogers, C. (1959). Towards a theory of creativity. In H. H. Anderson (Ed.), *Creativity and its cultivation* (pp. 69–82). New York: Harper.

31. Davis, G. (1986). *Creativity is forever* (2nd ed.). Dubuque, IA: Kendall-Hunt. p. 2.

32. Seligman, M. E. P. (1998). *Learned optimism* (2nd ed.). New York: Pocket Books.

33. Emmons, H., & Alter, D. (2015). *Staying sharp: 9 keys for a youthful brain through modern science and ageless wisdom.* New York: Touchstone.

34. Bernstein, M. (1988). *Charles F. Kettering—A self-starter who gave us the self-starter.* Retrieved on November 23, 2016, from www.daytoninnovationlegacy.org/kettering.html.

35. Lewin, K. (1947). Frontier in group dynamics II. Channels of group life; social planning and action research. *Human Relations, 1,* 143–153.

36. Currey, M. (2013). *Daily rituals: How artists work.* New York: Alfred A. Knopf.

37. Ibid.

38. Illinois Mathematics and Science Academy. *IMSA's mission and beliefs.* Retrieved on August 29, 2016, from www.imsa.edu/discover/profile/mission_and_beliefs.

39. K. Wild, personal communication, June 12, 2016.

40. *Keen IO Secures $14.7M in Series B financing to accelerate the adoption of its leading cloud analytics platform and intelligence API.* BusinessWire. Retrieved on August 29, 2016, from www.businesswire.com/news/home/20160629005355/en/Keen-IO-Secures-14.7M-Series-Financing-Accelerate.

41. Kinni, T. (2016, June 8). *My company is my therapist.* Strategy+Business. Retrieved on August 29, 2016, from www.strategy-business.com/blog/My-Company-Is-My-Therapist?gko=5540b.

42. Kegan, R., Laskow Lahey, L., Miller, M. L., Fleming, A., & Helsing, D. *An everyone culture: Becoming a deliberately developmental organization.* Retrieved on August 29, 2016, from https://hbr.org/product/an-everyone-culture-becoming-a-deliberately-developmental-organization/14259-HBK-ENG.

43. Wild, personal communication, June 12, 2016.

44. *Lead with your strengths.* Gallup Strengths Center. Retrieved on August 29, 2016, from www.gallupstrengthscenter.com.

45. *Team.* Keen IO. Retrieved on August 29, 2016, from https://keen.io/team.

46. Wild, personal communication, June 12, 2016.

47. Ibid.

48. Ibid.

Chapter 5

1. Thum, M. (2014). *The 3 most inspirational Zen stories.* Retrieved July 19, 2014, from http://myrkothum.hubpages.com/hub/3zenstories.

2. *History of the graphical user interface.* (2014, February). Wikipedia. Retrieved February 14, 2014, from http://en.wikipedia.org/wiki/History_of_the_graphical_user_interface.

3. Estrin, J. (2015, August). *Kodak's first digital moment.* Retrieved November 23, 2016, from http://lens.blogs.nytimes.com/2015/08/12/kodaks-first-digital-moment/?_r=0. See also *Digital camera inventor explains how technology took down Kodak.* (2013, May). Huffington Post. Retrieved February 14, 2014, from www.huffingtonpost.com/2013/05/21/digital-camera-inventor-kodak-bankruptcy_n_3315622.html.

4. *Eastman Kodak.* (2014, February). Wikipedia. Retrieved February 14, 2014, from http://en

.wikipedia.org/wiki/History_of_the_graphical_user_interface.

5. Collins, J. C., & Porras, J. I. (1994). *Built to last: Successful habits of visionary companies*. New York: HarperCollins.

6. Scott, G. M., Leritz, L. E., & Mumford, M. D. (2004). The effectiveness of creativity training: A meta-analysis. *Creativity Research Journal, 16,* 361–388.

7. Kim, K. H. (2011). Creativity crisis: The decrease in creativity scores on the Torrance Tests of Creative Thinking. *Creativity Research Journal, 23,* 285–295.

8. Scott et al., *Effectiveness of creativity training*.

9. Ibid., p. 382.

10. Grivas, C., & Puccio, G. J. (2012). *The innovative team*. San Francisco: Jossey-Bass.

11. Brown, T. (2009). *Change by design: How design thinking transforms organizations and inspires innovation*. New York: Harper Business. See also Kumar, V. (2013). *101 design methods*. Hoboken, NJ: Wiley.

12. Jobs, S. (n.d.). *Steve Jobs quotable quote*. Retrieved on November 28, 2016, from www.goodreads.com/quotes/457177-design-is-not-just-what-it-looks-like-and-feels.

13. Parnes, S. J., & Noller, R. B. (1997). *Guide to creative action*. New York: Scribner.

14. Parnes, S. J., & Meadow, A. (1959). Effects of brainstorming instruction on creative problem solving by trained and untrained subjects. *Journal of Educational Psychology, 50,* 171–176.

15. Gabora, L., & Kaufman, S. B. (2010). Evolutionary approaches to creativity. In J. C. Kaufman & R. J. Sternberg (Eds.), *The Cambridge handbook of creativity* (pp. 279–300). Cambridge, UK: Cambridge University Press. p. 286.

16. Ibid., p. 285.

17. Kelley, T., & Kelley, D. (2012, December). Reclaim your creative confidence: How to get over the fears that block your best ideas. *Harvard Business Review*. Retrieved on May 27, 2016, from https://hbr.org/2012/12/reclaim-your-creative-confidence.

18. Osborn, A. F. (1953). *Applied imagination: Principles and procedures of creative problem-solving*. New York: Scribner.

19. Dyson, J. (2014, January 24). *Failures are interesting*. Science Friday. Retrieved on May 27, 2016, from www.sciencefriday.com/segments/james-dyson-failures-are-interesting.

20. Collins & Porras, *Built to last*, p. 140.

21. Ibid., p. 148.

22. Scott et al., *Effectiveness of creativity training*.

23. Brady, D. (2012, October 26). Julie Corbett: Bottles inspired by the iPhone. *Bloomberg Businessweek*. Retrieved on November 23, 2016, from www.bloomberg.com/news/articles/2012-10-25/julie-corbett-bottles-inspired-by-the-iphone.

24. Murray, D. K. (2009). *Borrowing brilliance: The six steps to business innovation by building on the ideas of others*. New York: Gotham. p. 172.

25. Morsani College of Medicine, Department of Molecular Pharmacology and Physiology. *Dr. Dominic D'Agostino*. Retrieved September 5, 2016, from http://health.usf.edu/medicine/mpp/faculty/24854/Dominic-DAgostino.aspx.

26. *Most weight squatted in twenty-four hours*. Retrieved September 5, 2016, from www.youtube.com/watch?v=ZV5A8Oj8_ME.

27. *Starving cancer: Dominic D'Agostino*. TEDxTampaBay. Retrieved September 5, 2016, from www.youtube.com/watch?v=3fM9o72ykww.

28. *Otto Warburg—Biographical*. Nobelprize.org. Retrieved September 6, 2016, from www.nobelprize.org/nobel_prizes/medicine/laureates/1931/warburg-bio.html.

29. Boston College, Morrissey College of Arts and Sciences. *Dr. Thomas Seyfried*. Retrieved September 6, 2016, from www.bc.edu/schools/cas/biology/facadmin/seyfried.html.

30. D'Agostino D. P., Olson J. E., & Dean J. B. (2009). Acute hyperoxia increases lipid peroxidation and induces plasma membrane blebbing in human U87 glioblastoma cells. *Neuroscience, 159*(3), 1011–1022.

31. Dominic D'Agostino, personal communication, December 17, 2014.

32. Schwagler, N. (2013, February 5). *USF disease warriors explore new use for research*. 83 Degrees. Retrieved September 5, 2016, from www.83degreesmedia.com/features/researchers020513.aspx.

Chapter 6

1. Spector, R., & Richardson, J. (2000). *Amazon.com: Get big fast*. New York: Harper Business.

2. Ibid.

3. Mithen, S. (1996). *The prehistory of the mind: The cognitive origins of art and science*. New York: Thames and Hudson.

4. Suri, J. F. (2005). *Thoughtless acts: Observations on intuitive design*. San Francisco: Chronicle Books.

5. Trifilm. (2009, April 22). *A Trifilm story: The Q-Drum* [Video file]. Retrieved November 18, 2016, from www.youtube.com/watch?v=XQ_n5y3-Xnk.

6. Klein, G. (2013). *Seeing what others don't: The remarkable ways we gain insights*. New York: PublicAffairs.

7. Gopnik, A., Meltzoff, A. N., & Khul, P. (1999). *The scientist in the crib*. New York: Perennial.

8. Ibid.

9. Langer, E. J. (1989). *Mindfulness*. Reading, MA: Addison-Wesley. See also Langer, E. J. (2009). *Counterclockwise: Mindful health and the power of possibility*. New York: Random House.

10. Garcia, T. (2016, May 3). *Amazon accounted for 60% of U.S. online sales growth in 2015*. MarketWatch. Retrieved November 18, 2016, from www.marketwatch.com/story/amazon-accounted-for-60-of-online-sales-growth-in-2015-2016-05-03.

11. Chaplin, J. (2007). *The first scientific American: Benjamin Franklin and the pursuit of genius*. New York: Basic Books.

12. Navarro, J. (2010). *Louder than words: Take your career from average to exceptional with the hidden power of nonverbal intelligence*. New York: HarperCollins.

13. Navarro. J. (2010, October 13). Benjamin Franklin & nonverbal communications: Lessons on nonverbal communications from America's foremost entrepreneur. *Psychology Today* (para. 5).

14. Spradley, J. P. (1980). *Participant observation*. New York: Holt, Rinehart and Winston.

15. Ibid.

16. Hardy, S. (2006, November 15). *Creative Generalist Q&A: Jane Fulton Suri*. Creative Generalist. Retrieved November 18, 2016, from http://creativegeneralist.com/2006/11/creative-generalist-qa-jane-fulton-suri.

17. Dewey, J. (1991). *How we think*. Buffalo, NY: Prometheus. (Original work published 1910) p. 94.

18. Getzels, J. W., & Csíkszentmihályi, M. (1976). *The creative vision: A longitudinal study of problem finding in art*. New York: Wiley.

19. Scott, G., Leritz, L. E., & Mumford, M. D. (2004). The effectiveness of creativity training: A quantitative review. *Creativity Research Journal, 16,* 361–388.

20. Dweck, C. (n.d.). *Carol Dweck*. Mindset. Retrieved November 18, 2016, from http://mindsetonline.com/abouttheauthor.

21. Dweck, C. (2006). *Mindset: The new psychology of success*. New York: Random House. p. 16.

22. Ibid., p. 11.

23. Dyer, J. H., Gregersen, H. B., & Christensen, C. M. (2009). The innovator's DNA. *Harvard Business Review, 87*(12), 60–67.

24. Lang, A. (2012). *The power of why*. Toronto, Canada: HarperCollins.

25. Torrance, E. P. (1965). Scientific views of creativity and factors affecting its growth. *Daedalus*, 663.

26. Ibid.

27. Bronson, P., & Merryman, A. (2010, July 10). The creativity crisis. *Newsweek*.

28. Torrance, E. P. (1995). *Why fly? A philosophy of creativity*. Norwood, NJ: Greenwood.

29. Ibid., p. 13.

30. Ibid., p. 119.

31. May, R. (1975). *The courage to create*. New York: Norton. p. 13.

32. Marsh, D. R., Schroeder, D. G., Dearden, K. A., Sternin, J., & Sternin, M. (2004). The power of positive deviance. *British Medical Journal, 329*(7475), 1177.

33. Spreitzer, G. M., & Sonenshein, S. (2004). Toward the construct definition of positive deviance. *American Behavioral Scientist, 47*(6), 828–847.

34. Merck. *Mission*. Retrieved November 28, 2016, from www.merck.com/about/home.html.

35. Christensen, C. M., Cook, S., & Hall, T. (2006, January 16). What customers want from your products. *Harvard Business School: Working Knowledge*. Retrieved November 18, 2016, from http://hbswk.hbs.edu/item/5170.html.

36. Oestreicher, K. G. (2011). Segmentation & the jobs-to-be-done theory: A conceptual approach to explaining product failure. *Journal of Marketing Development and Competitiveness, 5*(2), 103–121.

37. Dweck, *Mindset*.

38. Bennett, P. (2005, July). *Paul Bennett: Design is in the details* [Video file]. TED. Retrieved November 18, 2016, from www.ted.com/talks/paul_bennett_finds_design_in_the_details.

39. Spradley, *Participant observation*.
40. Smith, B. (2005, May). Travel? No trouble. *Time* Bonus Section. Retrieved February 15, 2015, from www.rideoncarryon.com/media.php.
41. Kelley, D., & Kelley, T. (2013). *Creative confidence: Unleashing the creative potential within us all*. New York: Crown Business.
42. Ibragimova, E., & van Boeijen, A. G. C. (2014). *From BoP to ToP and vice versa daily practices in settings with limited resources to inspire designers* (para. 11). Umeå Institute of Design. Retrieved from http://repository.tudelft.nl/islandora/object/uuid:f5b15e42-1a24-492f-a43d-fe957ade0045?collection=research.
43. Jean-Charles, Y. (2016, May). *Yelitsa Jean-Charles: How #blackgirlmagic can change the world* [Video file]. TEDx. Retrieved November 18, 2016, from http://tedxtalks.ted.com/video/How-blackgirlmagic-can-change-t.
44. Smedley, A. (2007). *Race in North America: Origin and evolution of a worldview*. Boulder, CO: Westview Press.
45. Ibid.
46. Rock, C. (Producer, Director). (2009). *Good hair* [DVD]. HBO Films.
47. Workneh, L. (2016). *How #BlackGirlMagic can help change the world*. Huffington Post. Retrieved November 18, 2016, from www.huffingtonpost.com/entry/how-blackgirlmagic-can-help-change-the-world_us_574efd56e4b0ed593f12dda9.
48. Ibid.
49. Sisson, M. (2015). *Self-cleaning services* [Video file]. ISSA. Retrieved November 18, 2016, from www.issa.com/video#275.
50. Ruiter, J. (2015, July). *Forest company has a magic NanoTouch*. Retrieved on November 28, 2016, from www.roanoke.com/business/forest-company-has-a-magic-nanotouch/article_48d47916-4ecc-5488-83ca-0a332f2d82e9.html.
51. *NanoTouch*. (n.d.). Retrieved on November 28, 2016, from www.nanotouchmaterials.com.
52. *NanoTouch materials benefits from $2 million grant to accelerate development of NanoSeptic self-cleaning surfaces*. BioSpace. Retrieved November 18, 2016, from www.biospace.com/News/nanotouch-materials-benefits-from-2-million-grant/380551.

Chapter 7

1. Wheatley, M. J. (1999). *Leadership and the new science*. San Francisco: Berrett-Koehler. p. 104.
2. Millar, G. W. (1995). *E. Paul Torrance: The creativity man: An authorized biography*. Norwood, NJ: Ablex.
3. Torrance, E. P. (1988). The nature of creativity as manifest in its testing. In R. Sternberg (Ed.), *The nature of creativity: Contemporary psychological perspectives* (pp. 43–75). New York: Cambridge University Press.
4. Mitchell, K. (2013, November). What innovation sounds like. *Inventors Eye, 4*(5). Retrieved November 28, 2016, from https://www.uspto.gov/custom-page/inventors-eye-what-innovation-sounds.
5. Ibid.
6. Treffinger, D. J., Isaksen, S. G., & Firestien, R. L. (1982). *Handbook of creative learning*. Williamsville, NY: Center for Creative Learning.
7. Maslow, A. H. (1968). *Toward a psychology of being*. New York: Van Nostrand Reinhold. See also Rogers, C. (2012). *On becoming a person: A therapist's view of psychotherapy*. Boston: Houghton Mifflin Harcourt.
8. Cohen-Meitar, R., Carmelli, A., & Waldman, D. A. (2009). Linking meaningfulness in the workplace to employee creativity: The intervening role of organizational identification and positive psychological experiences. *Creativity Research Journal, 21*, 361–375.
9. Maslow, *Toward a psychology of being*.
10. Orme-Johnson, D. W., & Farrow, J. T. (Eds.). (1977). *Scientific research on the transcendental meditation program: Vol. 1* (pp. 410–414). New York: Maharishi International University.
11. Boynton, T. (2001). Applied research using alpha/theta training for enhancing creativity and well-being. *Journal of Neurotherapy, 5*(1–2), 5–18.
12. Puccio, G. J. (2012, December). *Creativity as a life skill* (TEDx Gramercy). Retrieved February 15, 2016, from http://tedxtalks.ted.com/video/Creativity-as-a-Life-Skill-Gera.
13. Currey, M. (2013). *Daily rituals: How artists work*. New York: Alfred A. Knopf.
14. Bair, B., Smallwood, J., Mrazek, M. D., Kam, J. W. Y., Franklin, M. S., & Schooler, J. W. (2012). Inspired by distraction: Mind wandering facilitates

creative incubation. *Psychological Science, 23,* 1117–1122.

15. MacKinnon, D. W. (1978). *In search of human effectiveness: Identifying and developing creativity.* Buffalo, NY: Creative Education Foundation.

16. Martin, R. L. (2007). *The opposable mind: How successful leaders win through integrative thinking.* Boston: Harvard Business School Press.

17. Treffinger et al., *Handbook of creative learning.*

18. Murray, D. K. (2009). *Borrowing brilliance: The six steps to business innovation by building ideas on the ideas of others.* New York: Gotham Books.

19. Ibid., p. 67.

20. Basadur, M., & Thompson, R. (1986). Usefulness of the ideation principle of extended effort in real world professional and managerial creative problem solving. *Journal of Creative Behavior, 20*(1), 23–34.

21. Rao, J., & Watkinson, J. (2014, July 3). *Innovators' grit: The often long story to radical innovation.* Retrieved November 28, 2016, from https://innovationatwork .wordpress.com/2014/07/03/innovators-grit-the-often-long-story-to-radical-innovation.

22. de Bono, E. (1976). *The use of lateral thinking.* New York: Penguin.

23. Gonzales, D. (2001). *The art of solving problems: Comparing the similarities and differences between CPS, synectics and lateral thinking.* Unpublished master's project, the State University College at Buffalo, New York.

24. Horowitz, A. (2010). *Inside of a dog: What dogs see, smell, and know.* New York: Simon and Schuster. See also Horowitz, A. (2014). *On looking: A walker's guide to the art of observation.* New York: Simon and Schuster.

25. Horowitz, *On looking,* p. 20.

26. Mednick, M. T. (1962). The associative basis of the creative process. *Psychological Review, 69*(3), 220–232.

27. Gruszka, A., & Necka, E. (2002). Priming and acceptance of close and remote associations by creative and less creative people. *Creativity Research Journal, 14,* 174–192.

28. BBCHD Horizon. (2013). *The creative brain.* Retrieved February 16, 2016, from https://vimeo .com/64123432.

29. Bilger, B. (2008, September 15). The long dig: Getting through the Swiss Alps the hard way. *The New Yorker.* Retrieved February 15, 2016, from www.newyorker .com/magazine/2008/09/15/the-long-dig.

30. Benyus, J. M. (1997). *Biomimicry: Innovation inspired by nature.* New York: William Morrow.

31. Brown, S. L. (2009). *Play: How it shapes the brain, opens the imagination, and invigorates the soul.* New York: Penguin.

32. Brown, S. L. (2009, September 2). Let the children play (some more). *New York Times Opinionator.* Retrieved February 15, 2016, from http://opinio nator.blogs.nytimes.com/2009/09/02/let-the-children-play-some-more/?_php=true&_ type=blogs&_r=0.

33. The National Institute for Play. (n.d.). *The science. Pattern of play.* Retrieved November 2, 2014, from www.nifplay.org/science/pattern-play.

34. *Brian Regan: UPS* [Video file]. (2008, September 12). Retrieved November 28, 2016, from www .youtube.com/watch?v=0JhuAOg75c0.

35. Bridges, W. (2009). *Managing transitions: Making the most of change.* Boston: Da Capo Press.

36. Alan Alda Center for Communicating Science. Retrieved November 1, 2014, from www.centerfor communicatingscience.org.

37. Adelman, R. (2015, May). *A funny way to do business.* Retrieved February 15, 2016, from http://blog .getabstract.com/a-funny-way-to-do-business.

38. Brown, *Play,* p. 73.

39. *Treatments and side effects.* American Cancer Society. Retrieved November 28, 2016, from www.cancer .org/treatment/treatmentsandsideeffects/index.

40. Intezyne. Retrieved November 28, 2016, from www.intezyne.com.

41. Hollingsworth, J. (2011, June 14). Intezyne: Grad school lab mates hatch cancer-fighting bio-tech firm at USF incubator. *83 Degrees.* Retrieved November 28, 2016, from www.83degreesmedia .com/features/intezyne061411.aspx.

42. Hock, L. (2009, November 2). Young innovator of the year: Dr. Kevin Sill. *R&D.* Retrieved from www .rdmag.com/articles/2009/11/young-innovator-year-dr-kevin-sill.

Chapter 8

1. Sulloway, F. J. (2005, December). *The evolution of Charles Darwin.* Smithonian.com. Retrieved November 29, 2016, from www.smithsonianmag .com/science-nature/the-evolution-of-charles-darwin-110234034/?no-ist.

2. *Evolution of the dog.* (2016, August 13). PBS. Retrieved November 29, 2016, from www.pbs.org/wgbh/evolution/library/01/5/l_015_02.html.

3. Rowling, J. K. (2008, June 5). Text of J. K. Rowling's speech. *Harvard Gazette.* Retrieved November 29, 2016, from http://news.harvard.edu/gazette/story/2008/06/text-of-j-k-rowling-speech.

4. Kroll, L. (2012). 2012 billionaires list. *Forbes.* Retrieved December 9, 2016, from www.forbes.com/sites/luisakroll/2012/03/07/forbes-worlds-billionaires-2012/#58d02d019b13.

5. O'Connor, C. (2014, October 21). Spanx inventor Sara Blakely on hustling her way to a billion-dollar business. *Forbes.* Retrieved November 29, 2016, from www.forbes.com/sites/clareoconnor/2014/10/21/spanx-inventor-sara-blakely-on-hustling-her-way-to-a-billion-dollar-business.

6. Piaget, J. (1962). *Play, dreams, and imitation in childhood.* New York: Norton. p. 205.

7. Papert, S. (1980). *Mindstorms: Children, computers, and powerful ideas.* New York: Basic Books.

8. Ibid., p. 58.

9. Ibid., p. xix.

10. Cahen, H. (n.d.). *Design thinking for better innovation.* Retrieved November 29, 2016, from http://www.designthinkingblog.com/http:/www.designthinkingblog.com/design-thinking-for-better-innovation. Para. 3.

11. Ibid.

12. Ibid.

13. Paul, A. M. (2012, March 17). Your brain on fiction. *New York Times.* Retrieved November 29, 2016, from www.nytimes.com/2012/03/18/opinion/sunday/the-neuroscience-of-your-brain-on-fiction.html?pagewanted=all&_r=0.

14. Senge, P. M. (2006). *The fifth discipline: The art and practice of the learning organization.* New York: Currency.

15. Ibid., p. 15.

16. Waytz, A., & Mason, M. (2013). Your brain at work: What a new approach to neuroscience can teach us about management. *Harvard Business Review, 91*(7–8), 102–111.

17. Ibid., p. 105.

18. Murphy, R. (2010, October 6). Josh Cooley gives an in-depth look at Pixar's creative process. *Silicon Prairie News.* Retrieved November 29, 2016, from http://siliconprairienews.com/2010/10/josh-cooley-gives-an-in-depth-look-at-pixar-s-creative-process.

19. Ibid.

20. Dougherty, D. (2015, August 18). *The maker mindset.* Retrieved November 29, 2016, from https://llk.media.mit.edu/courses/readings/maker-mindset.pdf.

21. Van der Lugt, L. (2002). Functions of sketching in design idea generation meetings. In E. Edmonds, L. Candy, T. Kavanagh, & T. Hewett (Eds.), *Proceedings of the 4th conference on creativity & cognition* (pp. 72–79). Loughborough, UK: ACM Press.

22. Warfel, T. Z. (2009). *Prototyping: A practitioner's guide.* New York: Rosenfeld Media.

23. Ibid.

24. Puccio, G. J., & Cabra, J. F. (2011). Idea generation and idea evaluation: Cognitive skills and deliberate practice. In M. D. Mumford (Ed.), *Handbook for organizational creativity* (pp. 187–213). New York: Elsevier.

25. Ries, E. (2011). *The lean startup: How today's entrepreneurs use continuous innovation to create radically successful businesses.* New York: Random House.

26. Brown, T. (2008). Design thinking. *Harvard Business Review, 86*(6), 84–92.

27. Mumford, M. D. (2001). Something old, something new: Revisiting Guilford's conception of creative problem solving. *Creativity Research Journal, 13*(3), 267–276.

28. Puccio & Cabra, *Idea generation and idea evaluation.*

29. Cropley, D. H., Kaufman, J. C., & Cropley, A. J. (2011). Measuring creativity for innovation management. *Journal of Technology, Management, and Innovation, 6*(3), 13–29.

30. O'Quin, K., & Besemer, S. P. (2006). Using the Creative Product Semantic Scale as a metric for results-oriented business. *Creativity and Innovation Management, 15,* 34–44.

31. Cropley, Kaufman, & Cropley, *Measuring creativity for innovation management.*

32. Liedtka, J., & Ogilvie, T. (2011). *Designing for growth: A design thinking tool kit for managers.* New York: Columbia Business School.

33. Coughlan, P., & Prokopoff, I. (2006, Winter). Managing change by design. *Rotman Magazine,* 20–23.

34. Moule, J. (2012). *Killer UX design.* Melbourne, Australia: SitePoint.

35. Coughlan & Prokopoff, *Managing change by design.*

36. Dow, S. P., Glassco, A., Kass, J., Schwartz, M., Schwartz, D. L., & Klemmer, S. R. (2010). Parallel prototyping leads to better design results, more divergence, and increased self-efficacy. *ACM Transactions on Computer Human Interaction, 17*(4), Article 18.
37. Ibid.
38. Best, P. (2010). Branding and design innovation leadership: What's next? In T. Lockwood (Ed.), *Design thinking: Integrating innovation, customer experience, and brand value* (pp. 145–155). New York: Allworth Press. p. 153.
39. Robinson, K. (2006). *Ken Robinson: Do schools kill creativity?* TED Talk. Retrieved April 21, 2011, from www.ted.com/talks/ken_robinson_says_schools_kill_creativity.
40. Rodriguez, D., & Jacoby, R. (2007, Spring). Embracing risk to learn, grow and innovate. *Rotman Magazine*, 55–58.
41. Liedtka & Ogilvie, *Designing for growth.*
42. Ibid.
43. Cropley, Kaufman, & Cropley, *Measuring creativity for innovation management.*
44. Merlini, L. (2013, June 20). *Sir Ken Robinson on finding your passion.* Retrieved November 29, 2016, from http://blog.explo.org/education/sir-ken-robinson-finding-your-passion.
45. Cabra, J. F., & Uribe, D. (2013). Creative behavior. In E. Carayannis, I. Dubina, N. Seel, D. F. J. Campbell, & D. Uzunidis (Eds.), *Springer encyclopedia on creativity, invention, innovation, and entrepreneurship* (pp. 267–271). New York: Springer. See also Uribe, D., & Cabra, J. F. (2014). *TRYCycle: Creative behavior.* Santiago, Chile: IdeMax.
46. Brown, S. L. (2009). *Play: How it shapes the brain, opens the imagination, and invigorates the soul.* New York: Penguin.
47. Dweck, C. (2006). *Mindset: The new psychology of success.* New York: Random House.
48. Eliot, T. S. (1979). *Four quartets.* London: Faber. p. 240. (Original work published 1943)
49. R. Pressman, personal communication, April 18, 2016.
50. Ibid.
51. Check I'm Here. Retrieved November 29, 2016, from www.checkimhere.com.
52. Pressman, personal communication, April 18, 2016.
53. Ibid.

Chapter 9

1. Assayas, M. (2006). *Bono in conversation with Michka Assayas.* New York: Penguin.
2. Ibid.
3. Kotter, J. P. (1996). *Leading change.* Boston: Harvard Business Press.
4. Edwards, G. (2014). U2's "Bad" break: 12 minutes at Live Aid that made the band's career. *Rolling Stone.* Retrieved October 30, 2012, from www.rollingstone.com/music/news/u2s-bad-break-12-minutes-at-live-aid-that-made-the-bands-career-20140710.
5. Tyrangiel, J. (2006, December 26). The constant charmer. *Time, 166*(26), 46–62.
6. Pink, D. H. (2012). *To sell is human: The surprising truth about moving others.* New York: Penguin.
7. Schawbel, D. (2013, January 3). Daniel Pink says that in today's world we're all salespeople. *Forbes.* Retrieved November 29, 2016, from www.forbes.com/sites/danschawbel/2013/01/03/daniel-pink-says-that-in-todays-world-were-all-salespeople.
8. Ibid.
9. Gardner, H. (2004). *Changing minds: The art and science of changing our own and other people's minds.* Boston: Harvard Business School Press.
10. Shell, G. R., & Moussa, M. (2007). *The art of woo: Using strategic persuasion to sell your ideas.* New York: Penguin.
11. Mantelow, J., & Carlson, A. (n.d.). *Force field analysis: Analyzing the pressures for and against change.* Mind Tools. Retrieved December 18, 2014, from www.mindtools.com/pages/article/newTED_06.htm.
12. Dezieck, J. (n.d.). *Planning for change: The force field tool.* Learning & Development. Retrieved December 18, 2014, from https://hrweb.mit.edu/learning-development/learning-topics/change/articles/force-field.
13. Thompson, R. (n.d.). *Stakeholder analysis.* Mind Tools. Retrieved December 18, 2014, from www.mindtools.com/pages/article/newPPM_07.htm.
14. Mason, R. O., & Mitroff, I. L. (1981). *Challenging strategic planning assumptions: Theory, cases and techniques.* New York: Wiley.
15. Puccio, G. J., Mance, M., & Murdock, M. C. (2011). *Creative leadership: Skills that drive change.* Thousand Oaks, CA: Sage.

16. Pink, *To sell is human*, p. 4.

17. Fox, J. (2013, February 14). Why we're all in sales. *Harvard Business Review*. Retrieved November 29, 2016, from https://hbr.org/2013/02/why-were-all-in-sales.

18. Ibid.

19. Dan Pink's website presents a one-stop shop for all resources related to the author: www.danpink.com/resources.

20. Feloni, R. (2014, October, 16). Pixar's 22 rules for telling a great story. *Business Insider*. Retrieved November 29, 2016, from www.businessinsider.com/pixars-rules-for-storytelling-2014-10.

21. Hallen, E. (n.d.). How to use the psychology of social proof to your advantage. *Fast Company*. Retrieved December 18, 2014, from www.fastcompany.com/3030044/work-smart/how-to-use-the-psychology-of-social-proof-to-your-advantage.

22. Ibid.

23. Schein, E. (1999). *The corporate culture survival guide*. San Francisco: Jossey-Bass.

24. Elrod, P. D., II, & Tippett, D. D. (2002). The "death valley" of change. *Journal of Organizational Change Management, 15*(3), 273–291.

25. Ibid.

26. Kotter, *Leading change*.

27. Kotter, J. P. (1995). Leading change: Why transformation efforts fail. *Harvard Business Review, 73*(2), 59–67. p. 59.

28. Schein, E. H. (2010). *Organizational culture and leadership* (Vol. 2). Hoboken, NJ: Wiley.

29. Schein, E. H. (2009). *The corporate culture survival guide* (Vol. 158). Hoboken, NJ: Wiley.

30. Schein, E. H. (2013). *Humble inquiry: The gentle art of asking instead of telling*. Oakland, CA: Berrett-Koehler.

31. Moore, K. (2011, November 29). MIT's Ed Schein on why corporate culture is no longer the relevant topic and what is. *Forbes*. Retrieved November 29, 2016, from www.forbes.com/sites/karlmoore/2011/11/29/mits-ed-schein-on-why-corporate-culture-in-no-longer-the-relevant-topic-and-what-is.

32. Ibid.

33. Rickards, T. (1996). The management of innovation: Recasting the role of creativity. *European Journal of Work and Organizational Psychology, 5*(1), 13–27.

34. Rickards, T. (2007, September 3). Why innovation leaders should be controlled schizophrenics. *Leaders We Deserve*. Retrieved December 11, 2016, from https://leaderswedeserve.wordpress.com/category/innovation-leadership.

35. Shen, J. (2012, May 8). *Eleven compelling startup pitch archetypes (with examples from YC companies)*. The Art of Ass-Kicking. Retrieved November 29, 2016, from www.jasonshen.com/2012/eleven-compelling-startup-pitch-archetypes-with-examples-from-yc-companies.

36. Ibid.

37. Rickards, *Management of innovation*.

38. Keeley, L., Walters, H., Pikkel, R., & Quinn, B. (2013). *Ten types of innovation: The discipline of building breakthroughs*. New York: Wiley.

39. Horney, N., Pasmore, B., & O'Shea, T. (2010). Leadership agility: A business imperative for a VUCA world. *Human Resource Planning, 33*(4), 34–38.

40. Pink, D. H. (2012). *3 ABC exercises for newsletter subscribers*. Daniel H. Pink. Retrieved November 29, 2016, from www.danpink.com/newsletterbonus.

41. Keys, B., & Case, T. (1990). How to become an influential manager. *The Executive, 4*(4), 38–51. p. 48.

42. Duarte, N. (2011, November 21). *Nancy Duarte: The secret structure of great talks* [Video file]. Retrieved November 29, 2016, from www.ted.com/talks/nancy_duarte_the_secret_structure_of_great_talks.

43. Gardner, *Changing minds*.

44. Pink, *3 ABC exercises*.

45. Shell & Moussa, *The art of woo*.

46. MacArthur Foundation. (2014). *21 extraordinary creative people who inspire us all: Meet the 2014 MacArthur fellows*. Retrieved November 29, 2016, from www.macfound.org/press/press-releases/21-extraordinarily-creative-people-who-inspire-us-all-meet-2014-macarthur-fellows.

47. Puccio et al., *Creative leadership*.

48. Ibid., p. 210.

49. Feinstein, E. (2014, October 5). *An interview with MacArthur genius award winner Pamela O. Long*. History News Network. Retrieved November 29, 2016, from http://historynewsnetwork.org/article/157074.

50. Schawbel, *Daniel Pink says*.

51. Jones, D. (2010). *Finding the right answer* [Video file]. Retrieved November 29, 2016, from www.youtube.com/watch?v=5rDeK9vlUNs.

52. Kotter, *Leading change*.

Chapter 10

1. Blackburn, S. (1996). The brahmin and the mongoose: The narrative context of a well-travelled tale. *Bulletin of the School of Oriental and African Studies* (University of London), *59*(3), 494–507.

2. Goleman, D. (1994). *Emotional intelligence: Why it can matter more than IQ*. New York: Bantam.

3. Lynn, A. (2003). *The EQ difference: A powerful plan for putting emotional intelligence to work*. New York: AMACOM Books.

4. Weber, T. E. (2010, June 6). *Regrets from the man who fired Steve Jobs*. The Daily Beast. Retrieved November 30, 2016, from www.thedailybeast.com/articles/2010/06/06/why-i-fired-steve-jobs.html.

5. Smith, C. (2010, June 7). *John Sculley explains why he fired Steve Jobs*. Retrieved December 1, 2016, from www.huffingtonpost.com/2010/06/07/john-sculley-on-why-he-fi_n_602590.html.

6. Murphy, M. (2015, June 22). *Why new hires fail (emotional intelligence vs. skills)*. Leadership IQ. Retrieved November 30, 2016, from www.leadershipiq.com/blogs/leadershipiq/35354241-why-new-hires-fail-emotional-intelligence-vs-skills.

7. Lopes, P. N., Grewal, D., Kadis, J., Gall, M., & Salovey, P. (2006). Evidence that emotional intelligence is related to job performance and affect and attitudes at work. *Psicothema, 18*(1), 132–138.

8. Ibid.

9. Gentry, W. A., Weber, T. J., & Sadri, G. (2007). *Empathy in the workplace: A tool for effective leadership*. A Center for Creative Leadership White Paper. Retrieved November 30, 2016, from www.ccl.org/wp-content/uploads/2015/04/EmpathyInTheWorkplace.pdf.

10. Zhou, J., & George, J. M. (2003). Awakening employee creativity: The role of leader emotional intelligence. *Leadership Quarterly, 14*, 545–568.

11. Lynn, *The EQ difference*.

12. Datar, S. M., Garvin, D. A., & Cullen, P. G. (2010). *Rethinking the MBA: Business education at a crossroads*. Boston: Harvard Business Press.

13. Walton, D. (2012). *Emotional intelligence: A practical guide*. New York: MJF Books.

14. Datar et al., *Rethinking the MBA*.

15. Grow, B., Foust, D., Thornton, E., Farzad, R., McGregor, J., & Zegel, S. (2007, January 14). Out at Home Depot. *Bloomberg Businessweek*. Retrieved December 15, 2016, from www.bloomberg.com/news/articles/2007-01-14/out-at-home-depot.

16. Brady, D. (2007, January 14). Being mean is so last millennium. *Bloomberg Businessweek*. Retrieved December 15, 2016, from www.bloomberg.com/news/articles/2007-01-14/being-mean-is-so-last-millennium.

17. Datar et al., *Rethinking the MBA*.

18. Burkhardt, T. A. (2013). Analyzing the postwar requirements of jus ad bellum. In F. Allhof, N. G. Evans, & A. Henschke (Eds.), *Routledge handbook of ethics and war: Just war theory in the 21st century* (pp. 120–141). New York: Routledge.

19. Avolio, B. J., & Bass, B. M. (2002). Still flying high after all these years at Southwest Airlines. In B. J. Avolio & B. M. Bass (Eds.), *Developing potential across a full range of leadership cases on transactional and transformational leadership* (pp. 13–15). Mahwah, NJ: Erlbaum.

20. Ackoff, R. L., & Vergara, E. (1988). Creativity in problem solving and planning. In R. L. Kuhn (Ed.), *Handbook for creative and innovative managers* (pp. 77–89). New York: McGraw-Hill.

21. Ware, B. (2012). *The top five regrets of the dying: A life transformed by the dearly departing*. Carlsbad, CA: Hay House.

22. Creative Oklahoma. (2016). *E. Paul Torrance*. Retrieved November 30, 2016, from http://stateofcreativity.com/dr-e-paul-torrance. Para. 6.

23. Craske, M. G., Rauch, S. L., Ursano, R., Prenoveau, J., Pine, D. S., & Zinbarg, R. E. (2009). What is an anxiety disorder? *Depression and Anxiety, 26*, 1066–1085.

24. Layton, J. (2005, September 13). *How fear works*. How Stuff Works: Science. Retrieved January 12, 2015, from http://science.howstuffworks.com/life/inside-the-mind/emotions/fear.htm.

25. Dugan, R. (2014, November). *From mach-20 glider to hummingbird drone* [Video file]. Retrieved January 12, 2015, from www.ted.com/talks/regina_dugan_from_mach_20_glider_to_humming_bird_drone.

26. Ibid.

27. Miller, C. (2012, August 12). Motorola set for big cuts as Google reinvents it. *New York Times*. Retrieved January 12, 2015, from www.nytimes.com/2012/08/13/technology/motorola-to-cut-20-of-work-force-part-of-sweeping-change.html?_r=5&ref=technology&.

28. Pfeffer, J., & Sutton, R. I. (2000). *The knowing–doing gap: How smart companies turn knowledge into action*. Boston: Harvard Business School Press.

29. Zhou, J., & George, J. M. (2001). When job dissatisfaction leads to creativity: Encouraging the expression of voice. *Academy of Management Journal, 44,* 682–696.

30. *Edward de Bono on failure* [Video file]. (2010, June 13). Retrieved November 30, 2016, from www.youtube.com/watch?v=XNbfrdiUg_M.

31. *Mistake? Nearling!* Retrieved February 16, 2016, from www.nearling.com.

32. Wilkinson, A. (2015). *The creator's code: The six essential skills of extraordinary entrepreneurs*. New York: Simon & Schuster.

33. Walters, H. (2013, October 16). *Why we need creative confidence*. Retrieved January 12, 2015, from http://ideas.ted.com/2013/10/16/david-kelley-on-the-need-for-creative-confidence.

34. Jacob, J. (2011, September 4). "Step-by-step, ferociously," says Bezos, undaunted by Blue Origin space ship failure. *The Economist*. Retrieved November 30, 2016, from www.ibtimes.com/step-step-ferociously-says-bezos-undaunted-blue-origin-space-ship-failure-308884.

35. Dugan, *From mach-20 glider to hummingbird drone*.

36. Lassiter, J. B., III, & Richardson, E. W. (2014, March). *Airbnb*. Harvard Business School Case 812–046.

37. Thomas, O. (2013, February 22). Airbnb finally lands the Zappos veteran it's eyed for years. *Business Insider*. Retrieved January 27, 2015, from www.businessinsider.com/airbnb-finally-lands-alfred-lin-2013–2.

38. Lassiter & Richardson, *Airbnb*, p. 9.

39. Arrington, M. (2009, March 16). *Y Combinator gets the Sequoia Capital seal of approval*. TechCrunch. Retrieved January 27, 2015, from http://techcrunch.com/2009/03/16/y-combinator-gets-the-sequoia-capital-seal-of-approval.

40. *How design thinking transformed Airbnb from a failing startup to a billion dollar business*. (n.d.). First Round Review. Retrieved January 27, 2015, from http://firstround.com/article/How-design-thinking-transformed-Airbnb-from-failing-startup-to-billion-dollar-business.

41. Steinmetz, K. (2014, April 20). Major reservations: Why cities are worried about Airbnb. *Time*. Retrieved January 27, 2015, from http://time.com/64323/airbnb-san-francisco-new-york.

42. Coldwell, W. (2014, July 8). Airbnb's legal troubles: What are the issues? *The Guardian*. Retrieved January 27, 2015, from www.theguardian.com/travel/2014/jul/08/airbnb-legal-troubles-what-are-the-issues.

Chapter 11

1. *Herb Peterson*. Wikipedia. Retrieved March 14, 2014, from http://en.wikipedia.org/wiki/Herb_Peterson.

2. Kroc, R. (1977). *Grinding it out: The making of McDonald's*. Chicago: St. Martin's.

3. Nicastro, K. (2014, March 12). *McDonald's looks to breakfast to wake up sales*. Medill Reports Chicago. Retrieved March 14, 2014, from http://news.medill.northwestern.edu/chicago/news.aspx?id=228937.

4. Trefis Team. (2012, March 29). McDonald's secret weapon is breakfast but others are catching on. *Forbes*. Retrieved March 14, 2014, from www.forbes.com/sites/greatspeculations/2012/03/29/mcdonalds-secret-weapon-is-breakfast-but-others-are-catching-on.

5. Sternberg, R. J., & Lubart, T. I. (1995). *Defying the crowd: Cultivating creativity in a culture of conformity*. New York: Free Press.

6. Ibid., pp. 42–43.

7. Ibid., p. 3.

8. Simonton, D. K. (1997). Creative productivity: A predictive and explanatory model of career trajectories and landmarks. *Psychological Review, 104,* 66–89.

9. Sternberg & Lubart, *Defying the crowd*, p. 9.

10. Karp, H. B. (1996). *Change leadership: Using a Gestalt approach with work groups.* San Diego, CA: Pfeiffer.

11. Sternberg & Lubart, *Defying the crowd*, p. 67.

12. Faris, S. (2011, April 11). Nokia's lifeline? *Time.* Retrieved December 2, 2016, from http://content.time.com/time/magazine/article/0,9171,2062469,00.html.

13. Kuittinen, T. (2014, July 1). *Nokia's destiny: From boots to phones to . . . boots.* Retrieved December 2, 2016, from http://bgr.com/2014/07/01/nokia-future-analysis-smart-shoes.

14. Blau, J. R., & McKinley, W. (1979). Ideas, complexity, and innovation. *Administrative Science Quarterly, 24,* 200–219.

15. Karp, *Change leadership*, p. 16.

16. Fritz, R. (1991). *Creating: A guide to the creative process.* New York: Fawcett Columbine.

17. *Top ten Steve Jobs quotes.* (2016, February). Move me quotes and more. Retrieved February 16, 2016, from www.movemequotes.com/top-10-steve-jobs-quotes.

18. Devlin, M., & Chaskel, S. (2010, December). *From fear to hope in Colombia: Sergio Fajardo and Medellín, 2004–2007.* Retrieved December 2, 2016, from https://successfulsocieties.princeton.edu/sites/successfulsocieties/files/Policy_Note_ID116.pdf.

19. *Medellín violence statistics.* Retrieved May 5, 2016, from http://colombiareports.com/a-violence-statistics.

20. Long, W. R. (1990, July 15). *Lawlessness rampant in streets of Medellín, world's cocaine capital: Colombia: An anonymous warning tells citizens to be indoors by 9 p.m. to avoid "being surprised by killer bullets."* Retrieved December 2, 2016, from http://articles.latimes.com/1990-07-15/news/mn-259_1_cocaine-capital.

21. Fisher, R., & Ury, W. (1981). *Getting to yes: Negotiating agreement without giving in.* New York: Houghton Mifflin.

22. S. Fajardo, personal communication, July 13, 2015.

23. Ibid.

24. Devlin, M. (2009, November 3). *Interview of Sergio Fajardo Valderrama.* Innovations for Successful Societies. Retrieved May 6, 2016, from https://successfulsocieties.princeton.edu/sites/successfulsocieties/files/J30_GT_MD_Fajardo_web.pdf.

25. Fajardo, personal communication, July 13, 2015.

Index

judgment, managing and deferring, 86–87, 92, 98
    novelty seeking, 94–95, 98–99
    strategic approach to, 129
Dixon, Jenny, xiii
DNA, creativity in our, 106–107
Doblin consulting group, 166–167, 167 (table)
Dobrev, Stanislav, 58–59
Dog breeding, 139
Do-it-yourself (DIY) movement, 115
Domain-specific thinking, 5–6
Domestication of chickens, 22
Dougherty, Dale, 144
Douglass, Frederick, 192
Duarte, Nancy, 168
Dugan, Regina, 185, 186, 192
Dunbar, R., 27
Durrieu, F., 63
Dweck, Carol, 112–113, 115
Dyer, Jeffrey, 113
Dylan, Bob, xiii–xiv
Dyson, James, xiii–xiv, 95–96, 204

Early human species, 2–4
Eastern thinking, 125–126
Ecologic Brands, 97
Edison, Thomas, 188–189, 204, 205
Education, 27–28, 38–39, 40–44
Egg McMuffins, 196–197, 202
EI. See Emotional intelligence (EI)
Einstein, Albert, 96
Ekvall, Göran, 56–57
Elaboration, 23
Eliot, T. S., 151
Email pitches, 160–161
Embedding strategy, 115–116
Eminent creativity, 11–12
Emotional intelligence (EI)
    abilities, 179–181
    affirmative self-talk, 187–188
    Airbnb case study, 192–195
    barriers to creative thinking, 182–183
    creative confidence, 188–189
    definitions, 177
    fear, 183–187, 192–193
    learning from failure, 190–192
    observers' using, 110
    research support of, 178–179
    transformational leadership, 181–182

Empathy, 180
Empathy maps, 118
Employment. See Workplace issues
Enculturation, 25–27
Energy levels, 51
Entrepreneurship
    creative thinking connected to, xiii–xiv, xv
    defined, 72
    importance of failure to, 145–146
    locus of control and, 63
    serial opportunists, 105
    visualization and, 123–125
    willingness to acquire new mental models, 140–141
    See also specific entrepreneurs
Environment for creativity, 56–59, 167, 201
Epileptic seizures, 101–103
Ericsson, K. A., 30–31
Estay, C., 63
Estrin, Judy, 28
Ethnographers, 106, 110–111, 116
Evaluation of ideas, 146–147
    See also Judgment
Everyday creativity, 10–14
Everyday pitches, 161
Evolution
    anxiety and, 184
    creative explosion in modern humans, 4–6
    early species, 2–4, 106–107
    human intervention in, 139
    insight into creativity from, 8–10
    sexual selection and, 7–8
    wiring humans to be creative, 31–32, 106
    See also Darwin, Charles
Experiment step of creative process
    about, 48, 90, 90 (figure)
    breeding ideas through, 139
    Check I'm Here case study, 152–155
    developing ideas, 148–149, 150–151
    failure and, 139–140
    idea valuation skills, 149
    mental models, 140–143
    prototypes, 141–142, 144–145, 146
    serious play, 143–144
    sketching, 144
    tricycle metaphor, 150–151, 151 (figure)
    validation, 145–147

humans as intrinsically creative beings, 107–108, 108 (figure)

NanoTouch Technology case study, 120–122

power of observation, 90, 108–111, 116, 118

problem definition, 111–115

Universality of creative process, 89

University of Auckland's Creative Thinking Project, xiii

University of Oklahoma, 112

Uribe, Diego, 150–151, 151 (figure)

Ury, William, 208–209

Valéry, Paul, 183

Validation, 145–147

See also Experiment step of creative process

VanGundy, Andy, 60–61

Vergara, E., 29

Vision/visualization, 123–128, 206

Visual thinking mindset, 142

Volatility, uncertainty, complexity, and ambiguity (VUCA), 167

Wagner, Tony, 33, 55

Walton, David, 179–180

Warburg, Otto, 102

Ware, Bonnie, 184

Warfel, Todd Zaki, 144–145

Water carrier problem, 107, 108 (figure)

Watkinson, Jim, 128–129

Waytz, Adam, 143–144

Weapons of early humans, 3–4

Well-being (psychological), 75

Wheatley, Meg, 123

Why Fly (Torrance), 114

Wild, Kyle, 81–84

Wilkinson, Amy, 188

Workplace Basics, 71 (table)

Workplace issues, 33, 70–72, 71 (table), 79–80, 178, 190–191

World Economic Forum, xiv, 71 (table)

Wright brothers, 205

Xerox, 87, 97

Y Combinator (YC), 193–195

Yes-And thinking, 35–39, 37 (figure), 98, 134, 167

Yes-But thinking, 35–36, 38–39

Yorton, Tom, 134

Zhou, J., 178–179

Zuckerberg, Mark, 53